COUNCIL AND COMMUNE

Council and Commune
The conciliar movement
and the fifteenth-century
heritage

Antony Black

Burns & Oates · London
The Patmos Press · Shepherdstown

262
B62c

First published in Great Britain in 1979
by Burns & Oates 2-10 Jerdan Place,
London SW6 5PT and in the United States
of America by Patmos Press, Inc.

ISBN (UK) 0 86012 877 5

ISBN (USA) 0-915762-08-0

Library of Congress Catalog Card Number 79-89220

Typeset by 🅰 Tek-Art, Croydon, Surrey,
and printed by Billings and Sons Limited, Guildford, London and
Worcester for Burns & Oates

To my parents

Acknowledgments

I am grateful to John Bochel, James Cameron, Ian Machin, Michael Masterson, Walter Ullmann and Michael Wilks for having read and commented on all or part of various versions; to Miss Angus, Mrs Jack, Mrs Robertson and Miss Tindal for typing; and to the inter-library loans department of Dundee University Library for their courteous assistance.

Note: I have used the author-date system of reference for all secondary sources; full details are in the Bibliography.

CONTENTS

Ragusa's use of history − the university consilia *(1440-4) − the realist-organic view of the Church-in-council*

JUAN DE SEGOVIA

The 'collegiate' model − ruler and ruled − fictional theory of government and law − civic republicanism

Identification of Church with council − absolute collegiate sovereignty − parliamentary monarchy

CONCLUSION

Parliamentarism − society as an organic whole − the collective-distributive distinction: conciliarism and contractarianism − the idea of the commune.

(a) Early-modern conciliarism *(b)* The council today

ABBREVIATIONS

MOCC	*Magnum Oecumenicum Constantiense Concilium*
OC	Gerson, Jean. *Oeuvres complètes*
OO	*Opera omnia*
PC	Valois, N. *Le pape et le concile*
RHE	*Revue d'histoire ecclésiastique*
RQ	*Römische Quartalschrift*
SCH	*Studies in church history*
SHA	*Sitzungsberichte der heidelberger Akademie der Wissenschaften, phil.–hist. Klasse*
SM	*Sacramentum mundi*
TEP	Ailly, Pierre de, *Tractatus de ecclesiastica potestate*
TP	Segovia, Juan de, *Tractatus super presidentia*
VL	Codices Vaticani latini
ZK	*Zeitschrift für Kirchengeschichte*

PREFACE

The council, or representative assembly of the Church, and the commune, or small internally self-governing association, acquired a prominence in late-medieval theory and practice which has hardly been rivalled since and which is not without significance for the present day. And, as often happens in movements of revolution or opposition, the smaller, more fraternal body was taken, by those championing the sovereign council against the sovereign pope, as a model for the larger representative body, and sometimes for the Church as a whole. The core of this book concerns the use and development of communal ideas by the conciliarists; they constructed a political ideology to suit their case which bears comparison with that of contemporary Florence, of mid-seventeenth-century England or of revolutionary France. Yet, partly because their movement ended in failure, the conciliarist heritage, both political and ecclesiastical, has been largely lost, and has to be recovered by the historian. The contributions of Marsiglio and Cusa to political thought have long been recognized: I propose that Segovia and Velde made no less significant contributions and deserve a place in the annals of political thought.

This book, then, is about the political ideas of the mid-fifteenth-century conciliarists, especially of Juan de Segovia, set in the context of both history and theology. The special *Gestalt* of ideas that comprised conciliar theory in its final phase during the Council of Basle (1431-49) — and not during this final phase alone — included two major thrusts of social and constitutional argument. First, a far-reaching theory of social holism was developed. Neo-Platonic philosophy suggested the idea that the council was a visible manifestation of the invisible essence of the Church. The notion of the Church as a metaphysical whole was revived, in order to

1

argue that the Church as a whole is prior in being to any of its 'parts', and that therefore the council is prior in jurisdiction to the pope; in organic terms, the whole body performs acts that no single 'member' can perform. Far from being related to nominalism, therefore, conciliarism in its final phase – and, again, not in its final phase alone – was closely related to philosophical realism. This comes out most clearly of all in the works of the Netherlander Heimerich van de Velde (de Campo), a famous realist philosopher, whose ecclesiological works are here fully examined for the first time.

Secondly, the conciliarists developed a distinctive political theory centred upon the idea of the guild-like commune, the Christianized *collegium*.[1] This was the culmination of an epochal movement in medieval ecclesiology, political theory and organizational practice; its chief exponent was the Castilian theologian Juan de Segovia. He proclaimed a theory of direct democracy which was at once an idealization of the medieval corporation and a strong anticipation of later notions, in particular of Rousseau's. The theoretical writings of Segovia, which are also here fully expounded for the first time, were soon forgotten and had little if any influence. Was this persistent re-emergence, then, of the ideal of direct democracy due to underlying features of European political culture – in the self-governing towns, for example? Or is it a characteristic of a certain type of association – the guild or commune – in any culture? I hope here to provide material for an answer to the first question. The second, more elusive question I hope to return to later.[2]

Segovia emerges as the chief theoretical exponent of Basle conciliarism. What his colleagues stated piecemeal he elaborated into a far-reaching, if sometimes inconsistent, set of reflections. He fully appreciated the close connections between conciliar theory and civic republicanism (currently being expounded by the Florentine humanists); his notion of rulership places him in a tradition of Christian republicanism which may be said to culminate in Milton. His remarks on secular monarchy link him to Erasmus and Bodin. His reflections on the artificial character of governmental and legal entities revealed the potential of the legal fiction for political theory, as this was to be developed, for instance, by Hobbes and Kelsen. His development of the distinction between society 'taken collectively' and society 'taken distributively' in some respects anticipated the dialectic between 'civil society' and 'the state of nature' that we find later in theorists of the social contract. Throughout, the continuity between late-medieval and early-modern political thought is so apparent as to render the customary dividing-line ('Renaissance', 'Reformation', c.1500) in important respects meaningless.

These phenomena can only be understood if they are placed in the

2

context, first, of the circumstances and events in which they arose; and, secondly, of earlier arguments and the intellectual tradition within which Segovia and others were operating. The conciliar movement was a distinctive episode in the theory and practice of church organization: the age-old conciliar tradition was here developed in a unique historical milieu penetrated by communal (i.e., collegiate, corporational) notions of society and government. The council of Basle was a decisive moment in the history of Europe, a fascinating example of the interaction of idealism and intrigue. Its internal structure was a marvellous example of the late-medieval talent for constitutional adaptation and creation, of which one finds parallel instances in the towns and city-states. (It was, moreover, the only medieval council, perhaps the only Catholic council of any period, at which heretics — the Hussites — were permitted to speak and debate). By examining the political culture of the late Middle Ages, the major conciliar thinkers of the period 1378-1418, the situation facing the men of Basle, and their specific and deliberate strategies, I hope both to have provided an integral portrait of conciliarism, and to have pinpointed the exact intentions of the Basle theorists, and the nature of their original contribution.[3]

These intellectual phenomena are also discussed critically as political conceptions and ideals in their own right. For example, the use of a communal model for a large, heterogeneous society posed special problems which the conciliarists, like some later parliamentarians, failed to resolve. The problem of how exactly the council represented the Church was acute; and the conciliarists did little more than develop a theory of symbolic representation based on a holist interpretation of the organic analogy. Here one may learn something of how ideas, evoked to support a cause, are imperfectly worked out because to do so would have legitimized more than was originally intended (people seldom persist in being inconsistent without a reason).

My attention was first drawn to this field by Professor Walter Ullmann, whose approach to the study of ideological history retains for me, despite very considerable disagreement, an irresistible fascination. His method is a particular version of what Weber called 'interpretative understanding (*Verstehen*)', of the attempt to discover the inner logic of diverse utterances, and by connecting them to an abstract model to explain why certain expressions and ideas so often appeared in conjunction, and what particular 'subjective meaning' they had for their exponents. Ullmann has used this approach with marked success in examining, for instance, the Roman-law context of papal monarchy. Yet such isolation of a key pattern is a notoriously tricky business, and Ullmann like others has often failed to do justice to the coexistence of different strands within the same thinker or ideology. Latterly, he has fallen into the trap of trying to explain too much by means of two simple models – the 'descending' and 'ascending' 'theses of government'.[4] He rigorously places the conciliarists in the latter category, which I fear obscures as much as it clarifies; I have therefore avoided these terms. Professor J.G.A. Pocock's adaptation of the Kuhnian 'paradigm' as a tool for understanding the history of political ideas in the context of their authors' general conceptual framework[5] has enormous potential, though it too runs the risk of undue isolation of specific themes. I did not consciously employ this approach here, though I would like to think that some implicit reference to paradigms has emerged. It would be worth pursuing the thought that what the conciliarists lacked was a paradigm of the republic[6]; what they certainly possessed was a paradigm of the commune. (I hope the reader will not find me a Newtonian writing after Einstein). The author to whom I feel the greatest debt is Otto Gierke; his erudition has never been rivalled, and his interpretations remain always suggestive. He it was who first elucidated medieval corporation theory (the communal model) and pointed out its manifold influence[7].

NOTES

1. The Roman-law term for a small, internally self-governing association.
2. In a book provisionally called 'Community and its modes: Guild and State in political thought'.
3. Cf. Skinner (1969); I became familiar with Professor Skinner's ideas on method after finishing this book; I hope I have observed some of his caveats.
4. Ullmann (1966), 19ff., 288ff.
5. Pocock (1972), 1ff.
6. Cf. Pocock (1975), 49ff.
7. Gierke, trans. Maitland, 64-5, 69, and *DGR* iii, 416-501; but see also Ullmann (1966), 215ff.

Interpretations of the conciliar movement

The conciliar movement has now engaged the attention of historians for nearly one hundred and fifty years, systematic study coming at first mainly from Germany (Marx could quote d'Ailly).[1] Interest focussed on its place in diplomatic and political history. Its role in the history of political ideas was first staked out by Gierke; he placed the conciliarists among those who, he thought, by putting forward a theory of popular sovereignty without regard for the real personality of the group unwittingly prepared the way for state absolutism.[2] It was no coincidence that an English historian, J.N. Figgis,[3] first claimed the conciliarists for the parliamentary, constitutionalist tradition, their contribution to which has remained a focus for many subsequent studies.[4] The conciliarists did indeed produce remarkable anticipations of later theories of constitutionalism and representation. If we compare what happened at Constance and Basle with what happened in England some two hundred years later, we cannot fail to be struck by numerous parallels;[5] Basle in particular was a moment of intense constitutional experiment and upheaval, though it ended not in compromise but in collapse. The legacy of these councils has come to be widely regarded as one of the transitions from medieval to modern constitutionalism and democracy.

Yet this parliamentarian approach (which I myself adopted in *Monarchy and Community*), reflecting as it does the ideological concerns of modern scholars, has led to a partially false view of the movement itself. The conciliarists did indeed appeal, as did papalists, to principles which they held to be generally applicable to any human polity. But any thorough examination of their works shows that they regarded themselves, for the most part, primarily as theologians. They drew *most* of their arguments from biblical, patristic and canonist sources, and most of what they said was intended to apply specifically, sometimes exclusively, to the Church. No doubt, even when they addressed themselves thus specifically to the Church, it is possible to say that they were doing political theory, inasmuch as they were thinking about a constitutional structure, about the relationship between rulers and ruled in a particular society. But, except when they talked explicitly about secular government or about government in general, their work was not *just* political theory. Just as much, often more so, it was theology. While the boundaries between these fields are notoriously unclear, one must pay at least as much attention to the theological as to the political elements in these writers. The danger is that, by classifying them as 'political thinkers', one may seriously misunderstand their own purpose, or imply that their reflections and arguments were extraneous to theology proper. Rather, their primary concern, like that of most Christian theologians, was with the deposit of faith; this they sought to interpret and apply with whatever tools seemed appropriate, which inevitably, in their endeavour, included political theory.

Professor Brian Tierney's study of the origins of late-medieval conciliar theory in earlier canon law[6] has done much to redress this imbalance. But it has led — though not in Tierney's own work — to another imbalance, namely an exaggeration of the canonist at the expense of the theological elements in conciliar theory, with the implication that their theory stemmed primarily and essentially from canon law. Since the sources of these two fields overlap so much it is, again, difficult to draw a boundary, but it must be emphasized that, at least from c.1408 onwards, their ideas owed at least as much to a study of scripture as to a study of canonist commentaries. Several leading conciliarists, notably Gerson and our two protagonists here — Segovia and Velde — made the explicit claim that they were replacing reliance on civil jurisprudence, for which they blamed the canonists in general, with reliance on scripture. And it is probable that, in the case of Gerson and the Basle thinkers at any rate, they learnt their corporation theory at least as much from contemporary institutions as they did from the lawyers themselves. In general, however, Tierney's study has undoubtedly given us a much sounder appreciation of the nature of conciliarism, by showing that it sprang in part from a Catholic tradition that was already in existence.

The most recent trend in conciliar studies, inspired by movements in ecclesiology today, seems to me to bring us closer to the spirit of the majority of the conciliarist themselves. Karl Rahner and Hans Küng take our authors quite seriously in their own field, as theologians, while both they and historians such as Paul de Vooght[7] see the movement, and in the case of Küng and de Vooght the decree *Haec Sancta* in particular, as legitimate expressions of Catholic ecclesiology. This is another case of modern scholars approaching the conciliar movement from the point of view of its 'cultural significance' for them. On account of the nature of the sources themselves, it is probably less misleading to start from an ecclesiological than from a parliamentarian angle. But the ecclesiological historian has his own confessional and personal prejudices to contend with;[8] from the historical viewpoint, any such 'approach' can only serve as a way into the material.

Having said this, I have in this study once again focussed upon the political ideas of the conciliar movement. In fact, political philosophy, dealing with the nature of power and authority in general, and ecclesiology, dealing with the Church as a unique institution based on revelation, are very often so intertwined in the conciliarists' minds that they could not be separated in exposition; this is particularly so with the two major figures dealt with here, Segovia and Velde. Where they could be separated, I have followed the course of the political argument; and the reader should be aware that there is a great deal of conciliarist argument which I have referred to only in passing. The themes of organic community and communal decision-making have, I would like to think, become central to this study because they are the central themes, as regards political philosophy, in the actual sources. In selecting such political-philosophical themes, I have been fully aware of, and tried to take account of, the conciliarists' own theological orientation. Indeed, I became so impressed by the volume and quality of the purely ecclesiological material, and by unmistakable parallels with ecclesiology today, that, while the focus of this book is upon political ideas, I have devoted a postscript to the ecclesiological heritage of the conciliar movement.

The Council of Basle arrived relatively late on the scene of political history. Johann Haller pioneered the field with his splendid collection of sources in *Concilium Basiliense,* but never wrote his projected history of the Council; his *Papsttum und Kirchenreform* stops short at 1418.[9] His insights into the Council were published in short articles; valuable partial studies were produced by his followers and have constantly been added to. Haller viewed Basle with a certain scepticism, while acknowledging that it was an important chapter in the *Vorreformation.*[10] Valois' authoritative account was largely concerned with diplomacy; his Roman Catholic ('Vatican I') perspective led him too to see Basle in rather a poor light. To my mind the best studies remain those of Pérouse and Lazarus, neither of them intended as a complete history, for which, though the material is available, we are still waiting.[11]

In intellectual history, the theorists of Basle fared no better. To be sure, Nicholas of Cusa's *De concordantia catholica* has been exhaustively studied, primarily as a work of political theory;[12] the works of the canonist Niccolo de' Tudeschi (Panormitanus) have also become well-known.[13] But these men were in fact untypical of Basle as a whole. It is partly for this reason that I have here undertaken a full study of all the Basle theorists, including lesser writers and the documents of the Council itself. From this emerges a clear picture of Basle conciliarism as a specific body of doctrine. Lastly, while Segovia is well known as a historian of the Council of Basle itself,[14] I have here undertaken for the first time, so far as I know,[15] a full treatment of his ecclesiological and political ideas.

NOTES
1. *The eighteenth Brumaire of Louis Bonaparte* in *The Marx-Engels reader,* ed. R.C. Tucker (New York, 1972), 522.
2. Gierke trans. Maitland, 49-60.
3. Figgis (1916).
4. Notably by Oakley (1962, 1964a, 1969), Rueger, Tierney (1975).
5. Cf. Black (1969), 54f.
6. Tierney (1968).
7. *KK*; Bäumer (1968), Brandmüller (1967), Fink (1965), Hürten (1963), Küng (1965), Pichler, Vooght (1960b, 1963, 1965, 1968).
8. E.g. Jedin (1965).
9. Cf. Bilderback (1966), 16ff., 25ff.
10. Cf. below, pp. 47f.
11. Below, p. 31n.1
12. Below, p. 52f.
13. Below, p. 103n.1
14. Fromherz.
15. I have been unable to consult Vera-Fajardo; cf. Black (1970a), 22-34, 44-50.

The following distinctions within conciliar thought, which emerge during the book, may be mentioned at the outset for the sake of clarity. First, there were (*i*) electoral conciliarism, according to which the council represents the Church because it is in some way elected; (*ii*) episcopal conciliarism, according to which it represents the Church because it comprises the bishops; (*iii*) collectivist conciliarism, according to which it does so because it is a microcosm of the whole Church as a unified, organic entity. Second, there were (*a*) moderate conciliar theory which sees the council as an occasional legislature and emergency superior of the pope; (*b*) radical conciliar theory which sees the council as the normal, regular juridical sovereign in the Church. There were, naturally, many gradations and mixtures of these categories. By 'Basle conciliarism' I mean a combination of (*iii*) with (*b*) – whether my evidence sustains this definition is for the reader to judge. (I have adopted this classification, in preference to others, as particularly illuminating for the Basle material. Franzen's distinction between 'conciliars' and 'conciliarists' is similar to my distinction between (a) and (b)).

CHAPTER 1

INTELLECTUAL AND HISTORICAL BACKGROUND

The complex historical roots of the conciliar movement may be considered under the headings of theology, canon law, political theory and historical circumstance. In the spheres of theology and canon law, conciliarism was not the progeny of medieval ecclesiastical culture alone. It derived from the early Church the idea of synodal decision-making in the areas of doctrine and discipline. After Nicaea this became one normal method of settling disputes within the universal Church as well as within local or regional churches.[1] Side by side with this there developed the ecclesiastical authority of bishops, and, still more important, the authority of the great metropolitan sees, above all of Rome. The participation or subsequent assent of these was considered necessary for a council to qualify as a true general or ecumenical council. In the western Church, the view that the Roman see held a universal primacy of jurisdiction gained ground from early times, attaining classic expression in Leo I's claim to 'fulness of power'.[2] While many in the east ascribed the power to convoke councils to the emperor[3] — a claim to be revived in the west during the conciliar period — and asserted the approximately equal authority of all the major patriarchs,[4] the standard medieval doctrine in the west was that the pope convoked and presided over a general council, as well as ratifying its decrees.[5] But a general council was regarded on all sides as the proper forum for decision-making in the key area of doctrine; and it was this tradition of the 'legislative' and doctrinal supremacy of general councils that later clashed with the juridical claims of the Roman see. Provincial synods, moreover, and other local church councils met fairly frequently during the early and high Middle Ages in some parts of Europe.[6]

The Gregorian reform movement of the late-eleventh and early-twelfth centuries led to a further elaboration of the doctrine of papal supremacy and a more thorough implementation of it in practice. Western bishops were made more dependent on Rome; Latin canon law, employing the model of Roman-imperial law, was structured upon the principle of the monarchical sovereignty of the pope. Above all, the Gregorian period witnessed an increased insistence upon the subordination of secular to ecclesiastical power.[7] Nevertheless, until the early fourteenth century Latin general councils met relatively frequently and worked on the whole in harmony with the papacy. The canonists of the high Middle Ages did not produce an unambiguous theory of papal and conciliar authority; and their reservations and nuances made conciliarism legally tenable. In general, Gratian, the Decretists and, still more, the Decretalists resolved disputed questions of ecclesiastical right in favour of Rome, and emphasized both the supremacy of ecclesiastical over secular power and the supremacy of the pope or Roman see over all other ecclesiastical authorities.[8] But there were exceptions. For example, the canon *Si papa* (*Dist.* 40, c.6), which stated that the pope 'is to be judged by no-one, unless he is found to be deviant from the faith', forced them to consider the possibility of doctrinal error on the part of the pope. In such a case, according to one school of thought initiated by Huguccio, he automatically ceased to be pope, and cardinals or council could put matters right without overriding a true pope.[9] According to another school of thought initiated by Alanus, a heretical pope was actually to be judged as such by cardinals or council:[10] it was primarily this interpretation that gave conciliarism its foothold in canon law.

Tierney's thesis, that conciliarists drew extensively on some canonists' views of the correct relationship between head and members in lesser ecclesiastical corporations, has rightly won universal acceptance. These canonists held that (in Tierney's words) 'authority in a corporation was not concentrated in the head alone but diffused among the various members, that the power of jurisdiction, unlike the power of order, was conferred on a prelate by human delegation in the act of election'.[11] This corporational model, however, was derived by the fifteenth-century conciliarists as much from contemporary *practice* as from the canonist writings.[12] They also cited, in this connection, the synodal decision-making practices of many religious orders (some of which held a regular 'general assembly (*congregatio generalis*)'[13] — one of the terms used for a general council), and also the example of confraternities.[14] The universities themselves, through which most future church leaders passed, were an outstanding instance of corporational practices. At Paris, on which many other universities were modelled, decisions were taken by the teaching body by faculties and in a 'general assembly'; the *rector* was accountable and elected for short terms with few independent powers.[15] The general principle of such collegiate institutions was that all members legislated and elected officials saw to the execution of the rules. One may see here a confluence of the Christian notion of *koinonia*[16] (often expressed as 'the common life (*vita communis*)'), the Germanic *Gemeinschaft*[17] and the Roman *collegium*.[18] One must also note, à propos Tierney's thesis, that several leading conciliarists, including Gerson and our two protagonists here — Velde and Segovia — explicitly claimed that they were replacing reliance on civil jurisprudence, for which they blamed the canonists in general, with a return to scripture.[19]

Representative assemblies and constitutionalist practices in secular states provided a further model and precedent for the conciliarist programme. The idea that universal consent was necessary to validate legislative acts and to raise taxes, and that an assembly of notables and elected commoners embodied the consent of the whole community, so that it could at least share power with the prince, had taken firm root in political culture in many parts of Europe.[20] Just as papalists invoked the monarchical model of imperial Rome and, increasingly, of some contemporary states, so conciliarists appealed to parliamentarian and constitutionalist analogies in the secular sphere. But again a word of caution is needed.[21] While it was often held that the same norms held good for all organizations, whether secular or ecclesiastical, some conciliarists, notably Gerson and Segovia, rejected this analogy: just as they subjected canon law to scripture, so they affirmed that the Church's constitution, being based on revelation, was *sui generis.*[22]

An element in the general political culture which considerably affected conciliar thought was, once again, corporation lore, which had permeated some secular as well as ecclesiastical institutions. The prime example here was those cities, particularly German cities with a 'guild regime (*Zunftregierung*)' and occasionally some Italian cities, in which the citizens' assembly legislated and elected its magistrates on an accountable basis.[23] Thus Bartolus, who mentioned such constitutions with some approval, was cited alongside the canonist corporation theorists.[24] This civic-republican element became particularly important in the later phase of Basle conciliarism.[25]

The middle and later decades of the fourteenth century saw an increase in the number of guild-governed towns, the foundation of many new universities, and a multiplication of religious associations for both laymen and clerics: the last two phenomena continued well into the fifteenth century. The great schism coincided exactly with the rising of the *Ciompi* in Florence (1378). The Brethren of the Common Life and the Windesheim canons, two major reform-movements of the fourteenth century, both

11

espoused the collegiate ideal.[26] Thus conciliarism could appeal to the organizational instincts of many people in Europe, particularly in the towns of central Europe. Much as in a later age civic-republican principles challenged the monarchical conception of the large state, this communal undercurrent surfaced in the late-medieval church polity as a direct challenge to the monarchical *mores* of the papacy.

Theologians and publicists of the late-thirteenth and early-fourteenth centuries used materials provided by the canonists to construct more coherent and metaphysical theories of the church polity.[27] Depending on their opinions, they either built up theories of unlimited papal sovereignty or imposed more radical limits on papal power. Among those who pursued the latter course, Henry of Ghent (d.1293) and William Durandus the Younger (d.1330) insisted on the essential independence of the bishops, and ascribed final authority to the council *qua* assembly of bishops. Durandus anticipated the decree *Frequens* (1417) by advocating a constitutional law enjoining frequent councils to be held at regular intervals.[28] Marsiglio of Padua, in his *Defender of the Peace* (1324), argued that, just as the 'corporation of citizens (*universitas civium*)' was sovereign in the political sphere, so the 'corporation of faithful (*universitas fidelium*)' was sovereign in religious matters. He applied his famous model of civil authority to the Church.[29] Under the leadership of the secular rulers, the corporation of the faithful was to exercise juridical sovereignty in church matters: in the words of Gewirth, it must 'control excommunication, elect the priesthood to its posts, define articles of faith through the general council, elect the council, make binding all its decisions, and elect the pope'.[30] To prove this, he used collectivist arguments which would surface again during Constance and, still more, Basle: the whole is greater than the part, the collective wisdom and virtue of the many is superior to that of the expert few; Christ would never allow the 'greater part' of the faithful to err.[31] The council itself played a smaller part in Marsiglio's scheme than in that of later conciliarists; the sovereignty of the Church as a whole, including laity as much as clergy, was held in purer form and more systematically worked out by Marsiglio than by any later conciliarists.

The influence of Marsiglio on conciliarism is easily exaggerated.[32] Later conciliarists used him, alongside other sources, eclectically; none of them espoused his programme as a whole. In particular, they played down the role of the laity and the secular powers. But the Basle conciliarists surely had Marsiglio at the back of their minds when they said that the council was related to the pope as sovereign legislature to accountable executive, and that the pope could be *suspended* from his executive functions on suspicion of guilt, pending his trial;[33] and when they derived the council's authority from its representation of the Church as a whole rather than from the participation of the bishops.

William of Ockham (d.1349),[34] though not himself a conciliarist,[35] provided later conciliar theorists with important arguments, many of which he himself had taken from the canonists.[36] His definition of a council, with its suggestion that it include delegates from all ranks in the Church, was repeated by Gelnhausen and other conciliarists of the schism period: 'A general council is the assembly . . . of many or several persons, representing or acting on behalf of the various ranks, orders and sexes, duly summoned to attend or send proctors; and of persons of greater weight and ability from the whole of Christendom, to work for the good of the universal Church'.[37] He worked out in great detail the arguments in favour of the right of the ordinary faithful to convoke an emergency council without papal consent.[38] He suggested a two-tier method of electing the council: first, parishes or communities would elect an episcopal council or regional parliament; this would then send delegates to the general council.[39] The second stage was sometimes partially adopted in the early fifteenth century, when some states held national synods of clergy to work out a national policy: if it was decided to support a given council, then the senior clergy of the land would attend, in part as national representatives.[40]

But, unlike the mainstream conciliarists, Ockham denied that the council as such had of itself supreme legislative authority or fulness of jurisdictional power. These, together with doctrinal inerrancy, he reserved to the whole body of the faithful. Conciliar acts were only valid if subsequently endorsed by all the faithful.[41] For, just as Rousseau would deny that the general will could ever be represented, so Ockham denied that individual believers could alienate their doctrinal decision-making powers to a representative council.[42] He was thoroughly scornful of Marsiglio's majoritarian and collectivist arguments.[43] As Lagarde says, the council has for Ockham only 'an episodic and secondary role' and 'it is in vain that one would look (to him) for a coherent theory of the rights of a council'.[44]

The conciliar movement was strengthened and influenced by general historical trends of the period. Not only was it a reaction by some clergy against papal centralization. It also played into the hands of those who were seeking to establish the autonomy of the secular state in ecclesiastical matters, in particular of the French monarchy and the German princes.[45] Among the early theorists, John of Paris and Marsiglio combined conciliar ideas with theories of national and secular autonomy.[46] Secular rulers used the schisms of 1378-1417 and of 1439-49 to their advantage.[47] The conciliar period dealt a fatal blow to any surviving claims on the part of the papacy that it could oversee the norms or direct the policies of European states. The early-fifteenth century councils were, *de facto,* assemblies of secular as well as ecclesiastical leaders, and the princes used them as a forum for negotiation between themselves, or with a common enemy (such as the Hussites). Finally, the diplomacy engendered by the complex manoeuvres to end the schisms helped to develop channels whereby international relations could be conducted.[48]

The need for church reform added enormous impetus to the conciliar movement. Papal centralization, with its scope for nepotism, dispensations from canon law, and intervention in secular politics by means of appointments to benefices, was coming to be widely regarded as a major abuse in itself. Whereas previously reformers had looked to the papacy, and later would look to kings, as the instruments of reform, in the late Middle Ages they looked to a general council.

NOTES

1. *LTK* vi,525f.; *SM* ii, 8ff. A full study of the history of conciliar thought, which would mark out continuity and change between the early Christian writers, the medieval period and more recent developments, is urgently needed.
2. Ullmann (1965), 7-12.
3. Pelikan, ii, 168.
4. Pelikan, ii, 23, 162-5; *LTK* viii, 172ff.
5. *HbK* iii part 2, 206-14; Le Bras, 333ff.; Ullmann (1965), 182, 185, 362-3; Tierney (1968), 50, 54; cf. Héfèle-Leclerq v, 1316ff.
6. *SM* ii, 12-16; Héfèle-Leclerq iv-v; Fliche, 328, 391ff., 396, 406, 417, 421, 423.
7. Ullmann (1949); Ullmann (1965), 262ff., 413ff.; Fliche, 55ff., 179ff.
8. Buisson, 74ff., 131ff.; Tierney (1968), 28-9; Wilks (1963), 151-2.
9. Tierney (1968), 62-3; Tierney (1972), 50.
10. Tierney (1968), 58; Tierney (1972), 52.
11. Tierney (1968), 165, and also 106ff., 157ff.; cf. Gierke, *DGR* trans. Maitland 64.
12. Below, pp.55 at n. 7, 165f.
13. Le Bras, 486-9; Marongiu, 37-41.
14. Below, p.20 at n. 13. Cf. DLO 666-93.
15. Rashdall, i, 184ff., 299ff., 313ff., 402.; Cobban, 75ff.
16. The New Testament word implying a strongly-felt bond of spiritual communion.
17. 'Fellowship' again, implying strong mutual bonds, for instance of family or friends; a relationship in which participants feel, in Tonnies' phrase, 'essentially united' (below, p.161 n. 1); similar to Gierke's *Genossenschaft,* which describes the same relationship in a wider political context (in Maitland's words, 'Our German Fellowship is . . . a living organism . . . Itself can will, itself can act': introd. to his transl. of Gierke, p.xxvi).
18. Cf. Schnörr v. Carolsfeld; Gierke, *DGR* trans. Maitland, 37ff.
19. Below, pp.22 at n. 32, 61f., 128f.
20. Marongiu, 61-105; Cam et al.; Legarde (1958); Post, 163ff.; Gierke, *DGR* trans. Maitland, 61-7; Tierney (1968), 49.
21. As against, for example, Figgis, 56; Oakley (1969b), 368-70; cf. below, p.195ff.
22. Below, pp.50, 129, 151.
23. M. Weber (1958), 157-96; Clarke, 86ff.; Rörig, 154ff.; Petit-Dutaillis, 223-4, 313; Waley, 56ff.
24. Below, pp.99f., 102f., 158f.; cf. Woolf; Ullmann (1962), Ullmann (1966), 28ff.

25. Below, pp. 88f., 99-103, 172-5.
26. *DLO* 921-31; Lagarde (1937); Feine, 344ff.
27. Grabmann; Wilks (1963), 30-63, 254-87, 354-407; Tierney (1972), 58ff., 131ff.
28. Tierney (1972), 85, 155-7, 195; cf. below, p. 18.
29. Gewirth (1951); Quillet; Rubinstein. See esp. *Defensor pacis*, I. iv-vii, x-xiii; II. iv-xi. Cf. Ullmann (1966), 269ff., 288.
30. Gewirth (1951), i, 263, and 280-1; *Defensor pacis*, II, xv.4 and xxii.4-10.
31. *Defensor pacis*, I. xii.5 and xiii.4; II. xix-xx, esp. xx.4.
32. For example, by Gewirth (1951), i, 286.
33. Below, p. 51; on suspension of the civil *pars principans: Defensor pacis* I.xviii.3.
34. Lagarde (1963) v, 30-203; Scholz (1952); Morrall (1961); Tierney (1972), 205ff.; McGrade, esp. 48ff.
35. Lagarde (1960); Andres Hernansanz; McGrade, 19n., 30.
36. Tierney (1954), esp. p.68.
37. *Dialogus*, 603; cf. Gelnhausen, *Epistola concordiae*, 1217.
38. *Dialogus*, 603; Lagarde (1963), v, 60.
39. *Dialogus*, 603.
40. *DLO* 83, 127, 206, 233-5.
41. *Dialogus*, 830-1; Lagarde (1963), v, 73.
42. Lagarde (1963), v, 73.; cf. Rousseau, *Du contrat social*, iii, c.15.
43. Lagarde (1963), v, 57-8, 73, 315ff.
44. Lagarde (1963), v, 53, 82-3.
45. Arquillière (1911a, 1911b); Scholz (1903, 1911-14); Martin (1937); Tierney (1968), 77-9, 157ff.; McNeil (1938), 275-7; Wilks (1963), 517.
46. Leclerq; Ullmann (1966), 263-79.
47. Below, pp. 45-7.
48. Jacob (1963), 46-7; Mattingley, 67ff., 84ff.

The Great Schism and the Council of Constance

The great schism of 1378[1] thrust all these questions into the arena of European power politics. It produced an immediate flood of conciliarist writings, mainly from the university of Paris; which suggests that conciliarist ideas were already prevalent there. The influence of Marsiglio and still more of Ockham was now at its height. The canonist Conrad of Gelnhausen[2] argued that a council was superior to the pope and cardinals because it was less likely to err in faith.[3] He recommended that it be convoked by the French king, the emperor and other Christian princes.[4] The theologian Henry Langenstein[5] followed Gelnhausen on these points, adding that a council could not itself err in faith;[6] and he followed Ockham in suggesting that delegates be appointed by national synods.[7] In fact, both these authors used Ockham extensively,[8] as did Pierre d'Ailly in his conciliarist writings of this period.[9] Langenstein also used Marsiglio, though he adapted his ideas to fit in with a more clerical and episcopalist version of conciliar supremacy. The power of electing the pope — which was the starting-point for any discussion of the schism — belongs, he said, in a general way to the whole Church, but 'resides primarily with the corporation of faithful

15

bishops (*universitatem episcoporum fidelium*)'.[10] Therefore it is they who in the first instance have the right and duty to deal with a disputed election.[11] But, if they fail in their duty, the power of papal election reverts 'to the rest of the faithful', and 'the corporation of priests (*universitas sacerdotum*) would perhaps, with the consent of the people, elect one of their number (to have power) over all the faithful'.[12]

The attempt to resolve the schism by immediately calling a general council failed, as the two rival lines of popes – the Roman or Urbanist and the Avignonese or Clementine – established themselves.[13] In 1383 the French king, who supported the Clementine line, ordered Paris university to stop advocating a council; many conciliarist thinkers who were not of French birth moved elsewhere, thus contributing no doubt to the spread of conciliar doctrine. From 1398 to 1403 French court policy changed, in an attempt to force the rival popes to resign by a withdrawal of allegiance. During these years the French Church was governed by a national-conciliar regime; all prelates were to be elected by their chapters, and appeals were to terminate in a provincial synod. In practice, however, the king intervened in elections and appropriated church taxes.[14] All this was a *Vorspiel* for the Basle period. The idea of decentralization, proclaimed in the programme of 'Gallican liberties' (1406), was taking root; but in practice it played into the hands of the secular power.[15]

In 1409 the council of Pisa, convoked by some cardinals of each allegiance, vainly deposed the rivals and elected a new pope: the result was that there were now three instead of two claimants.[16] The following year Dietrich of Niem, a curial official, published a remarkable work.[17] Niem argued for conciliar sovereignty by, *inter alia*, distinguishing between 'the catholic Church', which consisted of all Christians (Greeks, Latins, barbarians, men and women, rich and poor), and 'the apostolic Church', which consisted of pope, cardinals, bishops, clergy. The catholic is related to the apostolic Church as genus to species, as juridical-legislative superior to executive organ; the apostolic derives its power from the catholic Church. 'The power of binding and loosing is entrusted to the (catholic) Church alone'; the apostolic church is 'as it were the instrument and operator of the keys of the universal Church and the executor (*executiva*) of its powers of binding and loosing'.[18] The council represents the catholic Church and is therefore superior to the pope. It alone can make and change laws.[19] Niem gave the power of convoking a council first to the emperor, then to the bishops, and only in the last resort to the cardinals, thus reversing the traditional canonist prescription for emergency convocation.[20] The emperor and other kings have the authority to promote, by means of a council, the 'public reformation' of the Church.[21] Niem stands in the somewhat 'anticlerical' tradition of German imperialism, and is the closest follower of Marsiglio in this period.[22] Velde was to adopt the distinction between the catholic and apostolic Church, but used it in a different sense.[23] Segovia had read Niem and used some of his arguments selectively;[24] but neither of these Basilians was directly influenced by Marsiglio, for both saw the Church in exclusively clerical terms.

The schism was finally resolved at the council of Constance (1414-18).[25] But this in turn gave rise to fresh aspirations for conciliar supremacy, which had been more clearly legitimized by the decrees *Haec Sancta* (1415) and *Frequens* (1417), and for reform, which that council itself failed to satisfy. The new, virtually undisputed pope, Martin V (1417-31), did his best to ignore the conciliar programme; this made almost inevitable a further, decisive conflict, which took place at Basle. Constance and Basle cannot really be considered in separation from each other; a survey of certain aspects of Constance and, more particularly, of its leading theorists is necessary, in order to understand Basle's point of departure.

First, Constance deposed two contenders for the papacy, and a third resigned; it arranged for the election of the new pope by a partly novel procedure decreed by the council itself. These facts themselves (together with the earlier deposition of two popes at Pisa) were of decisive importance, both psychologically and as precedents. Secondly, there were the two above-mentioned decrees. *Haec Sancta* declared that: 'This holy synod . . . having been legitimately assembled in the Holy Spirit, making up a general council and representing the catholic Church, has power immediately from Christ, which everyone of whatever standing or office, even if he is of papal standing, is bound to obey in matters pertaining to faith, the eradication of the said schism and the reformation of the said Church in head and members. Next, it declares that whoever of whatever position, standing or office, even if he is of papal standing, contumaciously refuses to obey the commands, statutes or ordinances or precepts of this holy synod or of any other legitimately assembled general council, which it has enacted or shall enact on the above-mentioned (topics) and matters pertaining thereto, unless he changes his mind, should be subject to suitable penance and duly punished, recourse being had to other legal means (*alia iuris subsidia*) if necessary'.[26]

The decree was a compromise:[27] both its authority and its meaning were debated during the Basle controversy and are being debated again today. Franzen and many others argue that it was intended as an *ad hoc* pronouncement, and that it was only the conciliarists, particularly Gerson and the Paris delegation, who saw it as a dogmatic definition of conciliar superiority.[28] (True, it was intended to give further credibility to the course of action which the council was about to undertake.) De

Vooght and Küng argue that it was intended as a dogmatic definition.[29] Tierney takes the intermediate view that it was intended as a binding constitutional statement, not a merely *ad hoc* one, but not as an article of faith, and that therefore, like *Frequens*, it was not 'irreformable'.[30] The Basle conciliarists generally held that it was a dogmatic definition *de fide*.[31]

By the same token that it had been so widely recognized, the council of Constance included men who conceived its role and function in very different ways. Some saw it solely as the means for ending the schism; the fact that the Urbanist pope resigned in 1415 meant that the council could be regarded as having scarcely infringed the principle of papal supremacy; for them, its proceedings were essentially emergency measures. Others saw it as a means not only of restoring unity but also of removing the causes of schism, that is reforming the Church centrally as well as locally. Some saw it as a means of redressing the imbalance in the Church's constitution brought about by excessive centralization. Conflicts within the council after the three claimants had been disposed of reflected these differences: some urged that the council itself should carry out reforms prior to electing a new pope who might obstruct them, others urged that a new pope must first be elected. The reformers were hampered by international conflicts of opinion; of their leaders, bishop Hallum of Salisbury died in 1417, and Gerson lost face in the dispute over tyrannicide. Their only major success was the passing of the decree *Frequens* (9 October 1417), which stipulated that councils should in future meet at regular, specified intervals, and at places determined by the preceding council, 'so that with this continuity a council will always either be in session or it will be awaited at the end of a certain current period'.[32] This was surely the most important step ever taken to impose a limit on papal power; in effect, it would make the Church a strictly constitutional monarchy. Few reforms were passed by the council as a whole. A series of concordats agreed between Martin V and the nations separately embodied some reform measures, but these had little effect; the papacy's subsequent policy of 'divide and rule' amply justified the fears of the reformers.

NOTES

1. *DLO* 3-45 *HbK* iii part 2, 490-516; Ullmann (1972a); Valois (1896); Prerovsky; Bliemetzrieder (1909); Fink (1962).
2. Kneer; Wenck; Cameron, 17-18, 21-39; Martin (1939), 59-65.
3. *Epistola concordiae*, 1210, 1214.
4. Cameron, 17.
5. Martin (1939), 66ff.; Ullmann (1972a), 181ff.; Cameron, 30ff.; *DLO* 493n.
6. *Consilium pacis*, Dupin, ii, 824.
7. Cameron, 33; above, p.13.
8. Cameron, 15, 17, 22, 33, 87; Martin (1939), 68; Ullmann (1972a), 181n.
9. Roberts; Oakley (1964a), 11-12, 199-203, 243.

10. *Consilium pacis, MOCC* ii, 32-5.
11. *Consilium pacis, MOCC* ii, 35.
12. *Consilium pacis, MOCC* ii, 35.
13. *DLO* 45-7; Fink (1962); Franzen in *KK* 3-35; Cameron, 14, 17-18, 26-7, 63-70; Rashdall, i, 571ff.
14. *DLO* 91ff.; Haller (1903), 226-68.
15. *DLO* 329-43; Haller (1903), 278-375.
16. *DLO* 145-54.
17. 'De modis uniendi ac reformandi ecclesiam in concilio generali'. Cf. Heimpel (1929); Jacob (1963), 37-8.
18. *De modis*, 70-2.
19. *De modis*, 87-8.
20. *De modis*, 85ff., 97-114.
21. *De modis*, 115ff., 131-2.
22. Sigmund (1962b); Camerson, 97-9, 103, 105, 111.
23. Below, p. 65.
24. Below, pp. 136, n. 33, 183n. 19, n. 25.
25. *LTK* vi, 501-3; *HbK* iii part 2, 545-72; *DLO* 165-215; *KK*; Loomis; Franzen (1965); Fink (1965); Crowder, 7-28.; Stuhr.
26. Mansi, xxvii, 590.
27. Franzen in *KK*, 98-104.
28. Franzen in *KK* 103ff.; H. Zimmermann in *KK*, 113-37; Riedlinger in *KK*, 214-40; Brandmüller (1967), Bäumer (1968), Gill (1964); Hürten (1963); Pichler.
29. Vooght (1960) and (1963); Küng (1965).
30. Tierney (1969).
31. Below, pp. 50f; Engels.
32. Mansi xxvii, 1159; *DLO* 198.

Gerson, d'Ailly, Zabarella

The conciliar theory of the men who inspired and led the conciliar movement in its one undoubted success, the reunification of the papacy at Constance, diverged in important respects from earlier conciliarism, and established most of the patterns of thought which the Basle thinkers would adopt and elaborate. Among them the most outstanding were cardinal Francesco Zabarella (1360-1417), the foremost canonist of his day,[1] cardinal Pierre d'Ailly (1350-1420), who started as a radical conciliarist at Paris, then supported the Clementine papacy, and finally threw in his lot with the Pisan project and espoused a decidedly moderate version of conciliar theory;[2] and, greatest of all, Jean Gerson (d.1429), Netherlander, eclectic philosopher, moral and mystical theologian, an ecclesiastic who combined principle with statesmanship.[3] As chancellor of Paris university, Gerson exercised an enormous intellectual and moral influence on his contemporaries and on the next generation.

These men differed both from their predecessors and from their successors, in that they effectively ascribed authority neither to the faithful at large nor to the council *per se,* but to the council as comprising the episcopate, or at least the senior ecclesiastical elements in the Church.

19

To be sure, they ascribe sovereignty to the 'corporation of the faithful' (Zabarella),[4] to the 'mystical body of Christ' (d'Ailly[5] and Gerson[6]), but primarily, it would appear, for the purpose of ensuring the convocation of a council.[7] The authority ascribed to the Church by d'Ailly and Gerson is the right to ensure its own unity by means of conciliar self-assembly. D'Ailly based this 'not only on the authority of Christ but also on the common law of nature (*communi iure naturali*)', according to which any animate being, if threatened with dismemberment, 'naturally assembles (*congregat*) all its members'. Similarly, this right belongs to 'any civil body or civil community or rightly ordered polity'.[8] But for the actual *exercise* of legislative or judicial authority, they make a practical equation between Church and council. Gerson makes this quite clear: the bishops, who are collectively 'incapable of deviation (*inobliquabilis*)' from faith and unity, comprise 'the assembled church'.[9]

Zabarella's application of canonist corporation theory to the Church as a whole would seem to have the same meaning: it is in the council that the Church exercises its powers 'as a corporation'. The only difference is that Zabarella the canonist will allow emergency convoking power to the emperor,[10] while Gerson the theologian reserves this for the bishops.[11] Gerson too drew analogies with contemporary corporational or communal practice: any corporation has the right of self-assembly and of controlling its ruler, 'as it was stated for chapter and dean, university and rector in their own way[12] . . . Any free association (*congregatio*), not subject to tyranny, has this right (*facultatem*) of assembling itself. This is clear in confraternities and many other charitable bodies (*conventionibus caritativis*)'.[13] Now, in these analogous cases the assembly literally contained all the members; and the emerging implication is that the council contains all members of the Church 'virtually'.[14]

The theory of the sovereignty of the Church, then, was used primarily to justify conciliar convocation without papal consent. To this end it was often employed in conjunction with the concept of equity (*epieikeia* extra-legal fairness),[15] which could be derived from the Gospels as well as from Aristotle. In both cases, the point was that positive law could be set aside, in emergency, in the community's interests. D'Ailly says that positive law cannot affect the right of self-preservation inherent in the Church, which is based on natural and divine law.[16] Niem concludes from the ancient-Roman adage 'let the people's safety be the supreme law' that 'if laws and rights are created for the sake of the republic, the republic itself is greater than any rights (*iura*)'.[17] Gerson ascribed the dispensation of equity to the Church itself: 'the Church will be the impartial, just and sharp dispenser of equity'.[18]

The council is not to be elected (as Marsiglio had said and others had hinted), nor are lesser clerics to be given an equal vote (as the Basileans were to argue). The council 'represents the Church' in a symbolic, quasi-mystical, 'absorptive' (Gierke) or indeed 'substitutive' (Trotsky) sense. As an anonymous writer at Constance put it: 'The pope, cardinals and other prelates are in power (*in virtute*) equivalent to the whole clergy and represent in effect (*in effectu*) the whole ecclesiastical polity . . . In what concerns faith and in related matters, they all collectively represent the whole corporation of faithful'.[19]

In order to make this point, Gerson drew a distinction between 'the Church considered dispersedly (*sparsim considerata*)' and 'its assembly and unification (*congregatio sua et unitio*) which takes place in a general council'. In the former sense, he says, the Church does not have the power mentioned in *Haec Sancta* 'except in a certain material or potential aspect (*nisi in quodam materiali seu potentiali*)'. On the other hand, in the latter sense, 'the Church's assembly and unification which takes place in a general council gives it as it were form (*dat quasi formam*), just as one finds in other communities. And the aforesaid ecclesiastical power of jurisdiction is founded on this unity or union (*unitate vel unione*); as the elevated Augustine seems to have noted when he said that the keys of the Church are given "to a unity (*unitati*)"'.[20]

The juristic version of Gerson's distinction, namely the distinction between the powers, rights and obligations or 'all as individuals (*omnes ut singuli*)' and those of 'all as a whole *(omnes et universi* or *ut universitas)*'[21] was used at Constance as a means of explaining away the texts on papal supremacy and papal immunity from judgment. An anonymous author said that 'the power of the pope was given to him by God . . . as regards the power of jurisdiction only, and also as regards individuals not the whole body (*quoad singulos, non quoad universos*)'.[22] Texts referring to the pope's immunity were intended to apply only to the Church at large, whether 'dispersim' or coniunctim', but not to the Church 'legitimately assembled' in a general council.[23]

The rejection of the theory that the Church's unity depended on the one pope (a theory rendered absurd by the circumstances) led gradually to the conception of the Church as a metaphysical whole rather than as a collection of individuals. 'Whenever any one thing is made up by an aggregation of many finite things or of many things that do not depend for their being and conservation on any one part of that aggregate, then indeed . . . power resides in the whole insofar as it is one (*potestas inest toti inquantum est unum*)'.[24] Such a notion could easily be derived from the organic analogy, and was implicit in Gerson's application of the matter-form distinction to the Church. This holistic conception of the Church, together with the collective-dispersed distinction,[25] was to gain enormous currency during Basle. But then it was to be combined with the notion of the council as an association of equals who derived their power not from their individual status but from their corporate membership of the council. This 'communal' notion of the council was only rarely voiced at Constance.[26]

For Gerson and his colleagues, on the other hand, the council has authority not only because it 'represents the church' but also because it comprises those who possess authority on their own account — though most especially when assembled together — namely (for Gerson) bishops, or (for Zabarella) 'prelates'.[27] Gerson understands ecclesiastical authority in an entirely traditional way, as located in the episcopate who, also in accordance with ancient tradition, make up the council.[28] (Segovia, after adopting the communal view of the council for some twenty years, eventually followed Gerson on this point.)[29] For both of these reasons, the council derives its authority directly from Christ: 'The assembled Church, standing in the place of the universal Church, is unswervable not only because it represents (*vices gerens*) the universal Church, but because it has the special privilege from Christ' (Gerson).[30] This was exactly in line with *Haec Sancta:* a council 'representing the catholic Church . . . holds power immediately from Christ'.[31] This may be related to Gerson's insistence that the disposition of Church authority should be based on theology rather than on canon law.[32] Ullmann's view that the conciliarists applied 'the ascending theme of government' to the Church,[33] while true of some earlier conciliarists, is not strictly true of Gerson and most of the Constance school; they combined ascending with descending claims (as did later advocates of the divine right of the people).

The conciliarism of Gerson, Zabarella and the later d'Ailly was episcopal rather than electoral with a mild admixture of ecclesial collectivism. When Zabarella said that 'the power itself is in the association itself as in its foundation',[34] when d'Ailly and Gerson said that the mystical body of Christ could ensure its own preservation in unity, they were sometimes justifying emergency means for conciliar convocation, sometimes speaking metaphorically. In equating Church and council they were continuing a canonist[35] and also a patristic tradition. The argument from popular or ecclesial sovereignty, then, was used by them primarily, and almost exclusively, as a conceptual basis for conciliar supremacy.

On the *scope* of conciliar authority, there was a crucial difference between the later d'Ailly and Gerson. They were both agreed, as were many at the time, that a council has authority to judge and depose a heretical or schismatic pope; but they were divided over whether it had *juridical* authority over the pope in matters of reform. As we have seen, the most crucial issue facing Constance in 1416-17 was whether first to elect the new pope or first to enact reform legislation.[36] If reforms were enacted first, the new pope might be held bound to implement them, in view of the wording of *Haec Sancta*. D'Ailly followed the cardinals in advocating an immediate election; Gerson was the chief inspiration of the reform party.[37] This partisan difference is closely related to the different views on the distribution of jurisdictional power which we find in d'Ailly's *Treatise on ecclesiastical power* (October 1416)[38] and in Gerson's *On ecclesiastical power* (February 1417).[39]

Superficially, their two statements look alike. They both (like John of Paris) ascribed to the Church the mixed form of government, the pope comprising the monarchical element, the cardinals the aristocratic, the council the 'timocratic' or 'political'.[40] They both used philosophical distinctions to explain the distribution of power between pope, Church and council. D'Ailly said that 'fulness of jurisdiction properly speaking resides solely in the Roman pontiff'. Just as 'virtue is in the soul or an accident is in the substance subjectively (*subiective*)', so too fulness of power is in the pope 'as in the subject receiving it and exercising it ministerially (*ministerialiter exercente*)'.[41] Gerson said that 'ecclesiastical power in its fulness is formally and subjectively (*formaliter et subiective*) in the Roman pontiff alone'.[42] D'Ailly ascribed fulness of power to the Church 'figuratively and . . . ambiguously (*tropice . . . equivoce*) . . . as in its object (*obiecto*), as an effect is said to be in its cause . . . as in the object that finally and causally contains it'. To the council he ascribed fulness of power 'as in a replica (*exemplo*), as a thing perceived is said to be "in the mirror" or a doctrine "in a book" . . . *representative*'; it is in the council 'as in an *exemplum* that represents it and canonically directs it (*regulariter dirigente*)'.[43] Gerson ascribed fulness of power to the Church and council 'materially or relatively (*respective*) . . . as regards its exercise or execution . . . its application to this or that person, and the regulation of its use, if perchance it is found to have been abused'.[44] The Church may 'apply' ecclesiastical power to one or another person 'through itself or through a general council'; the Church or council may 'regulate its use'.[45]

There are important differences between the positions outlined here. It is striking how little power d'Ailly really gives to Church or council in this passage. He gives them the role of 'canonically directing' the fulness of power: but what actual relationship between pope and council does this imply? Does it mean 'lays down moral guidelines', 'makes recommendations', or does it mean 'issues binding decrees' as to how papal power is to be used? I suspect that d'Ailly meant the former. In any case, he makes no mention of the council *exercising* fulness of power: that function is allotted to the papacy. Gerson, on the other hand, says that fulness of power belongs to the Church or council 'as regards its exercise or execution'. He also repeats d'Ailly's view on the council's 'regulatory' role, but adds the significant phrase that it may 'regulate *the use*' of fulness of power. All this suggests that the council's reforming power is mandatory rather than merely directive: Gerson had said earlier that a council is infallible in declaring not only truths of faith but also 'truths necessary or useful for the government of the Church'.[46] Zabarella also made his position clear on the council's right to issue binding rules on the use of papal power: 'I have often said that it is necessary that laws should be made in a general council that regulate the power of the pope in such a way that the power of other prelates is not drained away (*non absorberetur*)'.[47]

Further, Gerson lays more emphasis on the council's right to 'apply' ecclesiastical power to individuals, that is to decide who holds office, including the papal office. This was in part related to the current conflict at Constance over whether the cardinals or the council should elect the new pope; again, d'Ailly was siding with the cardinals, Gerson with the more conciliarist party.[48] It was also a clear statement of general principle on the council's power to elect and depose popes; in 1418 Gerson would argue that a heretical pope could not properly be considered deposed by the mere fact of his heresy, which would leave the matter open to subjective interpretation of a Wycliffite kind, but that for his judgment 'a human enactment is required'.[49]

We may say that by 1416 d'Ailly's position was virtually indistinguishable from that of Teutonicus and other Decretists who had given a council power to judge a heretical or schismatic pope.[50] Apart from that, the council for d'Ailly has become an advisory body. (He had been noticeably absent when *Haec Sancta* was promulgated.) It has no regular, normal jurisdictional power, but only an 'occasional', emergency power. This view was to be shared by Torquemada, a strong anti-conciliarist,[51] and by such moderate quasi-conciliarists as Rickel.[52] Gerson, on the other hand, wished to extend conciliar power, in accordance with *Haec Sancta*, to include the right to sanction a pope who is in need of reform or who obstinately refuses to reform the Church. His position was that conciliar reform decrees, which would normally have already received papal consent, bind future popes just as do their dogmatic pronouncements; if a pope infringes either, he may be brought to trial at a council.

Gerson's ascription of fulness of power to the pope 'formally and subjectively' must be taken as an abstract definition, as a purely 'analytical' statement: it did not mean that any particular pope had fulness of power vis à vis any particular council. In 1408-9, Gerson had emphasised the categorical distinction between offices and their individual incumbents:

the former are the 'essential' parts of the Church and are irremoveable, the latter are the 'fluid (*fluentes*)' parts and subject to change.[53] Thus individual popes may be sanctioned without affecting the integrity of the papacy; the council may oversee tenure of the papal office without infringing the divinely-instituted constitution of the Church. In *On ecclesiastical power* he repeated this view, and added that, since the papacy, cardinalate and so on are essential parts of the Church, 'if the general council represents the universal Church adequately and integrally, it must include the papal authority, whether there is a pope or whether he has ceased to exist through natural or civil death' (i.e. deposition).[54] This means that, if there is no pope, the council can exercise his authority in the interim: papal power is in principle detachable from the pope and may in some circumstances temporarily belong to a council. This again indicates that in Gerson's view ecclesiastical power belongs to the council in a fuller sense and on a more regular basis.

The promulation of the decree *Frequens* was achieved by the reform party, largely in order to ensure that reforms were carried out. Gerson's view of the council implied a much more regular role for it than councils had had in previous centuries; if we consider the frequency with which some provincial councils were held, he may be said to have applied a similar status and function to general councils vis à vis the universal Church. The collapse of the reform movement in 1416-18 and the subsequent failure of Martin V to undertake a serious reform programme led the conciliarists of Basle to take Gerson's views on the scope of conciliar power a great deal further.

NOTES
1. Ullmann (1972a), 191-231; Tierney (1968), 220-37; Merzbacher.
2. Oakley (1964a); McGowan; Roberts; *DLO* 895-6; Gilson, 799n.
3. *DLO* 837-68; Postumus-Meyjes, esp. 210-74; Morrall (1960); Pascoe; Connolly; Vooght (1968); Schäfer.
4. *Comm.*, fols. 109v, 110v; cf. Ullmann (1972a), 211; Tierney (1968), 225-7; 229. Cf. Frederick v.Parsberg, cit. Vooght (1965), 44; Escobar, below, p. 87, Tudeschi, below, p. 100f.
5. *MD* vii, 910; cf. *TEP* 949; cf. Oakley (1964a), 54-9.
6. *OC* vi, 131, 133.
7. Cf. *OC* vi, 217; *TEP* 953;*Acta concilii Constantiensis* ii, 45-6; Vooght (1965), 43.
8. *MD* vii, 910; *TEP* 956; cf. Gerson, *OC* vi, 137.
9. *OC* vi, 114-9, 132, 222.
10. Ullmann (1972a), 218-27; Tierney (1968), 218-21.
11. *OC* vi, 115-16; cf. d'Ailly cit. Oakley (1964a), 152.
12. *OC* vi, 233.
13. *OC* vi, 134.
14. Cf. below, pp. 184ff.
15. Ullmann (1972a), 182-3; cf. Tierney (1968), 19, 50-1.
16. *MD* vii, 910.

17. *De modis*, 74-5.
18. Postumus-Meyjes, 184-97; Martin (1939), 81-5; Morrall (1960), 88-90.
19. Anon., *de papae et concilii* . . ., 701.
20. *OC* vi, 217; cf. *ibid*, 115-16.
21. Cf. below, pp. 148ff.
22. Anon., *De papae* . . ., 702.
23. Anon., *Impugnatio* . . ., 293-4; *TEP* 956.
24. Anon., *De papae* . . ., 702; cf. *TEP* 957 ('Videtur esse ratio evidentie, quia omne totum sua parte maius est, loquendo de toto respectu suarum partium integralium'), 949, 951-3.
25. Below, pp. 138ff., 148ff.
26. E.g. Anon., *De papae* . . . 701.
27. Cit. Tierney (1968), 236.
28. *OC* vi, 114-9.
29. Below, p. 188.
30. *OC* vi, 116.
31. Mansi xxvii, 590.
32. *OC* vi, 227.
33. Ullmann (1975), 295. Cf. Ullmann (1966), 288ff.
34. *Comm.*, fol. 109v.
35. Tierney (1968), 48, 53, 152n.
36. Above, p. 18.
37. McGowan, 80; Cameron, 138-40.
38. Cf. Oakley (1964a), 117-29, 204-5; Cameron, 130ff.
39. Cf. Postumus-Meyjes, 293-6; Gierke, *DGR* trans. Maitland, 157; Cameron, 135ff.
40. D'Ailly, *TEP* 946, 957; Gerson, *OC* vi, 225, 247-8. Cf. Tierney (1975).
41. *TEP* 950-1; cf. Oakley (1964a), 148-9.
42. *OC* vi, 220.
43. *TEP* 950-1.
44. *OC* vi, 220, 232.
45. *OC* vi, 220, 229, 232; cf. Postumus-Meyjes, 229-38.
46. *OC* vi, 116.
47. Cit. Ullmann (1972a), 213.
48. McGowan, 82; Cameron, 124, 130, 133ff.; cf. *TEP* 935.
49. *OC* vi, 286-7.
50. Above, p. 10.
51. Horst.
52. Rickel, 567b, 577-8, 627a, 643.
53. *OC* vi, 132.
54. *OC* vi, 222.

CONCILIARISM DURING THE COUNCIL OF BASLE

CHAPTER 2

THE REVOLUTIONARY SYNOD

The council of Basle[1] was summoned in February 1431 by Martin V, in accordance with *Frequens*.[2] In the intervening years the council of Siena (1423-4) had been easily disposed of by Martin; this may have taught such Paris conciliarists as Ragusa and Beaupère (*Pulchipatris*) a lesson. Basle was a more secure location, being a free city on imperial territory; the emperor appointed a 'protector' for the council,[3] and its meeting-places were policed by the city magistrates. Martin died at the end of February, and was succeeded by Eugenius IV (Gabriel Condulmaro), a man of Venetian origin, who appears to have been pious but less statesmanlike than Martin; he was described as obstinate and rigid.[4] He immediately provoked a minor civil war in the Avignon area by appointing his nephew as bishop-ruler.[5] He remained throughout utterly convinced of the monarchical rights of the papacy, and tried to achieve 'not what he could but what he wanted';[6] but as time went on he employed some very able diplomats.

The council was opened in July by the papal legate in Germany, cardinal Giuliano Cesarini.[7] At first the response was extremely poor, but by the summer of 1432 a respectable number of prelates had arrived, and numbers continued to increase. One reason for this was fear of the Hussites, who had won a series of astounding victories culminating in the battle of Taus (August 1431), and whose arms and anticlerical propaganda posed a threat to neighbouring lands, and especially to the clergy.[8] The council offered from the start unequivocal resistance to Eugenius' attempts to disband, transfer or prorogue it[9]; the apparent inequity and — considering the Hussites — ineptitude of Eugenius won considerable support for it.

Bilderback considers that 'discontent with Rome was a more compelling reason for attendance' than fear of Hussitism.[10] As during Constance, many states adopted a coherent national policy towards the council; the decision of the French court, the emperor and a large number of German princes to support it ensured its continuation. These rulers, however, wished to bring Eugenius to his senses rather than to depose him. They therefore embarked almost immediately on a policy of conciliation between pope and council, and frowned on the radical conciliarism of the Paris-led majority of council members.[11] During 1433 secular pressure, the drift of high-level ecclesiastical opinion, even among the cardinals and the *curia*, combined with unrest in the papal states, forced Eugenius into recognising the legitimacy of the council since its inception, in terms free of any implication that such legitimacy derived from papal favour (December 1433). Eugenius' reconciliation was accepted by the council in February 1434.[12]

The council's legislative and governmental machinery

The truly revolutionary feature of the council of Basle lay in its establishment of new rules for membership, new internal procedures for decision-making, and its own judicial and administrative organs. Constance had been divided into 'nations', in which most of the discussion took place, and which voted en bloc.[13] Basle replaced this (at Ragusa's suggestion, apparently) by a division into 'deputations' or committees, dealing with faith, reform, peace and 'common affairs (*communia*)' respectively.[14] Almost any cleric, though very few not in priestly orders, could gain incorporation into the council with full, equal speaking and voting rights.[15] All members were granted freedom of speech and exemption from any jurisdiction but the council's own. Laymen themselves could not be incorporated; secular powers were incorporated through clerical proctors. These steps more or less eliminated direct secular intervention and reduced the senior to the same formal status as the junior clergy. Power was transferred to the majority, which consisted of a fairly stable group of pro-conciliar clergy; as at democratic Athens, rhetoric played an important role. Not only the pro-papal minority but also the major secular powers found the constitution objectionable.

This committee-system was orchestrated by a special committee known as 'the twelve';[16] elected monthly by each of the deputations in equal proportion, this group scrutinized the credentials of newcomers, assigned them to a deputation, assigned incoming business to the most appropriate deputation, and also prepared business which had been through the deputations for submission to the 'general assembly (*generalis congregatio*)' of the whole council. Both the twelve and the general assembly were chaired by the president of the council, who was elected; only two men held this office for long periods, Cesarini from 1431 to 1438, and Aleman from 1438 to 1449.

The deputations were the primary forum for discussion; an attempt was made to distribute members of each nationality and rank in equal proportion among the deputations, and also among the twelve.[17] All legislation had to go through the deputations, which met on three mornings a week, under the chairmanship of an elected president.[18] Voting was by a simple majority. If a motion passed the deputation to which it had been submitted, it was submitted to the other three deputations, which might also discuss it briefly. If approved by two or more deputations, it then went before the general assembly.[19] This met at least once a week, usually on Fridays. If a measure had been passed by three or four deputations, it was put to the vote without further discussion; if by only two, the general assembly discussed it again, the president having the power of closure. A two-thirds majority was required for a measure to pass the assembly; voting was secret. If a measure passed the assembly, it was put in the form of a decree, read out before the next assembly, and then ceremonially promulgated at a plenary session.[20] The assembly also received embassies and despatches – a typically republican practice.

There was, however, plenty of scope for unofficial meetings outside this formal framework, though legislation was enacted against them. For example, Segovia noted (à propos reform proposals) that 'from the beginning the ordinary and the exempt clergy held meetings separate from other members; the exempt did so particularly and more frequently'.[21] A nation-system continued to operate unofficially, and eventually obtained quasi-official recognition. It developed partly out of the need to promote national interests on questions of reform: each 'nation' elected a president.[22] Naturally, all such meetings influenced the formal discussion; Pérouse says that the nations in their 'semi-official' role exercised a 'profound though irregular influence' over the council.[23] The majority and minority factions held frequent meetings in the houses of prominent prelates in 1436-7. Formal 'extraordinary meetings' were also convoked from time to time. It must be said, however, that although Pérouse, Lazarus and Haller pioneered the field, the actual operation of Basle's decision-making machinery has never been systematically examined.

The Basle system obviously owed something to contemporary models. Universities were divided into faculties with elected deans, and governed by a 'general assembly' and an elected *rector*.[24] Some religious orders passed legislation by means of an international 'general assembly'. Many monastic, diocesan and collegiate chapters passed legislation by majority voting, and exercised more or less strict supervision over their *rector*. There was also the example of republican cities, many of which were governed by a lesser and a greater council, of which Basle itself was an instance. Such institutions provided part of the model for the council of Basle, and their corporational, communal practices were frequently invoked in Basilean writings. But the council's constitution was a novel combination of existing practices: for instance, both the specialised and the general deliberative bodies (that is, the committees or 'deputations' and the general assembly) were open to all members. Segovia was justified in calling it a new invention of his time.[25] As we shall see, the Basle theorists affirmed time and again that a council was a corporation, *collegium*, *universitas*, and that its affairs should be conducted in a spirit of fellowship, *caritas, koinonia.*[26]

Constance had condemned and burnt John Hus and Jerome of Prague. A further difference between Constance and Basle was the latter's admission of Hussite representatives to debate their case with Catholic theologians before the council – a step the like of which has still to be taken in our 'ecumenical' age. This was to some extent, it is true, forced on Basle by Hussite victories in the field; nevertheless one should note that Basle took a much more sympathetic view of the Hussites' demands than did Eugenius, and was ready to accept their main liturgical reforms, and that friendly relations developed between the two sides at the council.[27] It was a sign not so much of the Basileans' theological opinions as of their readiness to conduct religious affairs in a different spirit, by public debate between opponents. The whole committee-system was a machinery for such discussion.

Complicated though it was, the council's system appears to have worked well enough as regards the internal transaction of business; despite what critics have said, both then and now, about its ponderous procedures,[28] it was fully capable of reaching decisions. Its problems lay in getting the consent of the pope, princes and prelates that was necessary for the actual implementation of decrees; this was most evident in the case of reform decrees. And its diplomacy – as has often been noted of republics – was neither as elegant nor as efficient as that of its monarchical rival.

The most revolutionary step of all was the council's replication of the entire structure of the papal administrative and judicial machinery. Realizing perhaps that conciliar ideas might never triumph unless they grasped the central nerves of power, the Basileans attempted to establish conciliar control not only over doctrine but also over ecclesiastical jurisdiction. Thus not only did the council establish a 'tribunal on faith' comprising three 'judges of faith' (1432),[29] to be superseded by a 'consistory on faith' (February 1436) comprising eight theologians and four canonists, chaired by a single 'judge of faith' — Aleman himself, in fact.[30] It also set up a *rota*, a *camera* and a penitentiary,[31] and established courts to hear appeals on 'major cases' (such as disputed episcopal elections).[32] It administered its own treasury. And it instituted a chancery (1432) with power to issue Bulls and briefs, administered by a vice-chancellor[33] — a post also held by Aleman from 1434 onwards. This, then, was the substance and the policy behind the Basle conciliarists' claim that a council had 'fulness of power', constituting the Church's 'supreme tribunal'.[34] The ferocity of the future struggle owed much to the fact that, after the reconciliation with Eugenius in 1434, none of this machinery — surely indicative of a more far-reaching 'parliamentarism' than had hitherto been attempted in territorial states — was dismantled.

NOTES
1. There is no adequate history of the council; *DLO* 227-92 is fragmentary and biassed. For the internal history, see Pérouse, Lazarus; for the diplomatic history, Valois, *PC*. Haller intended to write the history and his extant works are full of deeply suggestive comment; a notable recent contribution is Bilderback (1966). The internal records are edited in *CB*, vols. i.-viii; Segovia's account is in *MC*, vols. ii.-iv. Cf. Meijknecht. I have been unable to consult the very recent work by Stieber.
2. *DLO* 222ff.; Brandmüller (1968).
3. Bansa; *PC* i, 142.
4. Dlugosc, book xiii, ch. 25; Gill (1961), 170, 172, 177.
5. *PC* ii, 2ff.
6. Dlugosc, book xiii, ch. 25.
7. Jacob (1968a).
8. Kaminsky; Leff (1967a), ii, 604ff.; Macek (1958).
9. *MC* ii, 47-62, 124ff.; Mansi xxix, 5-6, 21-2.
10. Bilderback (1966), 97, 171, 179; Bilderback (1967).
11. *MC* ii, 505.
12. *PC* i, 302ff.; Gill (1961), 56ff.
13. Gill (1971), 186-8.
14. *MC* ii, 126-8, 260-1; Lazarus, 111-15.
15. *MC* ii, 121, 414, 580, 651; Gill (1971), 191-2; Bilderback (1966), 76-7.
16. *MD* viii, 242-6; Lazarus, 181ff.
17. *MC* ii, 151; Lazarus, 159n.
18. *MC* ii, 212, 261.
19. *MC* ii, 262-3, 284; Lazarus, 135-51.
20. Lazarus, 151-7.
21. *MC* ii, 524.
22. Lazarus, 157-80.
23. Pérouse, 175.
24. Rashdall, i, 326-7, 402-10; below, p. 165. Cf. *MC* ii, 363, where Segovia says 'concilium generale ordinatum est velut studium generale'.
25. Below, p. 133.
26. Below, pp. 55, 88f., 100ff., 160.
27. Jacob (1949).

28. For example, Valois in *PC* i, 311-18; *DLO* 241-2.
29. *MC* ii, 223ff., 357; Mansi, xxix, 36ff.
30. *CB* iv, 55; Lazarus, 282ff.; Pérouse, 184ff.
31. *MC* ii, 219, 775; Lazarus, 243-71; *DLO* 244-5.
32. *MC* ii, 219, 825ff.; *MD* viii, 870-1; Lazarus, 272ff. Bilderback comments that 'the whole subject of the Council as a court is the largest virgin area of research left in the study of the Council, and it must be investigated before the Council can be understood in its entirety': Bilderback (1966), 116-7n.
33. *MC* ii, 357, 363; Lazarus, 185-233; Dephoff.
34. Below, p. 116n. 3.

Membership

In order to understand the nature of the council, a word must be said about its composition, especially about the formation of the majority group which was the vehicle for the doctrines of Basilean conciliarism. Overall membership of the council reached its peak just after the reconciliation with Eugenius and it only declined drastically after 1439.

April 1432	81
April 1433	c.420
February 1434	512
December 1436	355
Spring 1439	c.400[1]

First, let us consider the proportions of different strata of clergy.[2] As regards bishops and abbots, who alone had the vote at earlier councils (though there may have been some exceptions at Pisa and Constance), both Ourliac and Gill emphasise that they were neither numerous nor powerful at Basle; Gill calculates that at most they comprised one third of the council (this was in spring 1432).[3] Bilderback, on the contrary, whose study of the council's membership is by far the most thorough to date, points out that, in absolute terms, more bishops and abbots attended Basle between 1432 and 1437 than had attended the whole of the council of Constance, and that they formed as great a proportion of the whole council.[4] Gill also ignores proctorial representation of bishops and abbots, which, on the full information available for April 1433, would bring their proportion up to 56%[5] (bishops' and abbots' proxies had had the vote at earlier councils[6]). Thereafter, their proportion did indeed fall steadily: omitting proxies, they formed 26% in April 1433, 18% in February 1434, 15% in December 1436, and roughly 9% in 1439. The overwhelming difference between Basle and earlier councils was, of course, that the vote was not confined to bishops and abbots. Provosts, deans, priors, archdeacons, doctors and masters, rectors, vicars, canons, parish priests, *scolastici*,[7] brothers attended the council in large numbers and were incorporated as full voting members. For these we can give the following approximate proportions for April 1433: middle-rank clergy (provosts, deans, priors, archdeacons) 11%; university clergy (doctors and masters) 24%— allowing for those listed as proxies, this figure should probably be around 28%;[8] junior clergy (i.e. all other categories) 16%.[9] The proportion of middle-rank clergy remained constant until 1437 and declined thereafter. During the years 1432-7 the absolute numbers and the proportion of university clergy were probably about the same as at Constance;[10] thereafter their numbers and their proportion increased considerably. There was also a great increase in the numbers and proportion of junior clergy after 1437, so that from then on university and junior clergy comprised more than half the council; their proportion increased yet further after 1439.[11]

The following reasons may be suggested for these changes in the class composition of the council. By 1437 the Hussites had been pacified,[12] and questions of reform had divided the council. The rulers of France and Germany became increasingly unwilling to give the council whole-hearted support. The deputation-system alienated both senior clergy and secular rulers, because it denied them influence. The unprecedently long duration of the council proved both a bore and a financial strain, as indicated by the fact that, while the number of deans, provosts and priors changed little between 1433 and 1436, very few of those in attendance at these two dates were the same individuals.[13] The Greek question, and the development of a coherent majority group of radical conciliarists under French leadership which was unrepresentative of the Church as a whole but could dominate the proceedings through numbers,[14] were probably the most important factors in these changes.

Members of the religious orders comprised about 40% of the council in April 1433, made up of 90 abbots (53 by proxy), 5 generals, 11 provincials, 22 priors, and the rest university or junior clergy.[15] Hussitism and reform were among the issues that especially concerned them.[16] It appears that the older religious orders gave more support to the council than recently-founded orders, and were more inclined to support the conciliarist programme. A significant degree of support for Basle and its reforms came from the Carthusians ('numquam reformata quia numquam deformata').[17] Friars tended much more than others to be pro-papal; the Dominicans provided the outstanding champions of the papacy at this time: Torquemada, Kalteisen, Montenigro, Nieder, Hüntpichler.[18] The numbers of senior and middle-rank religious had already declined considerably by the end of 1436, when there were only 2 generals, 3 provincials, 28 abbots, 11 priors left;[19] by 1439 there were only 8 abbots.[20] This decline was probably largely due to the pacification of the Hussites, and in many cases, particularly among the friars and other exempt orders, dislike of the reform programme which sought to curtail their independence.[21]

National proportions are of special significance. One factor was distance: regions close to Basle were the most fully represented, while 'the outlying parts of Europe . . . were sparsely represented if at all'.[22] A great number came from Switzerland, Savoy, southern France and northern Italy.[23] Areas threatened directly by Hussitism were no better represented than others,[24] though Saxony appears to have been well represented in 1433, with no less than three provincials present.[25] From 1432 to 1436 France, the Low Countries and Germany were especially well represented; between 1432 and 1440 about 33% of the council were French, about 29% German.[26] England was severely under-represented, being pro-papal (partly because it already had greater ecclesiastical independence) and being alienated by the deputation-system which denied it the special power it had gained through the nation-system at Constance.[27] Political factors played an important part, notably in the case of Milan: Visconti saw the council as an ally, against Florence and the papacy, in the pursuit of his territorial interest in Italy. After 1437, non-Milanese Italians were almost entirely absent, and the proportion of Germans declined. France continued to be well represented, largely because of the conciliarism of Paris university. The significant new factor was that the depletion among bishops, abbots and middle-rank clergy from Italy and Germany was largely compensated for by newcomers of *all* strata, but with a preponderance of junior and university clergy, from the lands of the Basle allegiance. These comprised Aragon-Catalonia, Poland and Milan, whose rulers continued in the main to support Basle — Aragon and Milan because of political considerations in Italy; and also small territories such as Brittany, Savoy, Scotland and Switzerland.[28] In Brittany's case, this was a bid to retain ecclesiastical independence from France which gained the ear of the papacy on several episcopal appointments.[29] Scotland may have been motivated by hostility towards England. Savoy and Switzerland entered into almost a tacit alliance with Basle, the former providing the anti-pope Felix V, the latter being, among other things, a homeland of self-government. In addition, there was after 1439 a continual influx of doctors and masters from central-European universities.

NOTES

1. These and all the statistics that follow are based on Bilderback (1966), esp. 219-41; Gill (1971), 190-1; Lazarus, 346-56; *MC* ii, 151, 184, 355, 393, 650-1; *CB* i, 449; *CB* iv, 348ff.: *CB* v, 56, 79; *CB* vii, 445; *ASP*. On the sociology of the council, see Bilderback (1966) *passim*, and also Bilderback (1967)

and (1969); Gill (1971). Ourliac, on whom *DLO* 238ff. is based, is inclined to be unsystematic and biassed. Pérouse and Lazarus are extremely useful.

2. Study of this question is complicated by the fact that people might attend in a variety of roles, e.g. at once as canon, doctor and proxy. Some of the necessary background details have been provided in Stutt, Hanna, and Schofield (1961), (1966), (1967), (1971).

3. Gill (1971), 192; Ourliac in *DLO* 239.

4. Bilderback (1966), 177, and also 103-4, 226, 234.

5. Lazarus, 346ff.

6. Gill (1971), 177ff.; cf. Bilderback (1969).

7; Schoolmasters (?); they appear to have been attached to cathedral churches. Cf. Lazarus, 351.

8. Cf. *MC* ii, 355-6, 650-1.

9. Lazarus, 346-56.

10. Cf. Gill (1971), 181-2, 187-8.

11. Cf. Bilderback (1966), 240.

12. On this factor, cf. Bilderback (1966), 123-4, 138.

13. Lazarus, 346ff.; *CB* iv, 348ff.

14. Below, pp. 38ff.

15. Lazarus, 346-56, 358.

16. Cf. *MC* ii, 524.

17. Cf. Lazarus, 351; Jedin (1957), 37-8; *PC* ii, 263n.; V.Gerz-von Buren.

18. Jedin (1957), 34-5; *DLO* 788, 833; Frank.

19. *CB* iv, 348ff.

20. Computed from *ASP*.

21. Below, p. 40,; cf. Fromherz, 60, 89.

22. Bilderback (1966), 98.

23. Bilderback (1966), 203ff.

24. Bilderback (1967).

25. Lazarus, 350.

26. Computed from Bilderback (1966), 203, 211-15.

27. Zellfelder; Schofield (1961), (1964), (1966), (1971).

28. Bilderback (1966), 124, 147, 151-2, 160-1, 167; Bilderback (1969).

29. Bilderback (1966), 166ff.

The collegiate element

In view of the influence of collegiate-corporational ideas on conciliar theory during Basle, one must ask what proportion of the council came from milieux that would tend to encourage such ideas. One cannot compute this in exact terms; but one can perhaps say that provosts, deans, priors, university clergy, canons and *scolastici* would be used to collegiate forms of government. This would give a figure of approximately 40% for April 1433 and of more than 50%, rising steadily, from 1436.[1] The figure of 475 canons, as compared with 253 parish priests, who attended Basle overall,[2] rather suggests that, when the 'lower orders' swamped the council, they tended to be collegiate clergy; but how many of these were university clergy, and canons only in name and revenue, it would be difficult to know. Several council members had a collegiate mandate; we find certain canons, vicars, monks and brothers being incorporated as 'proctors of churches', 'proctor of the chapter', or 'for the chapter', 'for the order';[3] the large incorporation (82) of April 1434 included 13 'proctors of churches, of clergy (*cleri*) and of monasteries'.[4] The April 1433 list includes no less than 82 'other proctors having mandates'.[5] Several universities sent official delegations, consisting of one, two or more persons; by April 1433, Paris, Cologne, Vienna, Heidelberg, Erfurt and Avignon were incorporated in the council through proctors.[6] Such mandated members are significant for our understanding of the council as a representative body, since they were ordinary members of an ecclesiastical college or corporation, who had been specifically elected or deputed to represent that body at the council; they comprised the only elected element at Basle.

It is worth noting the number of clergy with civic connections. This is particularly striking, for April 1433, in the case of Germany; the number had fallen drastically by December 1436.

Town	1433	1436
Mainz	archbp, abt (1434), prior, *inquis* dean, canon, 2 *scolast.*	provost, *scolast.*
Cologne	archbp, provost, univ. deleg. (2)	rector, canon
Trier	archbp. 2 abts	—
Salzburg	archbp, abt proxy, 2 provosts, dean	—
Ratisbon	bp, abt (1434), dean	dean
Freising	bp, provost, canon, vicar	vicar
Lübeck	bp	bp, dean, 2 canons
Brixen	bp proxy, dean	canon, minor
Passau	bp, provost, minor	minor
Worms	bp, *scolast.*, minor	—
Bamberg	bp, abt, 2 canons, religious	minor
Havelberg	bp, proctor	provost
Newenburg	bp, provost proxy	—
Hildesheim	bp, *scolast.*, religious	—
Vienna	abt, provost, univ. deleg. (2)	minor
Mülbrunn	abt, 2 religious, proctor	abt
Gran (Hungary)	bp, archd., proctor	archd.[7]

A few towns were themselves incorporated through proctors.[8]

The council of Basle, then, comprised a unique gathering of clergy from the medieval ecclesiastical corporations. They came chiefly from France, Germany and the Low Countries. Some of them came from remote priories, many more from cities and the more urbanized parts of Europe, where the corporational mode of government affected secular as well as ecclesiastical life. It may well be that the presence of such a considerable body of men from collegiate instiutions, such as cathedral chapters, collegiate city churches, monasteries and friaries, had a significant influence on the council and also on conciliar thought. From provost to *scolasticus*, these men were seeped in the *moeurs* of collective, consultative and constitutional government. It would not be surprising if they invoked the model of chapter, college, cloister and university as the right pattern for the universal Church. The restoration of canonical elections[9] must have struck a sympathetic chord with them. So too must the whole notion of 'conciliar government' as it evolved at Basle; decision-making by a corporate body, to which executive officials were accountable was, after all, what they were accustomed to.

For the first and only time representatives of the infrastructure of ecclesiastical society wielded considerable influence at a general council. Against the pope, cardinals and princes they represented as it were the 'middle-class', workaday Church. At Basle, representatives of the subculture of the medieval Church that flourished at the local, capitular, urban level, laid claim to the overall organization of the Church, challenging the dominant culture of monarchical papalism. These men were reformers rather than revolutionaries; they wanted to fashion ecclesiastical government on a model that was already in existence, and to restore corporate discipline. They were not unfriendly to episcopal authority, but they wanted bishops to be elected by their chapters. Their concept of ecclesiastical order was traditional; they viewed the Hussites with disapproval and fear. They gave no consideration to the claims of the laity; they wished to maintain and restore 'the liberty of the Church' in the face of royal and princely, as well as of papal, encroachments. The council heartily disliked anything that smacked of the state-church or the Marsilian programme; it banned vernacular translations of the Bible and objected to laymen discussing articles of faith.[10] It exuded a Hildebrandine republicanism. There was much talk of the rights and status of priests, who were held to be of equal status with bishops in the council.[11] There were to be regular councils at the diocesan and provincial as well as at the universal level;[12] constitutional government was to function throughout the body of the church, with legislative power in the hands of priestly or episcopal synods; the general council itself was sometimes styled 'the college of priests (*collegium sacerdotum*)'.[13]

NOTES
1. Lazarus, 346ff.; *CB* iv, 348ff.

2. Bilderback (1966), 219.
3. *MC* ii, 184, 650; *CB* ii, 25, 136, 140; Lazarus, 351, 354.
4. *MC* ii, 650; cf. *CB* ii, 140; Bilderback (1966), 146ff.
5. Lazarus, 354-6.
6. Lazarus, 352; Kaufmann, i, 449-50, 463n.
7. Lazarus, 346ff.; *CB* iv, 348ff. In 1440 Cracow was represented by a bishop, archdeacon, 2 canons and a university delegation (*CB* indices).
8. *MC* ii, 355, 650.
9. Below, p. 41 at n.29.
10. *CB* viii, 79, 108, 126.
11. Below, pp. 69, 113, 187f.
12. Below, p. 41 at n. 32.
13. *MC* ii, 208, 390; cf. *ASP* 76-8.

The majority faction

We must now turn to the role of the majority group and the question of leadership within the council, which requires us to take up once again the sequence of events. From autumn 1431 to spring 1432 — the formative period for the council's organizational structure — the council appears to have been led and inspired chiefly by radical conciliarists, above all by the Paris university delegation. This was primarily due to the absence of senior prelates. In the main, however, they had the support of Cesarini and Sigismund. The Paris university delegation was small by comparison with Constance, but it consisted of determined men with a clearly-formulated policy.[1] Its chief member was Jean Beaupère (*Pulchipatris*), a theologian and former associate of Gerson; he had been beaten up by robbers while returning from the council of Siena. He played an outstanding role in the formulation of theoretical argument,[2] and in the formulation and execution of policy, including reform. Nicholas Lamy (*Amici*), Thomas Courcelles and Denis Sabrevois were also theologians; Courcelles took over the drafting of decrees in 1438.[3] All these four men had participated only a few months earlier (May 1431) in the condemnation of Jeanne d'Arc; Beaupère was rewarded for this by the English, and he conscientiously defended his view that she was hallucinated when the case was later re-examined under very different circumstances.[4] Guillaume Hugues was a canonist. Throughout the council, these Parisians appeared in important conciliar posts and took part in important ambassadorial missions, for example in attempts to persuade Eugenius to accept the reform decrees (1434-6).[5] Jan de Ragusa, who had represented Paris university at the council of Siena, and who went to Basle as a representative of Cesarini,[6] also played an important role in the opening stages.

When senior clergy began to arrive in larger numbers during 1432, the council's internal procedures had already been established, and the Parisians continued to be influential. This was partly because of their academic expertise, partly because of the prestige of Paris, where numerous clerical dignitaries had studied, and which was affectionately regarded as the 'mother' of several other universities. The leading role of the Paris doctors in matters of doctrine is indicated by a remark made by Ebendorfer, a representative of Vienna university, in 1433: 'The arguments of the French are as a shield to us . . . For this matter has been subtly disputed among those most scholarly men, and the arguments of each side have been discussed, many defending our cause, and many that our adversaries; to such an extent that the argument that this holy council is legitimately assembled has been well thrashed out by that school (sc. Paris), and has issued clearly from it (*ex ipsa scola . . . trita et lucida prodierit*) . . . Thus, if anyone has read their writings carefully, it is not surprising if they come to us and leave the path of (our) adversaries'.[6a] But from 1432 to 1435 the role of these men and their allies was offset by senior clergy and by the influence of the secular powers. This led to a series of compromises and facilitated the reconciliation with Eugenius; in the presidency debate of spring 1434 we find a coalition of moderate and radical conciliarists producing a compromise that still offended papal supporters.[7] The radicals were held in check by the moderating influence of Cesarini, the president of the council, and of the French and German rulers, who by no means shared the views of the French and German clergy at Basle.[8]

From at least 1435 onwards, however, a coherent majority group led by radical conciliarists and comprising an especially large proportion of French and, to a lesser degree, German clergy, came into being and began to dominate the council; these could count on support from the Milanese. Cardinal Louis Aleman[9] emerged as their leader. His marked personal hostility to Eugenius dated from Martin V's time,[10] and had been exacerbated by Eugenius' promotion of a nephew to the post of chamberlain (1431) which Aleman, as senior French cardinal, had reason to expect should be his.[11] Aleman was the only cardinal in Rome who refused to sign Eugenius' Bull of dissolution (November 1431); soon after his arrival at Basle (1434) he acquired the important posts of vice-chancellor and judge of faith.[12] He was to lead the conciliarist party from the mid-1430s till the end. He appears to have combined political and administrative ability with moral leadership, for his followers were anything but docile. Segovia described him as 'gentle of heart but tenacious of purpose'; he does not appear to have been personally ambitious.[13] Other leaders of the group included the patriarch of Aquileia (Ludwig von Teck),[14] and the archbishops of Lyons (Amedée de Talaru)[15] and of Tours (Philippe de Coëtquis).[16] During 1435-7 clergy of low status also became prominent in conciliar posts and delegations abroad, but several of the most active of them were well-connected persons. Johann Bachenstein, a canonist who became judge of faith, acted for Teck;[17] Jacob von Sirck came of good family and became archbishop of Trier in 1439;[18] Johann Grünwalder, a canon of Freising, was a bastard son of duke William of Bavaria.[19]

The strategy of the majority group from 1435 to 1437 was the implementation of the jurisdictional sovereignty of the council, the acquiescence of the pope in the doctrine of conciliar supremacy, and the implementation of reforms which would have removed effective control of church government from the Roman papacy.[20] National sentiment was also involved: the French-led majority resented the predominance of Italians at the *curia* and wished in effect to remove the papacy elsewhere. Coëtquis is quoted as saying: 'this time we shall either take the apostolic see out of the hands of the Italians, or else we shall so clip its wings that it won't matter where it resides'.[21] One observer spoke of an 'almost natural hatred' between the French and Italians.[22] Indeed, Pérouse viewed the majority strategy as specifically aimed at restoring the papacy to the Avignon area, where a pro-Basle faction, fanned by local resentment against Eugenius, was fostered by Aleman.[23] These ideological and nationalist factors were linked by the anti-Roman stance of Basle conciliarism.

The minority group, led by the new papal legates, supported by several cardinals, and with a hard core of Italians, was opposed to the majority on all these points, upheld the papal right to convoke, preside over and dissolve or transfer councils (except in exceptional circumstances), and wished to maintain the status quo prior to 1431 and, indeed, prior to the conciliar movement. Immediately after the reconciliation achieved between Basle and Eugenius in 1433-4, the presidency debate of February 1434[24] demonstrated that there was more form than substance in the agreement: it simply meant, in effect, that the controversy was for a while transferred to the floor of the council itself. Eugenius despatched cardinal Traversari, an astute negotiator, to Basle on a mission to detach the senior prelates from the conciliarist camp.[25] He held out promises of promotion and money;[26] indeed, both time and money were on the pope's side. Poggio and Monte were both employed in the defence of absolute ecclesiastical monarchy at the very time when they were defending Florentine liberty and republican government.[27] The conciliarists of the majority group, on the other hand, continued to operate the council as the focal point of church jurisdiction, and pressed ahead with reforms directed at the conciliarization and decentralization of Church government. They appeared set on a collision course.

The reform-programme itself included the abolition of annates (9.vi. 1435) and expectatives (24.i. 1438),[28] the abolition of all papal rights of appointment to ecclesiastical benefices, which were to be filled by capitular election (13.vii. 1433 and 24.iii. 1436),[29] and severe restrictions on appeals to the Roman courts (24.i.1438).[30] In Zwölfer's words, 'the entire previous system of papal centralization and fiscal control was done away with'.[31] In this way the Basle conciliarists tried to give – or restore – control of church government to the provinces and dioceses; it was also enacted that regular provincial and diocesan synods should be held (26.vi. 1433).[32] The council despatched embassies to Florence in a vain attempt to secure papal ratification and implementation of these decrees (1434-6).[33]

Meanwhile several senior prelates at Basle and some secular powers, notably Sigismund and Charles VII of France, were becoming disenchanted with the council. The deputation-system made it difficult for them to influence conciliar decisions. The council intervened in cases involving imperial jurisdiction. The prospect of a sovereign council with full legislative, administrative and judicial powers held no attraction for states capable of exercising their influence on the existing curial regime; and the council was beginning to appear less accomodating than the papacy. Basle's forlorn attempt to raise an indulgence on its own authority, to cover its diplomatic expenses (1436), alienated men of moderate opinion.[34]

The issue which finally split Basle was the venue of the proposed council of reunion with the Greeks. This had been under negotiation for some years. The Greeks refused, reasonably enough, to travel further than eastern Italy. During 1435-6 it became apparent, in a series of complex diplomatic manoeuvres, that the Basle majority would not agree to transfer the council to Italian|territory[35] . This *prima facie* unreasonable stance can only be understood in terms of their conviction that they needed a secure territorial base, free from papal power and influence, from which to execute their programme; and this meant keeping the council north of the Alps. Numerous locations were canvassed, Avignon, Savoy and Basle itself featuring prominently in the majority preferences. The breaking-point for many senior clergy and for men of moderate opinions on the pope-council issue was undoubtedly the majority's refusal to risk the success of their programme by agreeing to a transference to one of the cities agreeable to the Greeks. For such moderates, in short, reunion was a higher prize than conciliar government. This did not necessarily mean abandoning either reform or the doctrine of *Haec Sancta,* which Cesarini subsequently defended before the council of Florence.[36]

Of the rival parties within the council during 1436-7, Piccolomini, himself torn between conciliar republicanism and his ties with the Italian party, said: 'which side had the more honesty is another question . . . if you ask me, very few on either side were motivated by conscience alone'. One of these few, he said, was Juan de Segovia.[37] On 7 May 1437 two rival decrees, one to keep the council at Basle, the other to transfer it to Ferrara, were proclaimed amid uproar.[38] A sizeable and influential minority of prelates left Basle to take part with Eugenius in the council of Ferrara-Florence.

Their departure left the radical-conciliarist majority firmly in control of what was left of the council of Basle. Several university clergy of junior status now began to occupy positions of real leadership; many of them were soon to be made bishop or cardinal by the council. But at no time did the doctors — far less other junior clergy[39] — act as a group in isolation from others; they were to be found on both sides in all partisan divisions of the council, and some of them, especially junior clergy, were dependents or indeed servants of senior prelates of one faction or the other. Aleman remained the most dominant figure at Basle, becoming president in 1438. The next most influential leaders were, in addition to Teck, Talaru and Coëtquis, Niccolo de' Tudeschi, archbishop of Palermo, who had arrived in 1436 as one of two representatives of Alfonso of Aragon,[40] and also Johann Schele, bishop of Lübeck and imperial ambassador[41] ('who on account of his immoderate jests (*jocos immodicos*) became known as the council's comedian').[42]

NOTES

1. *MC* ii, 15; Lazarus, 352; *DLO* 248. On what follows see Champion, ii, 340-3, 378.
2. Below, p. 55.
3. *MC* ii, 1042.
4. Champion, ii, 341.
5. See data extracted from *CB* by Lazarus, 305ff. Beaupère, for example, was president of the committee on general matters in Nov. 1435, judge of faith in Feb. 1436, a member of the twelve in Oct. 1433, March 1436, Aug. 1436, Nov. 1439: Lazarus, 306, 313-6.
6. Below, pp. 106ff.
6a Cit. Jaroschka, 97n.
7. Below, pp. 54-6.
8. Wittram, esp. 83-4; *PC* i, 349ff.
9. *DHGE* ii, 86-7; Pérouse, *passim.*
10. Gill (1961), 33-4.
11. Pérouse, 28-9.
12. Pérouse, 186ff.
13. For his personality and leadership see Pérouse, 184ff., 205, 479-80, 498-9; Lazarus, 100ff.
14. *DLO* 118, 248.
15. *PC* i, 153ff.; ii, 119ff.
16. *PC* i, 241-2; ii, 218-19.
17. Pérouse, 383ff., 391ff.; Lazarus, 340; *MC* iii, 1281.
18. *DLO* 282, 289; *PC* i, 127-8; Chevalier, 2328.
19. Kallen, 6; Fromherz, 33n.
20. Cf. below, pp. 40f., 47f.
21. Piccolomini, *De rebus,* 188; cf. *CB* v, 158; *ASP* 151.
22. *CB* i, 435.
23. Pérouse, 197, 400-4; cf. *PC* i, 166ff., 289ff., *MD* viii, 163-4, 592ff.

24. Below, pp. 54-6.
25. Pérouse, 194ff.; *PC* ii, 391ff.
26. Cf. *CB* i, 428-36.
27. Black (1970a), 98-1 2; *Annales eccles.*, xxviii, 335-6; Baron (1966), 68, 407.
28. Zwölfer (1929), 194, 229ff., 244, 247.
29. Zwölfer (1929), 169ff., 215-42.
30. Zwölfer (1930), 4ff.
31. Zwölfer (1930), 51.
32. Zwölfer (1930), 43, 52.
33. Zwölfer (1929), 173-4, 235; cf. *MD* viii, 839ff.
34. *MC* ii, 885ff.; Pérouse, 193; *DLO* 267n.
35. Gill (1959), 21ff., 34ff., 45ff.; *PC* i, 378ff.
36. *PC* ii, 201ff.; Gill (1959), 313-4.
37. Mansi xxxi A, 225-6.
38. *MC* ii, 965; Mansi xxxi A, 229-30; *PC* 58-9.
39. Cf. Bilderback (1966), 37.
40. Below, p. 93.
41. G. Hödl.
42. Piccolomini, *De rebus*, 184.

The university men

The importance of the university doctors lay in their intellectual powers and their zeal for the cause as much as in their numbers. The policies of the majority faction being a mixture of theology and politics, it may be said, in very general terms, that, while clergy from the lands of the Basle allegiance provided the political element, certain intellectually prominent university clergy provided the doctrinal element in its leadership. The doctors owed their hegemony to their rhetorical and scholastic abilities; they served as both the spokesmen and the legitimisers of the Basle-conciliarist cause. For example, Segovia, a university doctor who after 1439 was effectively second-in-command to Aleman, had won widespread respect, from allies and opponents alike, for his personal and intellectual qualities.[1] Within the Basle committee-system the doctors were in their element; the faith committee became the theatre for the exposition and development of conciliar theory. It was such men, nurtured on the ecclesiological writings of Gerson, who developed a specifically Basilean version of conciliar theory. While Beaupère and the Paris delegation provided the most direct link with Gerson, it was now men from elsewhere such as Velde, Cusa and Segovia, who were the most original conciliar theorists.

On the other hand, the university clergy used their position within the council to promote their own interests. This was a manifestation of

43

guild-type self-interest as much as of personal ambition; if certain individuals of a rather mediocre nature (such as Johann Bachenstein) attained positions of eminence in the council, this was only after prolonged service, and in his case it was only with great difficulty (and disastrous consequences for the council) that he obtained a major benefice.[2] The reform decrees favouring university clergy came late in the day, which again suggests that the doctors did not dominate the council prior to 1437. On 24.i. 1438 it was decreed said that posts in the gift of metropolitan and cathedral Churches could only be filled by qualified theologians, and that graduates were to be given first consideration for the position of parish priest in towns and 'walled villages'.[3] It was stipulated (along lines suggested in an earlier reform proposal by Beaupère)[4] that the time of study could not be unduly shortened. Such measures were justifiable; not so the prevention of the promulgation of a decree against anyone holding a plurality of canonries or other minor benefices — a measure which would have eliminated a chief source of income for many doctors — after it had passed through all the necessary legislative stages (1441).[5]

Basle conciliar theory itself reflected the doctors' elevated view of their rightful position in the church: learning, wisdom, 'virtue' rather than birth, favour or connections, should determine ecclesiastical promotion and *doctores* have a special claim to participate in the supreme teaching organ of the Church.[6] Beaupère attacked the conferment of honorary degrees on youths of noble birth.[7] Both the theory and practice of Basle gave rather more prominence to theologians than to canonists. This is evident both in the qualifications for office stipulated in the reform-decree of 24.i.1438[8] and in the qualifications for membership of the council itself, which were lower for the theologians than for lawyers.[9] Moreover, the council appears to have attracted more theologians than canonists (46 as against 29 were present in April 1433);[10] while in the final conflict the council got more support from theology faculties than it did from law faculties.[11] Indeed, theologians played a far greater role in the exposition and development of conciliar theory during Basle than did canonists, a contrast with earlier periods which may be partly explained by the pro-papal stance of Bologna and most of Italy, which produced and trained so many of the canonists. Basle conciliarism was characterised by a reaction against the influence of canon law and a reassertion of the primacy of theology in ecclesiology. At all events, one facet of the council of Basle was that it comprised a revolt of the ecclesiastical intellectuals.

The programme of the majority remained to the end what it had always been. Thus, bearing in mind the formative influence of Beaupère and other doctors on that programme, there is some truth in Gill's view that the 'graduates' were the real leaders at Basle,[12] so long as one remembers that they were acting alongside senior prelates such as Aleman and Tudeschi. The development of a further majority-minority confrontation in 1438-9 is a fascinating reflection upon the dynamics of the council. This time, the majority were urging the immediate deposition of Eugenius for his non-compliance with conciliar doctrine and the reform decrees; the minority, led now by secular representatives such as Tudeschi and the archbishop of Milan, with some support from Schele and Coëtquis, urged delay in accordance with the pacifying and neutral policies of their rulers.[13] The majority now emphasized the need to maintain the 'liberty of the Church' from secular control, a view reflected in the deposition debate (May 1439)[14] and in conciliarist tracts from 1439 onwards. Eugenius was finally deposed in June 1439.[15]

NOTES
1. Below, pp. 121, 125.
2. Fromherz, 33n.
3. Zwölfer (1929), 196-7.
4. *CB* viii, 175-82.
5. Zwölfer (1930), 48ff.; Mansi, xxix, 410.
6. Below, pp. 111, 113; cf. Mansi, *Suppl.* vol. v, 180-2.
7. *CB* viii, 175-82; contrast decree of see of Mainz, March 1439, which makes office conditional on parentage: *DRTA* xiv, 115.
8. Zwölfer (1929) 196-7.
9. *MC* ii, 580: cit. Gill (1971), 191-2.
10. Lazarus, 352-4.
11. Below, p. 111.
12. Gill (1971), 194.
13. *ASP* 1-187 *passim.*
14. *ASP* 107ff., 123, 127, 141ff.
15. Mansi, xxix, 178-80.

Reform and the secular powers

After 1437 the conciliarist reform programme no longer coincided with the interests of most secular powers. There had indeed always been a variety of motives behind the reform measures. Idealistic conciliarists wished to decentralize church government, to restore to the local Church its proper degree of autonomy; had the programme succeeded, councils would indeed have become truly representative of the clergy at large. Many secular rulers, on the other hand, wished not only to decentralize but also partially to secularize (or 'nationalize') church government; they themselves wanted to control the local Churches, whose independence from the papacy was otherwise of little concern to them. Hence, the pragmatic sanction of Bourges (1438)[1] and the *Acceptatio* of Mainz (1439).[2] Basle became politically isolated, receiving positive support only from Poland

and a handful of small states. Its persistence in the new schism, dictated as this was by the deep-seated policy and ideology of the ascendant majority, alienated even Aragon and Milan.[3]

The council of Florence proceeded to hammer out a formula for reunion with the Greeks. This included a new definition of papal primacy.[4] The logic of events at Basle and Florence stimulated a new clarification and – for many – extension of the conception of papal monarchy; Eugenius and his supporters now claimed that a council was in virtually every respect subordinate to papal control.[5] Eugenius, meanwhile, courted the major secular powers. He used ideological arguments to convince rulers of the undesirable implications of conciliar doctrine if it were applied to secular régimes;[6] he promised to accommodate some of the ecclesiastical demands of secular rulers, such as a share in appointments and revenues, provided only that they would forswear conciliar supremacy.

Having adopted many of Basle's reform decrees on their own terms, the French and German powers refused to support Basle in the new conflict, indeed open schism, with Eugenius. They worked out, instead, a common policy of neutrality. This was partly designed to prevent the schism from taking effect within their territories; from 1439 onwards they studiously refused to acknowledge any further acts by either side against the other.[7] The council's new pope, Felix V formerly duke of Savoy (elected in 1440), was only recognised by a small number of states.[8] The secular powers' proposed solution to the schism was that a 'new, third council' should be arranged to mediate between the contestants.[9] This policy, thrashed out by the French and German powers in response to the events of 1437-9, was later adopted by other rulers as well: it came to nothing, foundering on the very nationalistic interests which largely inspired it. The neutrality lasted until 1447-8, when, following a series of annual debates in the Reichstag in which conciliarist and papalist theory was expounded with every conceivable nuance,[10] the struggle was concluded by means of concordats between the papacy and individual states.[11] So ended the last great medieval church council, and with it an epoch in the history of Rome and of Europe. Aided by renaissance scholar-diplomats, the Italian grip on the central government of the Church, though reduced by concessions, was at least partially secured for almost another century. After Basle, there were no further serious attempts to transfer ecclesiastical government to a general council, and not until Trent did the papacy undertake a large-scale reform programme for the Church as a whole. So far as the immediate future was concerned, one may almost say, using the jargon of another age, that ecclesiastical reformism was played out and the way was open for revolution.

The failure of large-scale Church reform, which led directly to the

Protestant Reformation, was due in part to the way the issue had become entangled in ecclesiological controversy and power politics (to the reformers' urgings some conservatives would reply that what was being asked was not 'reformatio' but 'deformatio'). But could it have been otherwise? The political reason for the failure was that as things stood the secular states must necessarily have been partners to the success of any such movement, and the Basileans steadfastly rejected the notion of such a partnership. Haller said that 'even a blind man with a stick could perceive that an ecclesiastical administration such as the council had worked out would increase greatly the power of the state in ecclesiastical matters'.[12] Yet it is not true, as Haller went on to say, that at Basle 'all knew what they were doing, and when they played into the hands of the secular states through the reform decrees of the council, we must assume that they did not intend something else'.[13] Had that been their intention, they might well have succeeded. That the council's conscious aims were not achieved is a measure of the gap between theory and practice in the late-medieval Church. On the one hand, the Basileans lacked a political power-base from which to construct their ideals (though certain rulers, such as the Duke of Savoy, came close to playing the role later to be adopted by Luther's princely protectors – a peril of which the papacy was not unaware). On the other hand, one of the most significant things about the conciliar movement during Basle is that it neither had nor sought popular appeal.[14] The fate of the Basle reforms, as revealed in the pragmatic sanction of Bourges, the *Acceptatio* of Mainz and the subsequent concordats, hinged on the fact that, in late-medieval Europe, the logic of ecclesiastical decentralization led almost inexorably to the state-church.

The historical consequences were momentous. Not only was the Church left unreformed. The aspirations of all those who pinned their hopes on a general council were disappointed; the gap between what many believed to be constitutional justice and existing forms of church government widened. This was particularly significant for the middle clergy of Germany; areas such as Saxony, Switzerland, southern France, above all the German and Swiss cities, which had sent numerous supporters to Basle, would be fertile ground for the sixteenth-century Reformers. Secondly, both the neutrality and the concordats laid the foundations for the future state domination of the Church. As Haller said, with only slight exaggeration: 'The principle *cuius regio, eius religio,* the Protestation of Speyer, and the protection of Luther from papal ban and imperial outlawry would have been impossible had the concept of ecclesiastical territorial autonomy not been held for three generations in Germany, just as it had been in England and France, as a customary element in public law and in the dominant concept of the state. We can see, then, that the council of Basle is not a blind alley, that it does not hang from a dead trace. The way of historical development leads directly from Basle to Wittenberg and Worms'.[15]

Thirdly, when the Reformation did break out, why did so many years elapse before a council was convened? It has been suggested that 'If a parliament of Catholic Christians had met before the condemnation of Luther's theses (1520) and Luther's excommunication (1521), or even just afterwards, it is probable that the schism would have been avoided. Rome refused to take the initiative to save the situation; and the familiars of Leo X and Clement VII all stated that no council could revoke a solemn doctrinal condemnation'.[16] This at first sight rather daring hypothesis is made more credible if we recall the difference between the attitudes of Basle and Eugenius towards the Hussites.[17] In any case, that the papacy held such a view of councils was partly due to the hardening of attitudes and doctrine in response to the conciliar movement; and the tardiness in convoking a council was largely due to the experience of the fifteenth century.[18]

NOTES

1. *DLO* 352-60; Martin (1939), iv, 294ff.; Valois (1906) *passim;* Héfèle-Leclerq, vii part 2, 1056ff.
2. Werminghoff; Hürten (1959).
3. *MC* iii, 125-43, 148-9; *PC* ii, 121-2, 139n.; Preiswerk; Kuchler; Bilderback (1966), 147.
4. Denzinger, 253; Gill (1959), 412ff.
5. Boularand; Hofmann; Black (1970a), 60-80.
6. Black (1970a), 86ff., 93ff., 105ff.
7. *MC* iii, 245ff.
8. Cognasso; *PC* ii, 183.
9. Bäumer (1965); *MC* iii, 139ff.
10. Black (1970a), 94ff., 112, 114, 116, 119ff., 124.
11. Mercati, i, 168ff.; *DLO* 422-3; Bertrams; *PC* ii, 326; Toews; Jedin (1957), 47ff.
12. Haller (1910), 25; cf. Bilderback (1966), 121-2, 173, 179-80.
13. Haller (1910), 25.
14. Cf. Black (1966), 87n.
15. Haller (1910), 26.
16. Delumeau, 5.
17. Above, p. 27.
18. Jedin (1957), 166ff.

CHAPTER 3

FORMATION OF
BASLE CONCILIARISM (1431-4)

1431-4 were the decisive years for the development of Basle conciliarism. The assertion of the council's right to resist dissolution by the pope was accompanied by an assertion of the outright, unlimited sovereignty of the council. One may, indeed, see a certain parallel here with the development of thought during the English and French revolutions. So far as doctrinal *decrees* were concerned, the output of Basle consisted almost entirely of reiterations of *Haec Sancta* and *Frequens*.[1] The most important addition was the rejection of the pope's right to dissolve a council unilaterally; this was related to the notion of the council as a sovereign corporation.

'It has not been, is not and will not in the future be either right or possible for the council to be dissolved, transferred to another place, or prorogued till another time, by any person, with whatever authority he is invested, even if he is in the papal office, without the deliberation and consent of the same council of Basle'. (15 February 1432).[2]

Similarly, Basle affirmed (26 June 1434) that a council held power 'immediately from Christ' whether or not papal legates were present.[3] The most controversial doctrinal decree was that of the 'three truths of the catholic faith' (15 May 1439):

'It is a truth of the catholic faith that the holy general council holds power over the pope and anyone else. The Roman pontiff of his own authority cannot dissolve, transfer or prorogue the general council when lawfully assembled without its own consent, and that is part of the same truth. Whoever obstinately opposes these truths must be deemed a heretic'.[4]

This was designed to justify the imminent deposition of Eugenius. It made explicit the fully *de fide* nature of *Haec Sancta* in the view of the Basle conciliarists.[5]

NOTES
1. 1st. session, 14 December 1431 in *MC* ii, 45ff.; 11th session, 27 April 1432 in *MC* ii, 713; 18th session, 26 June 1434 in *MC* ii, 713.
2. Mansi xxix, 21-2, *MC* ii, 214ff.; cf. Mansi xxix, 5-6, *MC* ii, 47ff.
3. *MC* ii, 713.
4. Mansi xxix, 178-80.
5. Cf. Vooght (1965), 105ff., 163ff.

The council's unlimited jurisdictional sovereignty

The official conciliar letters *Cogitanti* (3.ix.1432)[1] and *Speravit* (16.vi. 1433)[2] were fine statements of conciliar theory. The council, it was said, acts with the authority of the Church, whose decrees and customs are as unchallengeable as scripture.[3] Councils are incapable of error; rejecting the analogy between the pope and the emperor or other secular rulers (currently being emphasized by Monte, Roselli and others),[4] Basle affirmed that 'the body of the Church is not to be compared with other political bodies of cities or associations, because in the midst of this body is Christ, who rules it lest it err'.[5] History was invoked: 'we have often experienced and read that the pope . . . has erred; but we never read that the rest of the body erred when the pope did not'.[6] Relying on *Mathew* 18: 15-20 and the collective-dispersed distinction,[7] the council argued that jurisdiction was given 'to the unity of the faithful, not to individuals'; the notion of societal unity was used here specifically to counter the papal-monarchical argument that conciliar or ecclesial sovereignty implied a 'plurality of princes (sovereigns)' — and was therefore both impractical and contrary to the cosmic principle of unity.[8] Cesarini, who played a large part in drafting *Cogitanti*, made similar assertions in debates with Eugenius' envoys in July and October 1433.[9]

First, then, the council applied the teaching of *Haec Sancta* and *Frequens* to the crisis of 1431-3; Basle had been legitimately assembled, it was dealing with matters of faith (sc. Hussitism) and reform, and therefore the pope had no power to dissolve it, and was obliged to recognize it. In answer to citations from canon law and the canonists by Eugenius' spokesmen, Cesarini replied that not only could contrary texts be cited, but the ambiguities of canon law on this point had been finally resolved, since 'this matter is found to have been decided by the holy fathers in the council of Constance'.[10] (Cesarini, incidentally, regarded the respective powers of council and pope as matters of faith not of positive law.)[11]

Similarly, Heinrich Toke, a canon of Magdeburg representing the archbishop, said that, while the papal right of dissolution had previously been 'doubted and disputed on all sides', it had now been 'once and for all decided by the authority of the council of Constance'.[12]

Secondly, the Basle conciliarists were now affirming that the council held unlimited sovereignty in the Church: it could issue binding decrees on faith and reform, it was also the final court of appeal and could take over the papal executive functions as well if need be. This was the crucial point. Apart from the question of dissolution, the council's right to suspend the pope from office and assume his executive functions pending his trial – a claim possibly derived from Marsiglio[13] – was the most controverted question, and was justified in several Basilean tracts of 1432-4.[14] Cesarini himself justified Basle's establishment of a chancery with power to issue bulls and its assumption of powers previously belonging to the papacy in the collation of benefices and the settlement of disputed episcopal elections.[15] Christ, he said, is like a king who goes away leaving his affairs to be looked after by a servant (the pope); but, if the servant conducts himself badly, he is subject to correction by the queen (the Church) – an analogy that frequently appears in Basilean writings.[16] Cesarini argued that the council's jurisdictional supremacy derived from its dogmatic supremacy.[17]

NOTES

1. *MC* ii, 234-58.
2. *MC* ii, 373ff.
3. *MC* ii, 241.
4. Black (1970a), 86-7.
5. *MC* ii, 244-5.
6. *MC* ii, 243.
7. Above, p.21.
8. *MC* ii, 243-4, 381.
9. *MC* ii, 381, 492; cf. *MC* ii, 475-96, *MD* viii, 643-64.
10. *MC* ii, 381; cf. Mansi xxix, 512ff., esp. 525-6.
11. *MC* ii, 411; cf. Vooght (1965), 105ff., esp. 114.
12. *MOCC* vi, 20; cf. Mansi xxx, 814-22.
13. Above, p.12.
14. Toke, *Questio mota* and *Questio disputata*, esp. fol. 160v; Grünwalder, no title; Dionysius, *Conclusiones*; Anon, no title (all written in 1433). Cf. Kallen, 6-7.
15. *MC* ii, 480-1.
16. *MC* ii, 480-1; cf. Velde, below, p.75.
17. *MC* ii, 492-3.

Nicholas of Cusa

A brief word must be said about the special place of Nicholas of Cusa's

51

'Catholic concordance (*De concordantia catholica*)' — written in 1432-3 — in the conciliarism of this period.[1] Cusa is by far the best known conciliarist of Basle, yet I would suggest that Velde and Segovia rank beside him in originality of thought (though not in coherence), and that Segovia no less than Cusa drew out the implications for general political theory from conciliar doctrine. Cusa had been Velde's pupil at Cologne[2] and was friendly with both him and Segovia.[3] But as a conciliarist Cusa was *sui generis*; he does not conform to the pattern of Basle conciliarism either in his general conceptions or in his specific conclusions about immediate questions. After 1434 he became increasingly alienated from the majority group, supported Cesarini's line of moderation and conciliation, and eventually voted — unlike most Germans — for the minority decree of 1437.[4]

Cusa's central theme of concordance had two aspects: in the tradition of Abelard and Gratian, it meant the search for an inner harmony underlying apparently contradictory authoritative texts, and in the tradition of Albert the Great and Ramon Lull, both of whom Cusa became acquainted with during his year under Velde,[5] it meant the inner harmony and unity (or 'unanimity') of a hierarchically differentiated organism or society. This philosophical influence is clear from the outset, when he begins by applying to the 'mystical body' of the Church a series of typically neoplatonist triadic distinctions, for example between 'spirit', 'soul', and 'body'.[6] Cusa tries to show how the union of the different component parts of the Church — pope, patriarchs, bishops, priests, people — which ought to exist in Christ's mystical body can be realised in law and practice. Much of the character of Cusa's work is determined by the way in which he reinterprets the data of canon law, particularly the notion of 'consent' in the context of elections and legislation, in the light of this philosophical notion of the social 'concordance' of the Church. Nor must we forget that he was simultaneously preparing a legal case for an elected against an appointed archiepiscopal claimant.[7] The most distinctive feature of the work is the attempt to reconcile the notion of offices in the Church, divinely ordained according to the hierarchical model, with the idea that valid tenure of office requires the consent of those over whom it is exercised. True concordance, on which the validity of law and authority depends, exists when the divinely-created office is filled by someone chosen by and governing in accordance with the consent of his subjects.[8]

His distinctive theme is indeed *concordantia* (which he derived partly from Lull via Velde); from this central idea of concordance flow some of the divergences from other Basileans. For, on the one hand, he developed the case for elections throughout the ecclesiastical system far more vigorously than anyone else.[9] Both he and Velde would give the laity the role of electing parish priests,[10] which in Cusa's scheme meant that they formed in a sense the basis of the whole system: as he said, the priesthood *qua* soul of the Church derives from the people its 'motive, vegetative and sensitive power, which emanates from the potency of the material of the subjects through voluntary subjection'.[11] On the other hand, Cusa was unique among Basileans in maintaining that the consent of the Roman Church, at least in the sense of the Roman partriarchal synod presided over by the pope, is a necessary condition for valid conciliar legislation.[12] Further, he upholds the inerrancy of the Roman partriarchal synod;[13] while for him a general council is only infallible if it possesses a higher degree of unanimity than was required by other Basle conciliarists, and by the constitution of Basle itself.[14] For it is the consent of the different elements in the Church which gives councils their authority. What Cusa looks for is not a majority decision, but a deeper — and also potentially vaguer — spiritual unanimity, which may be either tacit or explicit.[15] While he takes the principle of consent much further than other Basileans in the case of elections, he gives less clear-cut powers to the council as such.

On the question of organic holism, Cusa, not unlike other Basle conciliarists, regarded the Church as a 'composite whole (*totum compositum*)',[16] but unlike them he retained the traditional distinction between the 'soul' and 'body' of the Church, identifying the soul with the priesthood, the body with the empire.[17] The influence of Velde may be detected in his speaking of the Church as having a 'substance' or 'nature',[18] and in his conception of triadic essences within, for example, the priesthood, corresponding to 'spirit, soul and body'.[19]

Cusa had been trained in canon law, and his work achieves a majestic interpenetration of the philosophical principle of *concordantia* with the canonical principle of consent. Yet he did not apply the corporational model of decision-making to the council. Some of his reservations about Basle's stance are characteristic of a canon-lawyer: for example, he is doubtful whether the council can suspend the pope from his functions.[20] He continued to deploy many of the same philosophical concepts after he had adhered to Eugenius in 1437.[21]

NOTES
1. Sigmund (1963), esp. 35-6, and (1962a); Heinz-Mohr; Meuthen (1962) and (1972); Vansteenberghe; Grass.
2. Colomer, 39-46; Sigmund (1963), 25-6.
3. Below, p. 125.
4. Sigmund (1963), 224ff.; Kallen, 80ff.
5. Colomer, 39-46.
6. *CC* (book) I, (ch.) ii, vi, viii; below, p. 76.
7. Sigmund (1963), 36, 219.
8. *CC* II, xiii.

9. *CC* II, xviii, xix.
10. *CC* II, xviii; below, p. 69.
11. *CC* II, xix at p. 205.
12. *CC* II, xi.
13. *CC* II, v at p. 107; of Sigmund (1963), 171.
14. *CC* II, xvii esp. at pp. 184, 190, xviii esp. at p. 194; Sigmund (1963), 181.
15. *CC* II, iv at p. 106, xvii at p. 194; cf. *CC* II, viii, x; Sigmund (1963), 172.
16. *CC* I Preface (à propos *I Cor*. 12:12); cf. below, pp. 64ff, 114, 138ff.
17. *CC* I Preface.
18. *CC* I Preface; cf. below, p. 66.
19. *CC* I, viii; II, r,vi. Cf. below, p. 76.
20. *CC* II, xviii at p. 198.
21. Sigmund (1963), 236ff.; Vansteenberghe, 65.

The presidency debate

The development in conciliar thought which had taken place by 1433-4 is best demonstrated by the debate on the presidency of the council (15-28 February 1434).[1] Following his capitulation, Eugenius had despatched three new legates, in addition to Cesarini, to the council, with Bulls of appointment making them joint presidents.[2] This act, designed to give Eugenius' supporters considerable control over the council, was contrary to provisions already made at Basle for the election of the council's president by the whole council, with specific and restricted powers. Segovia remarked, à propos Cesarini's temporary resignation from the presidency in 1432, that it was understood 'that it was in the council's power to set up a president for itself, and consequently ... that it was in its power ... to delimit his time and the mode of his presidency'.[3] A special commission was now set up to consider the matter. As reported by Segovia, this was intellectually the most impressive debate held at Basle: several treatises were written for circulation prior to the discussion. It soon became clear that the whole issue of conciliar and papal sovereignty lay not far beneath the surface of the dispute.

Three options were canvassed: acceptance of Eugenius' new legates as presidents 'on the strength of the Bulls', outright rejection of the legates' claim, and a compromise whereby they would be admitted as honorary co-presidents without coercive jurisdiction. Eugenius' position was defended by two Dominicans, Torquemada and Montenigro; the mainstream Basle conciliarists argued against the legates' admission; the compromise was supported by Cesarini, Cusa and the prior of St Benigne, Dijon – it also had the backing of the emperor, Sigismund. Cusa's contribution was an application of the views he had already expressed in the *De concordantia*: the difference between Cusa and the other conciliarists on this question was that Cusa held that the non-admission of the papal presidents would invalidate any future acts by the council.[4]

The conciliarist speakers were unanimous in maintaining that sovereignty lay wholly and inalienably with the council, which could also dispose of executive power.[5] They also held, on the basis of canonist corporation theory, that power was held by the council as a whole, not by the individuals composing it: there was in the council a 'common authority (*communis auctoritas*)'.[6] In defence of the council's majoritarian procedure, a cardinal cited his experience 'in many notable colleges; he had been a canon in chapters of cathedral Churches, a doctor in colleges of doctors, a counsellor of kings, a cardinal in the sacred college; and in his experience of these he had always seen this practice observed, that ... once the greater part ... were of one opinion, the smaller part gave way to them ... otherwise there would never be an end to the actions of any corporation'.[7]

Significant contributions were made to conciliar theory by Mathieu Menaye (or Menage)[8] and by Jean Beaupère.[9] Menaye defended the ascription of fulness of power to the Church-in-council by saying that the Church was 'a whole in respect of power' (or, 'a potential whole – *totum potestativum*'); fulness of power resided in it 'just as it is in the soul of a man, which can perform all the actions proper to men, not through one (power) but through all its powers'.[10] The organic analogy was further developed by Beaupère: he made two new points. First, he equated the Gersonian distinction between the Church taken collectively and the Church taken distributively with the distinction between the Church 'as a mystical body' and 'as a political body', itself a new application of organic terminology. Secondly, he identified the Church *qua* mystical body of Christ with the council *tout court*; the council, he said, was therefore 'immediately joined to Christ', receiving from him without intermediary the charismatic gifts of grace.[11] The pope was only head of the Church *qua* political body, not of the Church-in-council. These elaborations of the organic analogy, together with other refinements of conciliar theory introduced or re-stated during the presidency debate, were expounded in Segovia's official report for the four deputations.[12]

By now, therefore, conciliarists were claiming not so much that power should be divided between council and pope – the dominant theme at Constance – but rather that fulness of power resided in the council in the same unrestricted sense in which papalists, since Leo I, had ascribed it to the papacy. It is important to realise just what they were claiming. It was not only that the council is the Church's legislature, infallible in faith and morals; that the pope and others are bound to implement its decrees; and that a suspect pope may be suspended, pending his trial, and his executive functions may be assumed by the council. Crucially, they were claiming that the council, so long as it was in session, was the sovereign judicial court, the final court of appeal, in ecclesiastical matters. The regular convocation of councils prescribed by *Frequens* would ensure that this meant, in effect, that the council was the supreme organ of ecclesiastical jurisdiction. This was the difference between the 'occasional' supremacy of the council, as envisaged by those who saw a council in its more or less traditional role of deciding extraordinarily difficult cases, primarily of doctrine,[13] and the 'fulness of power' now claimed by the Basilean conciliarists, and already implemented by the council when it set up its own courts (from 1432), and forbade appeals from them.[14] This was, furthermore, the link between Basle's anti-papalism and its anti-secularism: it claimed for itself ecclesiastical jurisdiction in the traditional sense, and would not cede territory to the secular power.[15] The Basle majority seem to have sensed all along that there could be no reconciliation with Eugenius: their programme was truly revolutionary. It was a conscious attempt to transfer the central government of the Church from the Roman papacy to an (itinerant) council.

The constitutional theology behind this programme was that the council derived its power 'immediately from Christ', who functioned therein 'through himself'; the Holy Spirit was the true president of the council and inspired its acts. This was supported by scriptural argument showing that Christ gave his authority to the apostles or Church as a group; by precedents taken from the practice and theory of ecclesiastical and civil corporations; and by a constitutional philosophy, which affirmed the real unity of the whole church, the categorical distinction between whole and parts, and equated the council with the Church in its assembled or collective aspect.

The Basle conciliarists, then, had developed Gersonian ecclesiology to support the anti-papal stance which circumstances led them to adopt. The radicalization of conciliar theory was complete by early 1434. This ideology underlay the subsequent actions of the Basle majority and was restated by one writer after another. Its opponents would find themselves forced to quit Basle.

At the end of the presidency debate, the compromise solution suggested by Cesarini and demanded by the emperor was adopted. The papal nominees were admitted as honorary co-presidents alongside Cesarini, without coercive jurisdiction and 'saving the method of proceeding hitherto observed in this holy council' (26 April).[16] The new legates, incorporated on 14 April, were required not only to take the usual oath to uphold the decrees of Constance and Basle, but also specifically to observe *Haec Sancta*, which they had to recite in full.[17] Once again, the reconciliation was superficial: when *Haec Sancta* was re-promulgated on 26 June, the three legates representing Eugenius refused to take part in the session.[18]

NOTES

1. *MC* ii, 602-17, 629-36; cf. Kallen, 42ff.
2. *PC* i, 311-31.
3. *MC* ii, 122; cf. *MC* ii, 332, 470, and above, p. 29
4. *MC* ii, 612; Cusa, *De auctoritate*, 32; Sigmund (1963), 219.
5. *MC* ii, 606-7, 609, 610, 615-16.
6. *MC* ii, 607-8, 616; Kallen, 7.
7. *MC* ii, 629-30.
8. An obscure figure: cf. *PC* i, 385; *DLO* 320.
9. Champion ii, 340-1.
10. *MC* ii, 615. Cf. below, p. 65, 138ff.
11. *MC* ii, 609; cf. Codex Trevirensis 1205-503, fols. 173r-4v. D'Ailly had described the council as 'velut corpus mysticum': *TEP* 953; cf. *Acta concilii Constantiensis* ii, 405-6.
12. Below, pp. 119, 138ff.
13. Cf. Wilks (1963), 449-50, 505-6.
14. Above, p. 30f.; below, pp. 113 and n.3, 130; cf. Black (1966), 45.
15. Cf. Mansi, xxx, 843.
16. *MC* ii, 649-50; Mansi, xxix, 90.
17. *MC* ii, 647-8.
18. *MC* ii, 713; Mansi, xxix, 91.

CHAPTER 4

HEIMERICH VAN DE VELDE (1433–4): ORGANIC REALISM

Heimerich van de Velde (*Heimericus de Campo*)[1] was born in 1395 at the village of Sol in the Low Countries.[2] He studied at Paris university from 1410 to 1422, under Johannes de Nova Domo, a leading figure in the neo-Albertist movement in philosophical theology;[3] Heimerich was later to say of St Albert that he 'nourished me from my infancy'.[4] His studies at Paris coincided with the peak years of conciliar activity, and with the ascendancy within the conciliar movement of the university's chancellor, Gerson, another Netherlander, with whose writings on the Church Velde became familiar. In 1422, Velde moved to the university of Cologne where neo-Albertism was establishing itself in controversy with nominalism and Thomism, and he gave the Albertists his full support.[5] Velde became a life-long adherent of this school of neoplatonic realism, which viewed the universe as a series of emanations from the mind of God, so that the chief object of knowledge was the exemplars or universals pre-existing in the mind of God. The world of nature and man could be known by analogy with these or as particularizations of them. Symbols, artistic imagery and the sacraments themselves held a special place in this view of things as visible manifestations of the invisible order of reality;[6] Velde himself compared the Church-as-a-whole with the *mysterium artis*.[7] Velde, who was also attracted by Ramon Lull's metaphysical schemata, became one of the leading realist thinkers of his day. In 1425-6 he taught Nicholas of Cusa at Cologne, thus introducing to the field of philosophical theology a thinker who was far to outshine his master.[8]

In 1425, Velde became dean of arts. In August of that year he dedicated to Martin V a short ecclesiological work 'On the disordered condition of the Church and on the Bohemian heresy (*De incomposito statu ecclesie et de heresi Bohemorum*)'. It consists of two dialogues, the first between 'nature', 'reason' and 'truth', the second between 'a Bohemian' and 'a Romanist'. The work is studded with neoplatonic allegorical argument; it is also a characteristically northern-European complaint about ecclesiastical decadence, which Velde sees as partly responsible for the Hussite schism. If only the Church would give better rewards to men of learning and virtue it would not be in such a bad way.[9] He concludes with a plea for a hard-working graduate: 'but I am poor and have laboured from my youth, for from the sixth year of my infancy up to my thirtieth year which is now upon me I have sweated in the study of philosophy and theology'.[10] In 1428, Velde was made professor of theology, and in 1431 vice-chancellor. He held only one ecclesiastical benefice, the canonry of St Cecilia in Cologne; his plea to Martin V would appear to have been in vain.[11]

On 10 November 1432, the university made him one of its two delegates to the council; they were incorporated in December.[12] The official Basel records contain no further reference to Velde. He lodged for a time with the delegates of Vienna university, and Paris delegates later praised his work at the council. It is probable that he belonged to the faith committee, as most theologians did, and it is also probable that the remarkable collection of tracts entitled 'On Ecclesiastical Power (*De ecclesiastica potestate*)', which he composed in 1433-4, were written for circulation among his fellow-members. The praise given him by the Parisians implies that they admired his written contributions;[13] one of the tracts was written 'at someone's suggestion', and that 'someone' was almost certainly Nicholas of Cusa.[14] During 1433 he kept his principals informed on the Hussite negotiations, and on developments between Eugenius and the council, sending them copies of important papal and conciliar pronouncements.[15] He reflected that 'the whole occasion of the present disturbance is the comparison on sovereignty (*de superioritate comparatio*) which is un-resolved in the minds of many contestants on either side'.[16] By October, his colleague had left, and his correspondence from now on is largely concerned with his need for more money to keep himself at Basle.[17] Lack of funds, it would appear, compelled him to return to Cologne in February 1434, at which point the Paris university delegation at Basle wrote Cologne a letter praising Velde and supporting his pleas for money.[18] It is uncertain whether he returned to Basle; if he did, it was not for long.

For in 1435 Velde accepted the offer of a professorship at the university of Louvain, founded by Martin V in 1425 and constant in its adherence to the papacy. In 1437, when schism finally erupted, he sided with Eugenius, and wrote an 'apology' explaining 'why he parted company with the

59

council of Basle and adhered to Eugenius IV', which has been lost.[19] In October 1440 he attended a provincial synod at Cologne on behalf of the bishop of Liège; a piece written by him on this occasion indicates a clearly pro-papal development in his thinking. Velde here adopts the ancient distinction between priesthood and kingship as twin characteristics of the Christian community, but — rather than elaborating them, as was so commonly done, in terms of ecclesiastical and secular power — treats them as signifying collective and individual authority respectively. At an earlier time, he says, the priesthood had been 'universally united' and the kingship 'divided into parts', so that the 'synodical or senatorial royal authority of the priesthood overcame the power of the priestly kingship divided into parts, as the whole is above the parts'. But now the 'kingdom of the Church is universally united and the priesthood divided juridically through patriarchal, provincial and episcopal councils', so that the 'royal authority of the pope' is supreme, and the pope is 'regularly above the council'.[20] This notion of a historic evolution of the church constitution enabled him to account for the supremacy of councils at an earlier period. He still allowed for the 'occasional' supremacy of a council, but denied that this applied in the present case.[21] Rather, he supported the German princes in their plea for a new council to resolve the issues between Basle and Eugenius.[22] He also maintained a distinction between the power of dogmatic definition, which he ascribed to the council, and the power of ruling, which he ascribed to the hierarchy.[23] When pressed, however, he decided to 'declare himself' and said that 'the authority of Christ is greater in the pope than it is in the council'.[24] The rector of Cologne university, Tinctoris of Tournai (a former pupil of Velde), had him arrested for this contradiction of the university's teaching.[25] In a much fuller work written for the Reichstag of Frankfort (1446), 'The power of pope and general council (*Tractatus de potestate papae et concilii generalis)*', he developed his ideas further, and sought to reconcile the claims of pope and council through the dialectical metaphysics of neoplatonism. He expounded a remarkable theory of the dialectical development of the Church's constitution from democracy through aristocracy to monarchy, the final stage retaining elements of the earlier ones. It is a work of complex originality.[26] In practice, he still supported Eugenius in the current controversy, but also upheld the validity of *Haec Sancta*, and continued to advocate a new council, in order to resolve the doctrinal dispute and to restore unity. Velde remained at Louvain till his death in 1460.

Velde's *Ecclesiastical power* survives in a single manuscript, in a very difficult hand and not without mistakes; its language is idiosyncratic, its style obscure and its meaning often dense. No contemporary author explicitly refers to it; the manuscript came into the possession of Cusa, who added some notes in the margin. It has been studied by Colomer for its exposition of Lull's theory of knowledge (fols. 106-8) and for Lull's influence, via Velde, upon Cusa.[27] It consists of eight tracts. The first (fols. 89r–149r) and third (fols. 159r-69r) contain most of Velde's philosophical theology of the Church; this is also discussed in the seventh (fols. 177v-86r), which is followed by a set of arcane diagrams relating his ecclesiological theory to Lull's 'art of knowledge' (fols. 186v-8r). The second tract (fols. 149v-58v) is on papal and episcopal power. There are three short tracts (fols. 169v-70v, 170v-4r, 174r-7r) which add little to the others. The eighth tract (fols. 189r-94v) deals with the council's power to grant an indulgence.[28] Haubst dates the whole work between Easter 1433 and Easter 1434.[29] Refutations of the Bull *Deus Novit* in the latter part of the first tract[30] suggest that it was completed about October 1433. The short fifth tract was 'completed at Basle in February 1434'.[31] The seventh tract deals in the main with the legislative and executive powers of council and pope, and in particular with the 'invalidating clause', which was chiefly in dispute from December 1432 to July 1433;[32] but certain modifications of the radical-conciliarist views upheld in the earlier tracts suggest that it may have been written, or at least completed, after the preceding tracts.

Ecclesiastical power is surely unique in the history of ecclesiology. The reason why it was written and its practical conclusions are about the same as those of many other conciliarist tracts written in these years; but it has an intellectual momentum all of its own. It owes this to the originality of Velde's mind, and to the philosophico-theological sources he used; for he applied both neo-Platonic and neo-Aristotelian philosophy to the Church in an entirely new way. Velde upheld the primacy of scripture in the field of ecclesiology, particularly against the claims of the canon lawyers. In his work of 1425 he had said that the controversy between Bohemia and Rome should be settled by the Bible and not by 'doctors'.[33] At the beginning of *Ecclesiastical power*, he states that the main problem in the controversy between the Hussites, Eugenius and Basle is 'the contrary understanding of authorities' (i.e. biblical texts); and he proposes to resolve the problem by citing the texts used by each party to the dispute, so that 'set side by side they may become more clear'.[34] The pro-conciliar texts which he himself later uses to defend the conciliar case, include *Math.* 18:15-20; *Acts* 15 and 20:28; *I Cor.* 12:15-27.[35] Citing *Rev.* 1-2, he observes that, when the Spirit is said to be speaking to the seven Churches, this really means to the whole Church, because seven is 'the number of universality (*numerus universitatis*)'.[36] He later gives full rein to the allegorical method of scriptural exegesis.[37] In the seventh tract, quoting Christ's saying 'why do you break away from the commandments of God for the sake of your tradition?'

(*Mat.* 15:3), he issues a stinging attack on those who use 'the gentile fig-ments of human constitutions' as a means of interpreting 'the mysteries of the divine law' (i.e. of scripture).[38] He ascribes 'the lamentable state of the modern Church' to the undervaluing of 'the speculations of philosophy and revelations (*theophanias*) of theology' by men who prefer 'human wisdom' — that is, legal knowledge — which, he says, is 'foolish in the eyes of God'. The pro-papal case rests on 'the very numerous judgements of jurists'.[39]

The third tract is more philosophical in intention. He states it as his aim to deduce 'certain doctrinal syllogisms' from his long study of St Albert,[40] in other words to see what conclusions for ecclesiology can be drawn from it. As it turns out, this means that he wants to apply neoplatonic realism to the subject. He introduces the Pseudo-Dionysian notion of 'hierarchy' and triadic sets of 'exemplars', abstract concepts such as 'order, knowledge, action . . . being, living, understanding', which are conceived as ultimate realities because they exist in the divine mind.[41] But this does not exclude theology; in fact the council, the priesthood and the episcopate are dis-cussed most extensively in terms of Christology and sacramental theology.[42] This is because, in Velde's view, theology, philosophy and 'human prud-ence' (or law) are three stages of knowledge. In a passage reminiscent of Plato's allegory of the cave, he says that his task is to 'ascend stage by stage, through the medium of natural law, to one immediate and supreme exemplar; and so to rise up from shade through image to the unchallenge-able truth of the thing (*de umbra per imaginem ad irrefragabilem rei veritatem assurgere*)'.[43] He explains the three stages of knowledge further by saying that 'human prudence' or 'art' is the province of law; the 'hidden decree of nature (*dictamen occultum nature*)', that of philosophy; the theologian has access to the 'true judgements . . . of divine law', that is of scripture.[44] The three types of knowledge are interrelated because they correspond to three interrelated levels of reality or being: God, nature and human artifice. Since nature mirrors God, and art mirrors nature, inter-sections, cross-references and analogies can be found between the three levels of knowledge; such is the basis of Velde's approach. In the third tract, he states it as his intention to start with the highest level of knowledge and to work downwards: 'to descend by stages from primordial reasonings to natural ones, and from these to human reasonings; for nature is the image of divine reason, and art or human reason is the image of natural reason likewise. Thus God, nature and art are subordinated to one another (*de rationibus primordialibus ad rationes naturales, et de hiis ad rationes humanas gradatim descendere; ex quo natura est imago rationis divine, et ars seu ratio humana est imago rationis naturalis pariformiter. Sic deus, natura et ars subordinantur*)'.[45] By reading 'the Idea' for 'divine reason', one could make a parallel with Hegel. In both the third and the seventh tracts, then, we find theology and philosophy mingled together.

NOTES

1　His philosophy has been studied by Meerssemann and Haubst (1952); cf. Gilson, 802n.
2.　Black (1977a), 273-4n.
3.　Colomer, 8.
4.　*EP* fol. 159r.
5.　Keussen (1928), 62*, 240-1; Gilson, 532-4, 802n.
6.　Cf. Huizinga, 57f., 216ff.
7.　Below, p. 68 n. 6.
8.　Colomer, 8, 39-46. Another of his pupils was Johannes Tinctoris of Tournai, theology professor at Cologne 1440-69; Keussen (1928), 63*.
9.　*De incomposito*, fol. 58v.
10.　*De incomposito*, fol. 58v.
11.　Keussen (1928), 62*, Bianco, 823; Sigmund (1963), 25; Meerssemann, 15-16.
12.　*MC* ii, 285; Bianco (Anlage), 168; Keussen (1928), 234-43.
13.　Below, n. 18.
14.　*EP* fol. 177v; below, p. 80.
15.　Bianco (Anlage), 171-91.
16.　Bianco (Anlage), 181-2.
17.　Bianco (Anlage), 192-7; Black (1977a), 275-6.
18.　Bianco (Anlage), 199-200.
19.　Schulte (1877), 373.
20.　*DRTA* xv, 468-9.
21.　*DRTA* xv, 469.
22.　Above, pp. 46f.
23.　*DRTA* xv, 469.
24.　*DRTA* xv, 471.
25.　*DRTA* xv, 474.
26.　Black (1970b).
27.　Colomer, 25ff., 39ff.; fols. 106-8 are edited by Colomer, 121-4.
28.　Ed. Ladner (1977).
29.　Haubst (1952), 58n.
30.　*EP* fols. 135v, 136v, 148r.
31.　*EP* fol. 174r.
32.　Below, p. 80f.
33.　*De incomposito*, fol. 54v.
34.　*EP* fol. 89r; his 1446 work starts by observing that the main cause of the Basle-Eugenius schism is 'different interpretations of the decree of Constance' (i.e.*Haec Sancta*): Black (1970b), 79n.
35.　*EP* fols. 89r-v.
36.　*EP* fol. 89r.
37.　Below, pp. 75ff.
38.　*EP* fol. 185r.
39.　*EP* fol. 182v; cf.*I Cor*. 1:18-25.
40.　*EP* fol. 159r.
41.　For example, *EP* fols. 161r-2r; cf. below, p. 75f.
42.　*EP* fols. 159v-63v; cf. below, pp. 66f., 69f., 72f.
43.　*EP* fol. 183r.
44.　*EP* fol. 183r.
45.　*EP* fol. 159r.

In Velde's ecclesiology, as expressed in his works of 1433-4, we find the strong, collectivist version of the organic analogy, together with other holistic expressions of the nature of the Church, playing a dominant and all-pervasive role in the defence of the specifically Basilean version of conciliar theory. I do not think we can say that he first elaborated a philosophical theology of the Church, by means of a disinterested process of thought, and was then led to conclude from such objective reflection that the council was superior to the pope. Rather, a study of his tracts clearly suggests that he was elaborating these holistic ideas about the Church with the specific purpose of defending conciliarism. He was indeed already a convinced neoplatonic 'realist';[1] but he would later use similar philosophical ideas to defend a more moderate version of conciliar theory, indeed at one point (in 1440) he upheld papal supremacy.

Velde expatiated on the Gersonian argument, used by most Basle conciliarists, that the Church collectively, i.e. the council, is superior to the Church dispersively, i.e. the pope and bishops.[2] While Zabarella and other jurists had argued the case for conciliar sovereignty in terms of the superiority of the whole corporation over its individual members, and Gerson in terms of the superiority of the collective over the dispersed Church, Velde argued in particular in terms of the superiority of the Church *qua* united body of Christ over the Church *qua* dispersed members, and in terms of the superiority of substance over accidents. His argument, proceeding as it does from philosophical realism, lays an exceptionally strong emphasis on the existential reality of the Church as a whole, an emphasis that is stronger in Velde than in any other conciliarist or indeed, I suspect, any other medieval writer. Theology and philosophy are intertwined; and one may detect in Velde's arguments some of the flavour of Flemish-Rhenish mysticism.

Velde argues from St Paul's organic analogy (which culminated in the statement that the Christian community was the body of Christ, *I Cor.* 12:12-27) that 'just as such limbs are joined up to one root principle of life (*connectuntur ad unum radicale vite principium*), which is the heart ... so all the members of the Church are coordinated in one original or root principle of mystical life (*coordinantur ad unum originale seu radicale vite mystice principium*), which is Christ'.[3] Referring to *Romans* 1:17 ('the just man lives by faith'), he says that the life-principle of this body is faith, which is also its unifying principle: 'faith, as the same apostle testifies, is the spirit of life unifying universally all the limbs (members) of the Church in the same way that the life of the heart flows into the other parts of the human body to give them life'.[4] Velde defends this collectivist interpretation of the organic analogy by appealing to Aristotle's doctrine that functions such as understanding or anger should be ascribed to the whole man and not to the soul alone; we should not say 'the soul of the man understands' but 'the whole man understands through the soul'.[5]

Velde employs other theological arguments to express his strongly holist view of the Church. Faith is the essential, generic quality of the Church, the common possession of which binds all Christians together as a unified whole. Faith constitutes the Christian people as a unity 'in being and power'; it is the 'form' of the Church[6]. 'By participation in one faith all Christians are one Church[7] . . . The universal or catholic Church was first created by the holy Spirit on the day of Pentecost in the being of a total mystical body *(in esse totius corporis mystici)*[8] . . . The holy Church is the assembly *(congregatio)* of the faithful, bound together in one baptism, one faith, one hope of their calling and one Spirit'.[9] Velde follows Niem in asserting the superiority of the 'catholic' Church (which, however, unlike Niem he uses merely as a circumlocution for the council) over the apostolic Church, which like Niem he identifies with the pope and hierarchy; for Velde the former refers to the Church *qua* unity, the latter refers to the Church *qua* diversity.[10]

The crux of Velde's argument is to say that the Church thus united is 'prior to itself' considered as a diversity of members; this he takes to mean that the Church assembled in council is superior to the various hierarchical offices taken separately.[11] There is a basic *connexio fidelium ad Christum* which is 'prior' to any other aspect of the Church; therefore, Christ is 'more intimately' present in the council than he is in the pope: 'and therefore the jurisdiction of the same Christ is more vigorous and more authoritative in the general council than in the supreme pontiff'.[12] All Christians depend on the Church for their 'being', that is for their essential nature as Christians, which they receive through baptism; for their 'nutrition', received in the Eucharist and confirmation; and for the 'discipline of faith', administered through the 'hierarchical illumination of the priestly order'. Since he is a Christian, the pope is 'legitimately subject to holy mother Church represented by a general council in these three respects'.[13]

The mystical body comprises not only the union of Christians among themselves but also the union of Christians with Christ, resulting in the binding- or joining-together of Christ and the Church, made up of the ministering and acting members like an organic body; this is called the mystical composition of Christ's body'.[14] This again supports the prevalent conciliar view that Christ presides directly at the council; as Velde puts it, 'Christ, as activator (*actor*) of the Catholic faith, resides in the midst of the universal council or Church'.[15]

Velde further develops the organic analogy by reference to the notion of the Church as the continuation of Christ's being on earth; Christ and the faithful share 'a common nature, that is humanity'. 'Christ, through the grace of the hypostatic union, is human nature . . . Through this putting on (or raising up — *assumptionem*) of human nature, God produces the Church (*sibi dispensat deus ecclesiam*). Therefore the general council of Christians is the formal and power-bearing college of Christ and the Church, naturally or matrimonially univocal in being, power and action (*generale concilium est formale et potestativum . . . Christi et ecclesie collegium in esse, posse, et agere naturaliter seu coniugaliter univocum*)'.[16] Velde argues that the two aspects of the Church's being, its essential unity and its hierarchical differentiation, correspond to the divine and human natures in Christ respectively.

NOTES
1. Above, p. 58.
2. Above, p. 21.
3. *EP* fol. 89v.
4. *EP* fol. 89v.
5. *EP* fol. 137r; cf. Menaye, above, p. 55; Aquinas, *In . . . Ethic.*, lect. 6.
6. *EP* fol. 89v.
7. *EP* fol. 89v.
8. *EP* fol. 92r.
9. *EP* fol. 159r; cf. *Eph.* 4:3-6.
10. *EP* fols. 159v, 178v, and 161r: 'Que ecclesia catholica coordinat sub una, reparata per gratiam dei incarnatam, formali natura, ecclesia apostolica distinguit et subordinat sub una principali talis nature hypostasi seu persona . . . Sicut natura subest forme, que est sue unitatis, veritatis et bonitatis actus seu endelechia, sic ecclesia apostolica materialiter divisa, deformata et deordinata' (that is, when not 'formed' or 'ordered' as an essential unity, i.e. outwith the general council), 'subicitur ecclesie catholice, per unum baptisma materialiter unite, per unam fidem formate, et per unam spem efficaciter per unum spiritum finaliter ordinate'. Cf. Niem, above, p. 16.
11. *EP* fol. 89v; cf. Black (1977a), 280, 284.
12. *EP* fol. 89v.
13. *EP* fol. 90r-v.
14. *EP* fol. 159v.
15. *EP* fol. 89v.
16. *EP* fol. 159v; cf Wilks (1963), 21 and Vatican II decree *Lumen gentium* i, 8; 'Just as the assumed nature inseparably united to the divine word serves (Christ) as a living instrument of salvation, so, in a similar way, does the communal structure of the Church serve Christ's spirit': *Documents of Vatican II*, p. 22.

Priority of the universal essence of the Church

Velde, then, conceives the Church as a deep and real, albeit invisible, unity; for him this unity comprises the very essence of the Church. Velde also expresses this in philosophical language. Gerson and others had already defined the council as the 'form' of the Church, or as the Church 'in act', while the dispersed Church had been called the 'material' Church or the Church 'in potency'.[1] Velde took this kind of argument a good deal further, once again in a more holistic direction. For him the Church is an ontological 'substantia', 'species' or 'natura', which has a prior existence as a whole; members of the Church are characterized by their participation in the qualities and gifts of this whole in a way logically prior to their characterization as functionally differentiated members.[2] For through their redemption by Christ they all possess a new common 'nature' as 'the assembly of men regenerated in their nature (*congregatio hominum in natura regeneratorum*)', united under a single law 'according to the instinct (*instinctum*) of that nature'.[3] 'The Church is the essential and intelligible gathering-together of Christians (. . . *essentialis et notionalis collectio*)'.[4] The language used once again implies the equation of the Church *qua* whole with the general council.

In one passage he combines this philosophical holism with a christological argument: 'The univocal, formative virtue (*virtus formativa*) of the divine and human natures demands that all Christians, regenerated through baptism in the same original justice and god-formed by the same *caracter*, should come together in one divine-and-human essential potency, proper or appropriated, that is substantially, intelligibly or causally established (*in una divina et humana conveniant potentia essentiali, propria vel appropriata, i.e. substantialiter, notionaliter seu causaliter instaurata*)'.[5]

It would seem that Velde views the relationship of the Church-as-a whole to its individual members as one of substance to accidents.[6] Applying this to the council, he says that, since 'the substance which immediately founds the authority of the council is the human species ruled, confirmed and ordained *Christiformiter*', and since Christ did not put on a derivative (i.e. accidental or subordinate) nature (*'assumpsit naturam non suppositatam'*), therefore, 'just as substance (nature — *natura*) is above accident (*suppositum*), so the general council is *substantialiter* above the pope'.[7]

He perceives that it is possible to compare the relationship between the Church understood collectively (or *ut universitas*) and the Church understood dispersively (or *ut singuli*) with the relationship between a universal and its particulars. (A slight anticipation of this may be found in Huguccio's definition of *universitas* (association, corporation).)[8] To define the Church as 'the God-formed human species' meant, for a realist, that its members derived their essence from this prior totality. Velde's view, then, stands in the sharpest possible contrast to the nominalist views of late-medieval lawyers, which were summed up by the influential Baldus when he defined a 'people' as 'a collection of men into one mystical body, understood as an abstraction, the meaning of which is determined by the mind (*hominum collectio in unum corpus mysticum et abstractive sumptum, cuius significatio est inventa per intellectum)*.[9]

Thus Velde, more than any other conciliarist, and perhaps more than any other late-medieval writer, takes literally the holistic implications of the organic analogy. Can we then say that Velde's theory provides a unique exception to Gierke's view that medieval thinkers failed to grasp that the community as such is a 'subject of right' with a 'really-existing group-personality *(Gesamtpersönlichkeit)*'?[10] Gierke ascribed their failure to the fact that (in Tierney's words), despite their reference to the Church as a 'mystical body', 'they did not conceive of it as a true corporation because they subjected it to (a) super-imposed hierarchical authority'.[11] Gierke observes wistfully that 'the thought might have occurred' in the course of their discussions of the organic analogy 'that the Personality of the Individual consists in a . . . permanent Substance within an Organism'.[12] Exactly this thought appears to have occurred to Velde. He sees the whole Church as having a 'real personality', which 'itself can will, itself can act'.[13] Yet Gierke's generalisation still really holds true. For when we ask how Velde's Church can will and act, the answer is only through the general council; real power and 'personality' are denied to the Church as a whole.

NOTES

1. Above, p. 21; cf. below, pp. 114f.
2. *EP* fol. 159v.
3. *EP* fol. 140r.
4. *EP* fol. 159r.
5. *EP* fol. 161r.
6. In an analogy with craftsmanship, he says the Church as a whole is above the pope 'sicut mysterium artis supervenit officium sui principalis instrumenti': *EP* fol. 136r.
7. *EP* fols. 136r-v. The usual meaning of *suppositum* is subordinate part or subject (also, hypostasis, hypothesis), but I take Velde frequently to be using it to mean 'accident'
8. Below, p. 139.
9. Cit. Gierke, *DGR* iii, 432; cf. below, p. 150f., 170f.
10. Gierke, *DGR* trans. Maitland, 68.
11. Tierney (1968), 136-8; cf. Gierke, *DGR* iii, 252.
12. Gierke, *DGR* trans. Maitland, 68; cf. *DGR* trans. Barker, 78.
13. Maitland, introd. to his transl. of *DGR* p. xxvi.

It is sometimes suggested that such holistic realism was a natural ally of papalism:[1] this is certainly not true of the fifteenth century. Not only does Velde link realism with conciliar supremacy; he sees it as having further levelling implications. Apropos the incorporation of all Christians into the single body of Christ through baptism and faith, he says: 'The gospel truth is equally necessary for all believers in Christ and therefore it shines in the Church without acceptance of persons . . . the pope is not prior to or more powerful than any Christian'.[2]

This spiritual and sacramental equality among Christians precedes, for Velde, their differentiation into separate functional roles and their hierarchical subordination to one another. All of the preceding arguments imply that the council, which possesses supreme ecclesiastical authority, derives its standing not from the hierarchy but from the Church-as-a-whole.

Like Marsiglio and Cusa, though not necessarily because of them, Velde also believes in the equality of all priests, in virtue of their having all received the same sacramental ordination: 'Just as a sign, exemplar or idea shapes (things to which it is applied) formally and, through the necessity of its form, univocally; so the power of ecclesiastical order shapes everything that is applied to it into Christ formally, equally and without exception of persons (*Quemadmodum sigillum, exemplar seu idea figurat formaliter et per sue forme necessitatem univoce, sic potestas ecclesiastici ordinis christiformat omne sibi applicatum formaliter, equaliter et sine personarum exceptione)*'.[3] All priests 'are established with equal power (*equipotenter*) in the power of ecclesiastical order or jurisdiction'.[4] Consequently, all priests have an equal right (*'eque legitimi'*) to participate in papal elections.[5] The view that the jurisdictional power of priests was equal to that of bishops, at least within the council, became a commonplace of Basilean doctrine, especially during and after 1439.[6] But Velde, as we have seen, also emphasizes the equality of all believers in virtue of their common baptism. And this leads him, like Cusa but unlike most Basileans, to extend the principle of electoral participation to the laity. 'Everyone is inspired by the holy Spirit to choose a pastor';[7] ecclesiastical elections should in general take place 'by the mutual consent of the clergy and the people'.[8] The principle of equality, which Velde thinks entails electoral rights, is closely related here to philosophical realism: it derives from the priority of the universal exemplar over its particular manifestations.

NOTES
1. Cf. below, pp. 82f.
2. *EP* fols. 89v-90r.

3. *EP* fol. 160v; but elsewhere he asserts the distinctiveness of episcopal power: *EP* fol. 163v.
4. *EP* fol. 161r.
5. *EP* fol. 161r.
6. Below, p. 113 at n. 4.
7. *EP* fol. 181v.
8. *EP* fol. 181v.

The church-in-council as an 'actual whole (totum actuale)'

We have already noted several instances in which Velde applies his holistic conceptions of the Church specifically to the case for conciliar sovereignty. We must now consider those parts of his argument where he refers more immediately to the council itself. Velde says that the Church's unity is visibly realised in a council, because there members of the Church are united under a single roof. For the organic relationship between Christ and Christians is not so fully realised when the latter are scattered as when they are gathered together. 'Such a social correlation (*correlatio socialis*) cannot be established between Christ and Christians taken as accidents (or subordinates — *supposite acceptos*), and therefore divided from each other . . . Such joining-together has to be established in a formal and univocal being that participates in humanity (*in esse formali et univoco participa-(n)te humanitatis*); but it is thus that they come together in a general council . . . The Church in a general council is actively associated (*actu sociatur*) with its head'.[1]

The council symbolizes the 'spiritual and mystical marriage between Christ and the Church'.[2] In a passage in the seventh tract, Velde speaks of the council as having the qualities of Christ's mystical body, and of the papal régime as operating in the Church *qua* political body. As the special visible manifestation of Christ's mystical body, the council possesses the 'evangelical . . . (and) catholic power of the holy Spirit'[3] — it being a commonplace of Basle conciliarism that the holy Spirit presides at the council.[4] This argument, reminiscent of Beaupère[5] — though whether actually influenced by him one cannot say — and also of Segovia,[6] derives special force from Velde's neo-Platonic ontology which emphasized the priority of what is inward and spiritual over the physical realm of outward appearances. This, then, becomes a further argument for conciliar supremacy: 'As the spirit precedes the body, so the mystical jurisdiction of the holy Spirit precedes the human and political jurisdiction of the apostolic lord. Therefore, the uprightness of justice (*sic*) originally existing between the exterior and interior man shows that in the general council the apostolic keys are subject to the synodal will of the holy Spirit;

whence it is that in the same council the authority of the whole college is greater than that of the apostolic see, if these powers are compared with one another'.[7]

In the philosophical sphere, Velde argues that the council, as a real, structured unity-in-diversity is a more direct expression of the Church's essence than is the pope: 'the substance which immediately founds the authority of the council is the human species ruled, confirmed and ordained *Christiformiter*[8] . . . the council is in itself a kind of actual whole (*quoddam totem actuale*), assembled or made up out of the originally correlative principles (*sic: principiis originaliter correlativis*) of the universal Church; but the pope is a kind of potential whole (*quoddam totum potentiale*)'.[9] Here he seems to be suggesting that the council actualises the full qualities and powers of the Church because it is a whole in a more literal sense than are the constituent parts of the Church outwith the council.

In calling the council 'a kind of actual whole', then, Velde was implying that it realizes the essence of the Church. This is partly, as has been said, because it is a more visible unity than the Church at large. But Velde also sees the council as realizing certain crucial moral and intellectual qualities to a higher degree than could the pope. Aristotle says that 'a crowd judges better than one man alone', the book of Wisdom that 'a large group of wise men is the health of the world'; consequently, 'the love of the holy Spirit collecting the Church's members in synodal unity is more universal, deep and pure than charity participated in or exemplified by any person'.[10] The council is greater than the pope in 'fecundity of goodness . . . duration, strength, fulness of knowledge, freedom of will, perfection of virtue, certainty of truth'; and therefore it excels him 'in dignity of substance, power and activity'.[11] The very act of assembling the Church together accentuates its most brilliant and essential qualities: 'In a general council all the particular parts of the Church are transformed to the inspiration of the Spirit, from clarity of faith to clarity of intellect, from the piety of dispersed charity to the exaltation of united charity (*a sanctimonia caritatis finaliter disperse ad anagogiam sursum unite*), and from the dissension of contrary opinions and affections to the consensus of a decision of synodal harmony (*consensum sententie synodaliter concordantie*)'.[12] Such passages express a belief in the accentuation of spiritual qualities by their being used collectively.

Order and jurisdiction

Velde was also arguing here that the constitutional superiority of the council over the pope derived from its moral or spiritual superiority. Like

71

other conciliarists, Velde gave a peculiarly collectivist twist to this characteristic mode of anti-papal argument in the late Middle Ages. The implied challenge to the person-office distinction, from which arguments for papal supremacy derived so much of their force, was carried further in Velde's conception of the relation between the powers of order and jurisdiction. In some medieval ecclesiology there had been a tendency to treat these as separable, and to elevate the power of jurisdiction above that of order when the relative constitutional standing of various church offices was under discussion. This was particularly true of papalists, since what differentiated the pope from other bishops was precisely the power of jurisdiction. It was said that Christ as king was superior to Christ as priest, and that the power of jurisdiction derived from Christ's divinity, the power of order from his humanity.[13] Velde's view is very different, in fact almost the exact opposite. Not only does he say that in the sacramental ministry the two powers are concurrent.[14] He makes the power of jurisdiction inferior to, indeed dependent upon, the power of order. His argument may be diagnosed as follows.

The fundamental quality of the Church is its relation to Christ, that is faith. This, together with all the other spiritual qualities of the Church and of the individual believer, is received through baptism and nurtured through the other sacraments.[15] The power to bestow these, that is the power of order, is therefore related to the inner life of the Church or of the believer; while the power of jurisdiction is concerned only with external matters. Therefore, he concludes, the power of order is superior, and the power of jurisdiction flows from it. He adds that the power of order stems from Christ's divine nature, that of jurisdiction from his human nature.[16]

This forms an integral part of Velde's argument for the supremacy of the council over the pope. For the council comprises the episcopate and priesthood in collegiate form: 'Although the council is not a priest according to the personal and implanted (*caracteristicam*) possession (*proprietatem*) of a particular ministry, and is not king or queen in the manner of a (particular) official agent, it is nevertheless the ecclesiastical college made up of priests and prelates or mystical kings, in the name or *virtus* of the universal priesthood of Christ in the royal power of the holy Spirit'.[17] While he does not here quite ascribe the power of order to the council as such, this nevertheless anticipated a later objection of Torquemada, that the Church *qua* corporation could not possess either ordinal or jurisdictional powers, since these could be ascribed only to individual persons.[18]

These arguments for the superiority of whole over part, of the spiritual over the external, and of order over jurisdiction are combined, furthermore, to establish the radical-conciliarist case that the power of the pope, which is primarily one of the jurisdiction, *derives from* the council. We have already observed Velde's argument that 'in the assumed nature of Christ' (that is, his human nature) 'spirit, soul and body are subordinated to one another', so that 'just as the spirit precedes the body, so the mystical jurisdiction of the holy Spirit precedes the human and political jurisdiction of the apostolic lord (sc. the pope)'.[19] 'The power of Christ and of the Church', he says, comes from all three persons of the Trinity and 'depends primarily on the gratuitous and free benevolence of the holy Spirit', which is 'the origin (*originativa*) of exterior jurisdiction'.[20] Ecclesiastical jurisdiction, he says – not unlike Cusa – 'depends partly on Christ, who preordains it essentially, intelligibly and causally (*essentialiter, notionaliter et causaliter*); and partly on the Church, actualizing it for government through the choice of election (*regenda ipsam per arbitrium electionis actuante*)'.[21] Finally, 'The general council depends originally in mind on itself and Christ; the pope (depends) on the same, *with the church mediating* . . . Ecclesiastical power descends from Christ, *the Church mediating*, onto the pope, at least as regards its apostolic or pastoral being'.[22]

NOTES

1. *EP* fol. 134v; for other conciliarists' use of *Math.* 18:19-20, below, pp. 130, 184.
2. *EP* fol. 181r.
3. *EP* fol. 181r.
4. Above, p. 55f; below, p. 160.
5. Above, p. 55.
6. Below, pp. 150ff.
7. *EP* fol. 181r; cf. *EP* fol. 168v: 'synodi ecclesiastici congregatio dependet essentialiter et per se a (word omitted – ? dispositione) fidei catholice, i.e. universalis inspirationis, i.e. spiritu sancto'.
8. *EP* fol. 136r.
9. *EP* fol. 109v; cf. *EP* fols. 137r, 178r-v; below, pp. 138ff.
10. *EP* fol. 92r; Aristotle, *Politics*, III, xi; *Wisdom* 6:24.
11. *EP* fol. 107r.
12. *EP* fol. 137r; cf. pope John XXIII in *Documents of Vatican II*, 711-12; Küng, 12, 31.
13. Wilks (1963), 375-7; Wilks (1957).
14. *EP* fol. 163v: 'in sacramentali ministerio simul ex potestate ordinis et iurisdictionis exercitio concurrit perfecta iustificationis sacramentalis origo'.
15. *EP* fols. 89v-90r.
16. *EP* fol. 160r.
17. *EP* fol. 186r; cf. *EP* fol. 163v: '(concilium) integretur ex christicolis sacerdotio regali fungentibus, i.e. tam clavibus ordinis tam potestate iurisdictionis ecclesie . . .'
18. Black (1970a), 55.
19. *EP* fol. 181r; cf. *EP* fol. 162v: 'potestas iurisdictionis apostolice subest catholice spiritus sancti gentes in unitate fidei congreganti providentie'.
20. *EP* fols. 160r-v.
21. *EP* fol. 161v.
22. *EP* fol. 177r; cf. *EP* fol. 160v: 'potestas iurisdictionis est secundum arbitrium ecclesie in virtute, sc. congregate, validabiliter, regulariter et ordinabiliter distributa finaliter sub uno ierarcha primario ordinate connexionis . . .'

73

Velde, then, employs a form of the theory of 'hierarchy' (or hierocracy), that power is concurrent with holiness, to establish conciliar supremacy. This was a reversal of the papalist theory of hierarchy – and indeed of the ecclesiological tradition that derived from pseudo-Denis in east and west – according to which authority inhered in the individual pope or bishop because he occupied a holy office established by God in accordance with the hierarchical model of the cosmos.[1] Velde conceives jurisdictional power as consequent on holiness; but holiness belongs primarily in an undifferentiated manner to the baptised community as a whole. Rather as the concept of sovereignty, elaborated in the context of absolute monarchy, was to be applied to the people or parliament, so here the concept of sacred authority, conceived for pope and bishops, was being applied to the believing community or general council. The community as a whole is conceived as the ultimate social reality of the Church, and therefore as the ultimate source of jurisdictional power. Velde retains the correspondence between the invisible and the visible cosmos. He conceives the celebration of a council as a quasi-sacramental act, realizing the qualities it symbolizes.[2] The philosophical theology which had been used to underpin the hierarchical-monarchical conception of church organization was transformed by Velde into a mechanism to support a constitutionalist, conciliarist, even to a certain extent an egalitarian view of the Church.

Velde concludes from this that the council alone exercises the full power of the Church-as-a-whole. Here again he made explicit something which other conciliar thinkers had implied without ever quite stating, as when Zabarella had contrasted the 'total power' of the whole association with the 'principal power' of the ruler. Velde says that the Church 'in the general council exercises the whole act of jurisdiction (*totum actum jurisdictionis*), not in the measure of its partial being which it has in the pope, but in the measure of the synodal being of the whole council'.[3] He says that, because the council is the 'actual whole of the Church, therefore 'its power is the integral capacity (*integra facultas*) of ecclesiastical jurisdiction'.[4] But on one issue Velde departs from standard Basilean doctrine: he witholds from the council the automatic guarantee of inerrancy. 'The judgements of general councils on faith and morals are still less like the true judgements of the Lord . . . only that is a general council in which is preserved the full and perfect gospel of the Christian Law'.[5] This is one of several points on which Velde holds a position different to that of the Basle majority but similar to that of Cusa.[6]

NOTES
1. Pelikan i, 344; Ullmann (1966), 46-7.
2. Cf. *Lumen gentium,* I i, and viii: *Documents of Vatican II,* 15, 22.
3. *EP* fol. 137r.
4. *EP* fol. 178r.
5. *EP* fol. 165r.
6. Above, p. 53.

A neoplatonic theory of government

Some other arguments of Velde in support of conciliar supremacy deserve
to be noted: they are in part allegorical, in part political and historical.
Velde argues for the superiority of the council, and in particular its right
to act as executive as well as legislature, by an allegorical interpretation of
the New Testament similes of the lord and his overseer, of the body, and
of the kingdom. Here he starts distributing triads in profusion. There are
what he calls 'three principles of government (*principia principatus*)':
'direction alone (*dirigens tantum*)', 'direction and execution', and 'execution
alone'. He applies these to his three similes, and then to the Church, in the
following manner:

direction alone	direction and execution	execution alone
paterfamilias	*materfamilias*	overseer (*dispensator*)
heart	head	limbs
king	queen	chief minister (*constabularius, princeps militum*)
Christ	'the Church or the general council representing it'	the pope[1]

The king-queen-chief minister analogy became quite a favourite with the
Basileans;[2] when it is used later by Cologne university,[3] the influence of
Velde may be suspected; no-one else makes quite such an elaborate job of
it as he.

Velde expounds the nature of ecclesiastical government on the basis of
an assumed triadic disposition of the universe, which derives from the
Trinity itself. Here he owes much to Pseudo-Denis, but as always Velde
develops the argument in his own way. He expresses the three principles
which the persons of the Trinity represent as 'being, life, intelligence
(esse, vivere, intelligere)'; in God, these 'follow one another according to
the order of the primordial reason of essential acts sprouting from a single

75

essence (*secundum ordinem rationis primordialis actuum essentialium ab una essentia pullulantium*)'.[4] Created things were established 'in being, living and intelligence all at once'; this was true of the angelic world, and of the 'greater and lesser worlds', that is of nature and humanity. Man is divided into 'higher reason, lower reason and sensual appetite (*ratio superior, ratio inferior et appetitus sensitivus*)', or 'spirit, soul and body (*spiritus, anima et corpus*)'; he possesses three kinds of virtue, 'divine, heroic and moral'.[5]

Since 'the primordial exemplar of all legitimate government is God', all forms of government follow the triadic pattern of 'being, living and intelligence'. This holds good for both ecclesiastical and secular government. In the Old Testament, it was found in 'the régime of Abraham, Isaac and Jacob', and in 'the ducal, judicial and regal rule of the Mosaic law'. In the New, it is found in 'the regal, priestly and pontifical' (he later substitutes 'ministerial') 'rule of Christ'. The same pattern is to be found in every government which 'figures' the 'perfect government (*principatus*)' of God; thus in secular government we have the following divisions (adapted from Aristotle):

royal	political	despotic
paternal	social	servile[6]

Velde assimilates the three good forms of government as defined by Aristotle (monarchy, aristocracy, polity) to three ecclesiological concepts derived from the New Testament (royalty, priesthood, ministry): 'The *genus* of secular human government is threefold, namely kingdom, aristocracy and polity or timocracy. Therefore, there is a threefold differentiation in the ecclesiastical hierarchy, namely royal or pontifical, priestly and ministerial'.[7]

He allots the various ecclesiastical offices to the three terms of the latter triad as follows:

type	royal	priestly	ministerial
presiding role	pope	archbishops	archdeacons
subdivisions	patriarchate	'archiepiscopal	'company of
	archiepiscopate	college of	deacons'[8]
	episcopate	cardinals or of	
		metropolitan	
		cathedral priests'	

Clearly, he envisages the three types of government in the Church as functioning side by side and simultaneously. Similarly, after subdividing secular government into royal-paternal, political-social, despotic-servile, he goes on to conclude that all ecclesiastical government must embody and give effect to each of these three types of order: it must embody freedom (royal-paternal type), legal obligation (political-social type), and coercive administration (despotic-servile type).[9]

Velde also maintains that these three forms of government go through a process of historical development, starting with the simplest and most subordinate which Velde calls the 'initial, indistinct stage'; progressing into the aristocratic; and finally developing into the 'royal priesthood'. 'The boy grows into a man, and likewise the disposition of the world when founded (? develops) into an ornate (? condition); also the old covenant was raised up from patriarchate to priesthood (*pontificium*) through the temporal kingdom; the royal priesthood (*sacerdotium*) of Christ in turn underwent growth from an initial undifferentiated state, through hierarchical differentiation up to the subjugation of the temporal empire'.[10] The organic analogy itself may have suggested the notion of growth. Velde was not alone in this period in conceiving the present constitution of the Church as the product of development out of a more 'indistinct' form.[11] (His theory may be contrasted with that of the Reformation and counter-Reformation theologians.) But this notion of growth is given a distinctively neoplatonic interpretation by Velde: there are *three* stages, and each higher one subsumes the lower, succeeding it temporally and superior to it in authority, but still including it.

This theory of ecclesiastical history was to be further developed in Velde's work of 1446.[12] There are similarities with Hegel's theory of history: the threefold stages, the 'synthesising' of the earlier stages in the later, and, underlying it all, the belief that history is a kind of exemplification of distinct ideas. The origins of Velde's theory are to be found in the Old Testament. St Bonaventure had expounded a Dionysian theory of history which may have influenced Velde,[13] and Joachim of Flora had elaborated a kind of trinitarian historicism.[14] That Velde was consciously using a Joachimite source is suggested by his going on to say, in a textually obscure passage, that according to the prophecy of Hildegard the Church was heading for a time of gross abuses and 'the miserable lapse of the priesthood'.[15] Velde saw in this, however, not an apocalyptic vision of the future, but rather an indication of the absolute necessity of councils and reform legislation.

Three forms of government, therefore, coexist in the Church. There is 'royal monarchy' with respect to Christ as the 'royal head'; there is the 'political government of the priests' who 'interpret the law'; and there is the 'ministerial, servile or despotic government, which is called apostolic'. This particular division comes early in Velde's first tract, and here he assimilates the priestly government to the council and the ministerial to the pope, thus giving the council clear superiority (in later passages he

77

applies the governmental forms to pope and council in a different way, as we shall see). Here, he concludes that 'the ecclesiastical hierarchy is a kind of pastoral or servile monarchy, related to the democratic or despotic régime, a civil government under one governing group (*civilis sub uno comitatu*)'.[16] (The 'servile monarchy' and the 'despotic régime' presumably refer to the pope, and the 'comitatus' to the council). Finally,

> 'As the whole is above the part *materialiter*, as the providence of the holy Spirit is above human providence *formaliter*, as the united virtue of an efficient (cause) is above the distributed virtue . . . so the political, priestly, judicial or aristocratic authority of the general council is above the apostolic, ministerial, ducal, democratic or despotic authority of the pope'.[17]

In later passages, on the other hand, Velde describes the council as the 'royal, priestly and pastoral college', and says that 'the ecclesiastical power which is hierarchically dispersed by Christ through the apostolic administration of his vicar (the pope), is formally collected in the council, established there both in its royal and its priestly aspects; and therefore it is more free, sublime, firm and strong (in the council) than in that natural and servile being which it has in the pope'.[18] In other words, he now conceives the council, not as representing *only* the priestly or aristocratic element in the Church, but as embodying *all three* aspects or types of ecclesiastical government. This makes an important difference; for while it may be thought to elevate yet further the dignity of the council, it also means that the papal element can be said to be an essential constituent part of the council. This forms a bridgehead to Velde's later ecclesiology, in which he tries to reconcile the claims of pope and council by adopting an intermediate position between the supporters of Basle and Eugenius;[19] it shows the growing correspondence between Velde's views and Cusa's.[20] In all of these passages, we find Velde again envisaging qualities or powers, such as royalty, priesthood, ministry, as belonging to the Church as a spiritual totality prior to their belonging to specialized personnel.

NOTES

1. *EP* fol. 90v; reproduced with variations at fol. 161v.
2. Above, p. 51.
3. *DRTA* xv, 466.
4. *EP* fol. 90v.
5. *EP* fol. 90v. Cf. *I Thess.* 5:23.
6. *EP* fol. 90v.
7. *EP* fol. 163v.
8. *EP* fols. 163v-4r.
9. *EP* fol. 90v.
10. *EP* fol. 163r; cf. fol. 177v: 'in hoc tempore ecclesiastice monarchie dum ecclesie dudum apostolici distincte et nedum actualiter subordinate sunt sub uno patriarcato capitali redeunte'.

11. 'Deus educavit ecclesiam, nam in principio quando ecclesia erat parvula . . .
    et indiscreta . . .', said Wyclif, with a different message in mind, however:
    Wilks (1969), 87n.
12. Black (1970b).
13. St Bonaventure, vis. iv, coll. iii at p. 250 (I am grateful to Professor Luscombe
    for this reference).
14. *DTC* viii, 1425-38; Cohn, 109-13; Leff (1967a), 73ff.
15. *EP* fol. 163r; Niem and d'Ailly also cited Hildegard: *DLO* 510-11.
16. *EP* fol. 91r.
17. *EP* fol. 92r.
18. *EP* fol. 161v.
19. Black (1970b).
20. Above, p. 52f.

Velde's attitude to the Basle majority's programme

Velde, then, at this stage in his career almost fully endorsed the general
ecclesiology of the radical conciliarists, among whom he was at this time
by far the most creative thinker. But did he support their policies, in
particular their claim that the council possessed full jurisdictional powers?
It would appear that all along he held an intermediate position on this
central issue. His practical ecclesiology was in fact remarkably close to Cusa's.

On the power to dissolve a council, Velde's views in the first and third
tracts[1] were identical with those of the radical conciliarists. Since the
council derives its power immediately from the Holy Spirit, the pope cannot 'convoke, regulate and dissolve such a council at will'.[2] He did not
actually deny this in the seventh tract, but stated something closer to an
intermediate, certainly a conciliatory position. He now said that the
convocation and dissolution of a council required the mutual consent of
pope and council: 'The mutual jurisdiction of the apostolic and of the
catholic Church must be preserved in the general council. Therefore it is
impossible . . . for any general council to be assembled or dissolved without the mutual authority of the holy Spirit (sc. the general council) and of
the pope'.[3] A council, then, can neither be convoked without
papal consent nor dissolved without its own.

On conciliar jurisdiction, Velde goes some but not all of the
way with the radical conciliarists. The pope is unequivocally subordinated to the council in the sense that he is bound to implement its decrees. He is 'bound to servile obedience to (the
council) as a son';[4] he must 'rule himself and others in accordance
with the synodal will'.[5] This clearly indicates that Velde supported
the radical-conciliarist view that the council, independently of the
pope, comprises the supreme legislative body and the pope, as
chief executive, is bound to carry out its legislation under pain of

constitutional sanctions.

But did he also agree with the radical conciliarists that the council possessed fulness of power in the sense of unlimited jurisdictional power – could it take over and operate the judicial and executive machinery of the Church? Velde says that the three areas of conciliar supremacy mentioned in *Haec Sancta* (faith, schism, reform) are not intended to exclude conciliar supremacy in other areas too: the key to Velde's view seems to lie in the ensuing statement that the council decides 'all cases concerning the whole mystical body of Christ in head and members (*casus universales totum corpus Christi mysticum in capite et in membris circumstante(s)*)'.[6] The phrase 'casus universales' tempts one to think Velde favoured conciliar involvement in the whole arena of ecclesiastical jurisdiction; but the succeeding phrase 'concerning the *whole* mystical body . . .' suggests rather that he was thinking not of judicial proceedings affecting individuals, but, once again, of general legislative enactments. In other words, he was saying that the council may issue binding decrees in any area of Church government, but nothing more.

Velde's views on the distribution of legislative and judicial-executive power between council and pope are most clearly stated in the seventh tract. If the above interpretation is correct, what we have here is clarification rather than a change of mind; but the clarification shows up divergences between Velde and the majority group, and also points of agreement between Velde and Cusa. There are clear indications that, in terms of practical ecclesiology, Velde held views similar to Cusa, especially in the seventh tract. We have seen, for example, that he did not think the council infallible,[7] and thought that conciliar convocation and dissolution required the 'mutual authority' of council and pope.[8] He also discusses the relationship between the council as legislature and the pope as executive in a markedly conciliatory manner. Having presented lists of pro-papal and pro-conciliar arguments, he says that 'clearly harmony (*concordia*) can be elicited from these'.[9] (Incidentally, he gives as a pro-papal argument, which he does not however accept, the idea that 'every power (*posse*), general or particular, among Christians seems to be implicit (*implicitum*)' in the papal power;[10] this sounds like the germ of Cusa's later theory of ecclesiastical power.)

The crucial point for discovering Velde's views on the practical relationship between pope and council is his discussion of their respective spheres of action in ecclesiastical appointments. During the first half of 1433 there was extensive debate at Basle as to whether the council might include in its decree on elections an 'invalidating clause (*clausula irritans*)', that is a clause which would invalidate in advance any papal nominations in contravention of the proposed decree. Opposition to this proposal was so great that the clause was omitted from the decree of 13 July 1433, and replaced with a requirement that the pope should swear to observe the decree.[11] Velde himself was an ardent advocate of reform: he condemned papal reservations and approved the radical-conciliarist proposal for a total ban on exemptions from canonical rules on qualifications for office.[12] On the one hand, he agrees with the radical conciliarists that a council possesses 'all manner (*omnimode*) of ecclesiastical power both in providing (to benefices) and in ministerially dispensing (from canonical regulations)'.[13] That is to say, it may lay down rules governing ecclesiastical appointments and enforce them through an invalidating clause: 'Even though the power of dispensation is entrusted to the said council and pope in common, nevertheless the council is greater than the pope in this, that it can lay down beforehand rules invalidating contrary dispensations *(prediffinire canones dispensationis contrarie irritativos)*'.[14] On the other hand, he says that 'the immediate and servile execution of particular ministerial functions does not suit *(congruit)* such a council, except through ministers subject to its universal jurisdiction, among whom the pope is chief *(princeps)*'.[15]

The distribution of governmental functions between council and pope indicated here was a compromise between radical and moderate views. Velde held that the council's function was legislative, the pope's executive, and that each should respect the boundary between their respective spheres of action. The council can on its own authority lay down general regulations on appointments and dispensations, and it may even enact an invalidating clause. But it may not appropriate, or intervene directly in, the pope's executive functions, that is his decisions on particular cases: it may not intervene in the adjudication of particular disputes. Further, from his metaphysical ecclesiology, Velde draws the practical conclusion that the council has jurisdiction over the pope: it may 'remove, suspend and regulate' the papal power;[16] indeed, conciliar jurisdiction extends not only to the individual pope but to the 'pope with the apostolic see'.[17] (He thus allows, unlike Cusa, that the pope may be suspended pending his trial, as well as be deposed after trial.) But Velde does not accept the council's claim to appropriate papal jurisdiction over individuals. It is the pope's function, he says, to exercise freely the fulness of jurisdiction over all others apart from himself, so long as he does not contravene conciliar decrees: and, Velde adds in a distinctively non-Basilean tone, to do so 'finally (*finaliter*)'.[18]

Velde's position, then, is the closest approximation to a genuine separation of powers between council and pope that we find in any Basilean; and it is clearly distinct on certain points from the radical-conciliarist position. With Velde, as with Cusa, there is more consistency than one might have expected between views expressed up to spring 1434 (when Velde clearly sympathised with what the council was doing) and views expressed thereafter. Velde's departure from Basle in 1434, and his subsequent support for Eugenius in 1437 and for a new council in 1446, were related to his disagreement with the radical conciliarists over the question of the council's unlimited jurisdictional powers in 1433-4.

NOTES

1. Cf. above, p. 61.
2. *EP* fol. 168v; cf. *EP* fol. 89r.
3. *EP* fol. 181r.
4. *EP* fol. 168v.
5. *EP* fol. 168v.
6. *EP* fol. 168r.
7. Above, p. 74.
8. Above, p. 79.
9. *EP* fol. 182r.
10. *EP* fol. 182v.
11. Zwölfer (1929), 170-3.
12. *EP* fols. 182r, 184v.
13. *EP* fol. 182r.
14. *EP* fol. 186r; cf. *EP* fols. 183v-4r.
15. *EP* fol. 182r.
16. *EP* fol. 161v.
17. *EP* fol. 168v.
18. *EP* fol. 186r; cf. *EP* fol. 183v.

Conciliarism and realism

In conclusion, Velde forces us to reconsider the relationships between realism and papalism, and between nominalism and conciliarism. Some scholars hold that realism (or neo-Platonism or Augustinianism) necessarily led to papalism, or at least that papalism naturally sought such allies. They suggest that it was no historical accident that so many defenders of papal monarchy viewed the Church-as-a-whole as some kind of real thing: the one idea led naturally to the other.[1] In our own day, a similar connection is often alleged between collectivism (or hegelianism or marxism) and totalitarianism. Nominalism, on the other hand (or Averroism or Aristotelianism), perhaps even Thomism, it is often said, undermined papalism by undermining the theory of the reality of the church-as-a-whole, which the pope was supposed to represent (in Wilks' words, 'The innate individualism of the theory of universals as expounded by Ockham threatened not only the papal monarchy but the whole theory of absolute rulership . . .').[2] These interpretations are quite untenable if applied to the first half of the fifteenth century: the situation there is exactly reversed. It was the papalists, notably Torquemada, who now used the nominalist view of corporations (which they could find in Baldus)[3] to say that the whole Church was not an entity to which authority could properly be ascribed.[4] In general, nominalism was used to support the fiction-theory of corporations, that they receive their being from the sovereign will; which, as Gierke saw, demolished corporate aspirations and cleared the ground for absolute monarchy.[5] We find the same in Hobbes.[6] It was the conciliarists who now used realist arguments; there is much more evidence of this in the 1440s.[7] Perhaps this goes to show that the relation between philosophical ideas and political programmes is mercurial. In any case, it is clear that quite different and indeed opposite constitutional conclusions were drawn from the same philosophical ideas; and this may warn us how perilous it is to conceive as logically necessary the ideological connections employed in politics.[8]

We may liken Velde to Hegel in that both conceive the essence of society as consisting in a spiritual principle within it, to which individuals are related as substance to accidents. We have noted a similarity between their theories of history. Both think in triadic terms; and Velde sometimes anticipates Hegel's dialectic by conceiving the third element as embracing and transcending the first two.[9] These similarities, which are embedded in their similar philosophies of mind and being, may be broadly related to their shared platonic and Judao-Christian heritage, perhaps even hypothetically to common patterns in European thought-processes. Velde, however, does not see conflict, whether physical or intellectual, as necessary to achieve transcendence. Rather, his synthesis is an application of the doctrine of 'the coincidence of opposites', which he himself had developed and which he passed on to Cusa.[10]

Velde shared the fate of Segovia, Cusa and other Basileans in gaining no disciples after 1449. We find a trace of his influence in a Cologne university statement of 1440,[11] but that is all. Whether this fate was deserved it is for the reader to decide. We may say that Velde's work shows that it was possible to develop a *philosophical theology* of conciliar supremacy, and that this could embrace those very aspects of ecclesiology which were generally underemphasized by writers of this era — that is, the non-juristic, non-hierarchical, the spiritual and theological aspects. These aspects are today once again the focus of ecclesiological thought. Velde used scriptural concepts and similes profusely, and in some ways more faithfully than others were doing. For example, rather than saying that the Church is a kingdom, and deducing therefrom that it must have a monarchical structure, he says that there is a kingly element in the Church; there are also priestly and ministerial elements. This in part anticipates Vatican II's decree on the Church (*Lumen Gentium*), which emphasizes the royal, priestly and prophetic aspects of *all* ecclesial activity.[12] So too does the entire playing-down of the significance of hierarchical distinctions, which Velde and many post-Vatican II theologians see as secondary to the inner unity of all the baptized.[13] The same may be said of Velde's subordination of the power of jurisdiction to the power of order, and of his emphasis on the ontological primacy of the spiritual, invisible community of believers. Velde's conception of the Church as 'the human species transformed by Christ' is both a continuation of patristic thought and an anticipation of more recent ecclesiology.

Nor is Velde's holism entirely peculiar to him. For the Christian-platonist fathers and many modern theologians likewise say that characteristics such as wisdom, and functions such as teaching or service, should be thought of as belonging to the whole Church rather than as the special prerogatives of certain individuals; this is glaringly obvious in the very concept of 'the apostolate of the laity' — an idea more radical than anything thought up by Basle. What remains peculiar to Velde is his notion of the Church as a substance in the neo-Platonic-realist sense, and the necessary connections he makes between this and the general council.

NOTES
1. Wilks (1963), 21, 33-4, 36, 41, 158, and esp. 526-7: 'Was the *Ecclesia* an ever-present reality? If so, its real presence could best be expressed in the person of the ruler . . . From this stemmed the idea that sovereignty was made actual in the papal vicariate of Christ'.
2. Wilks (1963), 107; cf. *ibid.;* 88-98.
3. Gierke *DGR* iii, 425ff.
4. Black (1970a), 54-5.
5. *DGR* trans. Maitland, 98.
6. Society attains a 'real unity' only by submission to a 'common power': *Leviathan*, ch. 18 at p. 112.
7. Below, pp. 113-15.
8. Cf. Gewirth (1961), esp. 130-2, 158n.; Ullmann (1966), 29.
9. Cf. Hegel, *Philosophy of right*, 179-80; Mure, 169ff. Cassirer (p. 39) noted the affinity between Cusa and Hegel: 'Hegel, whose basic thought Cusanus anticipates with remarkable clarity . . .'; cf. Black (1970b), 85-6.
10. Haubst (1952), 437ff.
11. Below, p. 114.
12. *Lumen gentium*, II, xiii; III, xxv-xxvii: *Documents of Vatican II*, 30-2, 48-52. Cf. below, pp. 218f.
13. *Lumen gentium*, II, ix; *Documents*, 25.

CHAPTER 5

ESCOBAR (1434-5): CONSTITUTIONALISM AND REFORM

Between 1434 and 1437 one important conciliar work was composed, 'Government of councils (*Gubernaculum conciliorum*)' by Andrés Diaz (or Didace) de Escobar (1367-1437?).[1] Escobar, a Portuguese Benedictine, had spent most of his life working in the Roman penitentiary, and in 1429 wrote a famous book on penance, the *Lumen confessorum*.[2] He had been at Constance when *Haec Sancta* was promulgated.[3] He held a succession of bishoprics; from 1428 till his death, he was titular bishop of Megara, to which in 1432 he added the abbacy of a Benedictine monastery in Oporto diocese.[4] This was possibly a reward for his assistance in Eugenius' negotiations during that year, when he made several trips to Basle.[5] It is not clear how long he spent at Basle, and his incorporation is not recorded. From 1434 to 1437 he was mainly engaged in curial business at Florence and Bologna.[6] The *Government of councils* was started in 1434 and finished late in 1435;[7] a reform proposal, dealing with every aspect of the Church from the *curia* to the laity, was appended to it.[8] The work was dedicated to Cesarini with the phrase 'to be sent' to him,[9] suggesting that Escobar was not at Basle when he completed it. In his dedication, he expresses a burning concern that the reforms that have been or are to be decreed will actually be put into effect.[10] Haller remarks caustically that Escobar himself was doing well enough out of the abuses he condemned.[12]

In the first eight books, the author contents himself with listing possible opinions on various aspects of the council and the Church's constitution. He generally expresses a tentative preference for the conciliarist opinion, but he always concludes by leaving the question open and submitting it for judgment to the Church and the Roman see.[13] In this way, after first

85

establishing that frequent general councils are necessary at the present time in order to reform the Church, he discusses the convocation, composition and procedure of the council. It is clear that his advocacy of frequent councils is inspired by his sense of the urgent need for reform, and this leads him to say that the method in which general councils are celebrated lies at the very basis of the Church's existence.[14] As in the case of Segovia, the example of representative institutions in the Hispanic peninsula may have led him in this direction.[15]

The ninth and last book, on the other hand, which deals with the dissolution of councils, adopts a completely different approach. It was written towards the end of 1435, after it had become clear that the pope was not going to accept or carry out the council's reform-decrees, particularly those on elections and annates.[15 a] This shocked and infuriated Escobar who, like Niem before him and Gozzadini after him, knew only too well the *mores* of the *curia*. His denunciation of papal abuses in book IX is as fierce as one might hear from a Beghard, a Hussite or a Protestant.[16] He now argued unreservedly that the council is above the pope, and asserted that the 'decree on the power of councils, affirmed and decreed in the holy councils of Constance and Basle' (sc. *Haec Sancta*) should be published time and again, and must be believed 'most firmly and without doubt, as one believes any article of faith contained in the apostles' creed'; anyone denying it should be condemned as a heretic.[17] If this doctrine is upheld, he says, councils will gain strength and 'with it every good thing will come for the Christian people'.[18] If it is not accepted, then councils are pointless and labour for reform will be in vain, since the pope will be able to annul whatever is decreed.[19] He therefore supports the extension of *Haec Sancta* to say that 'the power of the general council is greater than the power of the pope in authority, *jurisdiction and execution*'.[20] The pope, he goes on, must be made subject to correction and punishment by councils for refusing to carry out their decrees on reform, whether his disobedience is by word or example; the same strictures must apply here as in the case of the pope's heresy.[21] Escobar, then, is a classic example of a reformer driven to demand constitutional change.

In view of what is said in book IX, I think that we may take it that Escobar subsequently endorsed most of the conciliarist opinions which he had stated earlier in the work as only probable. Conciliar superiority (as he explicitly says in book IX) includes executive power; the council may execute its own decrees if the pope refuses to; indeed 'the general council can, through whomever it wills, execute and exercise all the functions of the papacy'.[22] He goes even further and says that the power of the *curia* to judge and make appointments should be automatically suspended during a council.[23] On the convocation of a council, he brings out very clearly the meaning of *Frequens* and the Basle decrees: 'The convocation of the council belongs to and ought to be carried out by general councils, in such a way that one council convokes another, and this one the next, and so on for ever'.[24] The council may only be dissolved by its own authority.[25]

On the question of voting rights at a council, he had previously given three opinions. One was that the pope alone had power to determine who could vote. Of this he remarks drily, 'this opinion pleases many doctors of canon law who are eager to please the Roman pontiff'.[26] A second view was that supreme ecclesiastical power (which includes the power to make decisions in councils) belongs to the episcopate; not indeed to the bishops as individuals scattered through their separate dioceses, but to the bishops collectively assembled, 'the company of bishops congregated for a general council'.[27] (This approaches the notion of episcopal collegiality.)[28] The third view was that anyone, clerical or lay, can participate in a general council, that 'all the faithful' should have a defining voice at the council, and that the council may admit anyone it chooses.[29] This, he comments, is the practice which has been adopted by Pisa, Constance and Basle – which are recognized as having been guided by the Holy Spirit.[30] He had concluded that 'this third opinion seems to be safer and holier and more above suspicion', but had left the question to be determined by Church and pope.[31] Though he does not specifically refer to the matter in book IX, he may well by then have supported this third opinion. He also gives sympathetic mention to the view, probably derived from Ockham, that as an alternative to specified individuals being summoned to attend in person or send proxies, 'from each region or nation a certain sufficient number shall be summoned, who will represent the bishops, abbots, and clergy of that region or nation'.[32]

As well as discussing these questions of constitutional procedure, Escobar makes a contribution, in passing, to the collectivist theory of conciliar supremacy and to the communal theory of the council itself; though some of his reflections are only stated as the opinions of 'modern men' or 'certain doctors'. He cites Zabarella's view that the pope stands to the Church as 'head of a corporation . . . in such a way that power itself is in the corporation itself, as in its primary foundation, but in the pope as in its principal minister'; and also Zabarella's analogy with the *civitas* (state or city), in which 'the rule of the city resides with the assembly of citizens or its weightier part'.[33] In defence of the idea that the council *qua* whole Church is superior to any individual parts of the Church, he cites the familiar holistic argument: 'virtue united is stronger than itself dispersed'.[34]

Escobar's chief contribution, however, lies in his evocation of the republican tradition.[34a] In defence of the inalienability of sovereignty from the whole Church, he cites (as Zabarella had also done) the populist interpretation of the *lex regia*. For, he says, the Church, like the Roman people, did not transfer all its power to Peter, but 'also retained (power) in itself, because it could not alienate the whole (power) from itself . . . From this some argue that the power of the people is greater than that of the magistracy itself'.[35] And in book IX he himself endorses the interpretation of Gerson given by Beaupère and Segovia to the effect that: 'this power of the Church . . . is in the universal Church intrinsically, necessarily, indefectibly and most fully'.[36] Like Beaupère, Segovia and others, he employs the terms 'political' and 'mystical' to define the difference between papal and divine headship of the Church: the pope is only the 'political, civil and ministerial, but not the mystical, real and essential head of the universal Church'.[37] In book IX, arguing that the council is self-substantive and so cannot be dissolved without its own consent, he appeals more explicitly to the idea of a republic, fusing it with the notion of the Church as a 'mystical body'. This time, he is explicitly stating his own views: 'The universal Church is a kind of mystical body, and a kind of republic (*res quaedam publica*) of the Christian people . . . That most holy republic is the universal Church . . . and therefore it is a common affair (*res communis*) of the Christian people; and a people is a grouping of the multitude, linked together by consent to law and community of interest, according to Plutarch; and the Christian people itself, assembled legitimately in the holy Spirit, makes (sc. celebrates and comprises) the holy general councils themselves'.[38]

The republican element in his thought also appears in his sympathetic and somewhat original statement of the communal or fraternal nature of the council. First, he argues that a *council* is the best vehicle for reform, because it encourages people to put common before private interests: 'For when, with private interests set aside, we are joined together and assembled by the charity of God Jesus in a council, when we put common things before private and not private before common, when we . . . direct all our intentions to the ultimate goal, which is Christ Jesus . . . then indeed "it is a good and pleasing thing for brothers to dwell together as one"'.[39]

He relates the argument for equality within the council to the theological values of fraternity and charity: 'All Christians are spiritual brothers, being regenerated by the same Father and mother' (sc. God and the Church) '. . . And therefore they should be like brothers in the flesh . . . Therefore they have an equal portion in (the inheritance of the universal Church which the universal council represents). Therefore all Christians should have an equal voice in (the Church) with a view to its salvation and government. Also, this fraternity among Christians is by reason of charity:

for all Christians should be of one will; and because charity makes every-thing be in common, and . . . puts common before private things . . . Therefore also there should be one charity, *one will, one intention* in the council'.[40] The principle of equal participation in public decision-making, in other words, is implicit in the Christian ethic. This passage shows how readily the notion of communal unity, so deeply engrained in late-medieval interpretations of the Christian ethic, could give rise to the notion of a collective will.[40 a]

This emphasis on republican ideas, which we also find in Segovia,[40 b] may serve to confirm our impression that Escobar was drawing, whether consciously or not, on the political culture of the Hispanic peninsula, with its strong civic tradition and its parliamentary-constitutionalist notion of the polity.[41] There is indeed a hint of Hispanic patriotism in Escobar, when he calls himself 'a poor Spaniard',[42] and when, in defence of the communal nature of the council, he cites 'our holy Spaniard, Isidore' to the effect that a council is 'an association of many faithful, assembled for one purpose and with one common intention'.[43]

This may not be unconnected with another view which we find in Escobar but in hardly any other conciliar writer of the Basle period: the advocacy of the right of kings and princes to carry out reforms if no-one else will. We may also suspect here the influence of Niem.[44] 'I, the poor Spaniard, see no other remedy in God's Church this side of God's command with a view to the reformation of the Church . . . than to continue councils'. Their decrees must be enforced if necessary 'by secular power and with an armed hand'.[45] In book IX, moreover, having asserted vehemently the authority of councils to coerce popes who will not carry out reforms or reform themselves, he links the right of secular intervention with an affirmation of Christian liberty — not, to be sure, altogether in Luther's sense of the term, for the emphasis is on the conciliarist notion of *con-situtional* liberty. 'If the universal Church is free with the evangelical freedom with which Christ liberated it,[46] namely from the servitude of sin . . . (and) if the pope tried to subject it to the servitude of sin by simonies, unjust promotions, tyrannies, undue exactions . . . prides, pomps, partialities and wars' — then indeed, to preserve this liberty, 'all kings of the earth should stand by, and all princes and all Christ's faithful should join together against the anointed of the Lord, against the vicar of Jesus Christ himself, and against whoever follows him in avoiding the reformation by councils'. They should resist him by all means, and withdraw their obedience from him.[47]

It is certainly surprising to find this author among those who sided with Eugenius in 1437.[48] It seems hardly likely that, after writing in this vein, he was swayed by papal gold. (He had pleaded poverty once or twice in his tract.)[49] An obvious explanation is that he thought that the opportunity of reunion with the Greeks outweighed other considerations. He may have been put off by the antics and composition of the majority party at Basle. Yet in an epilogue which may have been written early in 1437, he exhorts Cesarini to continue the council and pursue reform until it is carried out.[50]

It is still more surprising to find that, in his 'On the erring Greeks (*De Graecis errantibus*)' which he wrote at Ferrara in 1437, he argues against the Greek theory of the patriarchate by asserting papal plenitude of power, which includes the power to define faith.[51] Was this a piece of western chauvinism? Or had developments at Basle led him to change his mind? Whatever the reason, this was a bad omen for the cause of conciliar reform.

NOTES

1. Walters; Candal in *CF* iv, 1, pp. liiiff; Hofmann, 31-2; Schulte (1877), ii, 439-44. He was not, as was once thought, the author of *De modis*, written in fact by Niem: Walters, 21ff.; Sägmüller. *GC* is in *MOCC* vi, 139-334, printed from a copy written by a Benedictine of Melk between Christmas 1436 and March 1437; a copy was purchased by Torquemada: Hofmann, 31.
2. Walters, 18-19; *DLO* 660-1; cf. *DLO* 597.
3. *GC* 139.
4. *CB* i, 114n.
5. Candal in *CF* IV, 1, pp. lxxvff.
6. *CB* i, 114-15; Walters, 20-1.
7. *GC* 163-4, 269; Walters, 21-2.
8. *CB* i, 214-33; Candal in *CF* IV, 1, pp. lvff.
9. *GC* 140.
10. *GC* 139-40, 333-4.
12. *CB* i, 114-5; he wrote a defence of tithes: Munich, Staatsbibliothek, Clm 2509, fols. 220-30.
13. *GC* 142, 163-4, 269ff.
14. *GC* 229; cf. 274-5.
15. Below, pp. 191f.
15a Cf. *GC* 299-300, 319ff.
16. See esp. *GC* 319-26.
17. *GC* 330.
18. *GC* 299.
19. *GC* 299-300.
20. *GC* 300.
21. *GC* 320ff.; cf. *GC* 153.
22. *GC* 158; cf. above, p. 51.
23. *GC* 215.
24. *GC* 273.
25. *GC* 303-4; cf. *Avisamentum*, 215.
26. *GC* 256.
27. *GC* 248-53.
28. Above, p. 22; below, pp. 188, 216.
29. *GC* 257ff.; cf. Sägmüller, 570; also Ockham and Gelnhausen: above, pp. 13, 1:
30. *GC* 268.
31. *GC* 270.
32. *GC* 293; above, p. 3.

33. *GC* 260-1; Tierney (1968), 223.

34. *GC* 148-51; below, p. 157.

34a Flourishing in the Italian and German cities, republicanism upheld civic independence and free, i.e. non-tyrannical, government; this usually took a 'mixed' form, involving a meritocracy, a relatively wide degree of popular participation and 'rule of law'. Its theory derived mainly from Aristotle and Cicero; prior to Machiavelli it was not notably 'secular', though it was contemporaneously articulated most of all by the Florentine humanists: Baron (1966), Pocock (1975), 83ff.

35. *GC* 267; Tierney (1968), 224.

36. *GC* 309; below, p.144.

37. *GC* 305.

38. *GC* 328; cf. Sägmüller, 565.

39. *GC* 166, citing *Psalms* 133:1.

40. *GC* 265.

40a Below, pp. 158, 164.

40b Below, pp. 172ff.

41. Marongiu, 62-74; the Catalan estates would appeal to both Seneca and the principle of Christian charity: *Parlaments*, 183-4 (speech by bishop of Barcelona, 1442); the fourteenth-century Catalan publicist Eiximenis, discoursing on the ethic required by public office, emphasised the public good: Eiximenis, 39, 41 (citing *Rom.* 12), 44 (citing *I Cor.* 12), 46, 168; and the need for charity, 58. On the civic tradition, see Maravall, esp. p. 86; in the rising of 1520-1 the towns emphasised their concern for the 'bien publico': Maravall, 100, 104; and appealed to the principle of equality: Maravall, 238-9. Cf. Buisson, 348ff.

42. *GC* 275; cf. 164.

43. *GC* 170; cf. 140.

44. Above, pp. 16f.

45. *GC* 275.

46. Cf. Maravall, 176: the rebellious towns appealed to 'libertad cristiana'.

47. *GC* 322; cf. 320.

48. Walters, 25.

49. *GC* 164, 275.

50. *GC* 333-4.

51. Hofmann, 31-8.

CHAPTER 6

TUDESCHI (1437–42): THE LEGAL CASE FOR BASLE

In the second period of intensive literary activity on behalf of the council, from 1437 onwards, we find, in contrast to the first period, that the three most important conciliar theorists, Tudeschi, Ragusa and Segovia, all played a prominent part in the practical leadership of the council.

Niccolo de' Tudeschi, archbishop of Palermo[1] ('Panormitanus'), emerged as a leading spokesman for the majority group within the council between July and December 1437, following the departure of the minority group. In this period the case against Eugenius was being re-opened, starting with his citation (31 July) and culminating in his suspension (24 January 1438).[2] A major factor in Tudeschi's prominence at this stage in the council's history was his tremendous reputation as a canonist.

Tudeschi, born at Catania in 1386, was the son of a German noble who had settled in Sicily. As a young man he entered the Benedictine order, and went to study canon law at Bologna, where he was taught by Antonius de Butrio.[3] He was professor of canon law at Parma from 1412 to 1418, and then at Siena from 1418 to 1430. He participated in the council of Siena, and was opposed to its early dissolution;[4] about a year later, the city had to intercede with Martin V on his behalf in order for him to acquire the abbacy of St Mary of Maniaco in Messina.[5] This may in part explain the restrained and indecisive treatment he gave to the pope-council question in a *Quaestio* written in April 1426. While at Siena, he worked on his massive *Commentary on the Decretals*, which was finished, at the latest, in 1436.[6] By the time the council of Basle opened, he had established a reputation as the foremost canonist of his time. We may judge the width of his outlook by the fact that he wished not only to cross-fertilise the canon and civil laws, but also to introduce into canonistics a more thorough study of theology: his unfinished Commentary on the *Decretum* starts with an *apologia* for Aquinas' treatment of natural law.[7]

In 1431 Tudeschi moved from Siena to lecture at Bologna. In December 1432, he was called upon by Eugenius to join a delegation offering compromise terms to the council of Basle. The delegates arrived at Basle on 7 March 1433; Tudeschi was the leading spokesman in the presentation of Eugenius' case to the council.[8] In September, as Tudeschi was returning to Italy *via* Constance, he heard news of the spurious Bull *Deus Novit*, refused further service to Eugenius, and returned home to Sicily. In 1434 Alfonso V had him made archbishop of Palermo. When, in 1436, Alfonso decided to lend more definite support to Basle, in view of Eugenius' support for his rival in southern Italy (René of Anjou), he chose as his representatives Tudeschi and another canonist, Lodovico Pontano, formerly secretary to Eugenius, only 27 years old but already distinguished in his profession.[9] Towards the end of 1436, soon after his arrival at Basle, Tudeschi set himself the task of commenting on the *Decretum*; but he never got beyond the first *distinctio*.[10] He was swept up into ecclesiastical politics.

During the events that led up to the split of May 1437, Tudeschi and Pontano, who had already 'with more learning than sense' fallen out over precedence, apparently took opposite sides, Tudeschi supporting the majority, Pontano the minority.[11] Thanks to his reputation, Tudeschi rapidly rose to prominence within the majority faction: he was 'easily the prince of his party; the French followed him most of all; he won the greatest respect at the council, on account of his knowledge of both laws'.[12] Tudeschi's first major recorded speech was in support of the citation of Eugenius.[13] When Eugenius transferred the council to Ferrara, Tudeschi spoke in the general assembly in support of the majority view, already approved by the deputations, that the council should proceed immediately to the trial of the pope; this, he argued, it had the authority to do.[14] His next speech (20 December 1437), in reply to Cesarini's proposal that the council should seek a reconciliation with Eugenius, subsequently expanded in writing, was an impassioned defence of the whole conciliarist case.[15] He brought to bear the full weight of his legal learning to defend the view, which he had put forward in his *Commentary*, that decisions taken at a general council by a majority could not be impugned by appeal to the 'saner part (*sanior pars*)'. He produced a wealth of analogies with other ecclesiastical corporations to prove the point; and, as in his *Commentary*, he cited Bartolus. There was no basis (he argued) in the present instance for saying that the rights of the majority had devolved upon the minority.[16]

He ended by quoting Cicero on the blessedness of those who dedicate themselves to the service of the republic; how much more blessed are those who serve the cause of the Church.[17]

Tudeschi's stock at Basle rose to a peak after this contribution; though the subsequent departure of Cesarini was hardly a real cause for self-congratulation. It seems to have been the only occasion when Tudeschi abandoned himself to rhetoric which, together with his legal arguments, made a great impression. He was even made president for a short time, during which Eugenius' suspension and the council's final takeover of papal powers, including those of temporal government, were enacted.

During 1438-9, up to the deposition of Eugenius, Tudeschi became the intellectual leader of the new minority of secular representatives and their supporters. This group was advocating more or less what Cesarini had been advocating in 1437, namely a cessation of hostilities between pope and council. During the furious debates of April-May 1439, Tudeschi now argued that the council as then constituted did not have authority to try and depose Eugenius.[18]

After the deposition had taken place, Tudeschi returned to Palermo for consultation with Alfonso. He returned to Basle in autumn 1439. He spoke before the imperial electors in February 1440, but this work has been lost;[19] in November he accepted promotion to cardinal by Felix V. His most notable contribution to Basle conciliarism was a marathon address given at the Frankfurt Reichstag between 30 June and 2 July 1442; this was subsequently published, and appears in editions of his *Consilia* as '*Tractatus de concilio Basiliensi* (Tract on the council of Basle)'.[20]

The purpose of this speech was to justify the past actions and continued legitimacy of the council of Basle. Tudeschi justifies the stand of the majority party in 1437, and upholds the legitimacy of the majority decree (pp. 454-83); he disproves the validity of Eugenius' second transference of the council (pp. 484-95). Next, he comes to the question of the council's right to judge the pope: first, he discusses in general terms the power of a council to suspend and depose a pope, and argues that a council has such power if a pope commits certain crimes (pp. 495-524). He then proves that Basle had sufficient reason to depose Eugenius in 1439 (pp. 524-8); finally, he refutes the view, which had just been expressed by his opponent, Cusa, that Basle was wrong to flout the wishes of the secular powers, and that it ought first to have obtained their consent for so momentous a decision (pp. 535-8). In this last section, he was arguing exactly the opposite case to the one he had argued in 1439. This is Tudeschi's most decidedly conciliarist work.

The following year, Alfonso V having made peace with Eugenius in Italy and having withdrawn his support from Basle, Tudeschi obediently left the council and returned to Palermo (where he could not have been overjoyed to find that Eugenius had exempted his own chapter from his jurisdiction).[21] It is a sad postscript to the conciliarist theorising of the last great medieval canonist. When he died two years later, Piccolomini did not spare him, and wrote that his end had been 'like his life, gloomy'.

How sincere was Tudeschi's conciliarism? Certainly, he advocated different views on different occasions. In the *Quaestio* of 1426 he is on the whole pro-papal; in the *Commentary* he is somewhat more pro-conciliar than most canonists, but this is not saying a great deal since he does not follow Zabarella's conciliar theory here; in his later speeches and treatises he is definitely conciliarist. Yet even then he still propounded some different positions. We may note that in his *Commentary* he said that infallibility belonged not to councils but only to the whole Church, and that it might be retained by a single individual.[22] In his speech of 20 December 1437, on the contrary, he declared that, in the present case concerning Eugenius' denial of conciliar supremacy, the council cannot err because it is a question of 'faith and morals'.[23] In this speech he defends conciliar sovereignty in general on the grounds that a council comprises the bishops 'who have succeeded into the place of the college of the apostles';[24] he studiously avoids any discussion of the actual composition of the council of Basle. During the deposition debate of 1439, on the contrary, he defended the royal-episcopal minority on the grounds that a valid conciliar decree must have support of the majority of bishops within the council.[25] Then, in his 1442 speech, he mentions that there is canonical authority for lower clergy being summoned to attend a council, 'and they may be given the right to speak'.[26] He knew of course perfectly well that at Basle they also had the right to vote. But for the most part he defends the legitimacy of Basle's acts without specific mention of this topic. In the deposition debate of 1439 he argued that secular rulers had a right to be consulted on matters of faith.[27] In his 1442 speech he does not actually contradict this, but, in answer to Cusa's argument that, in deposing Eugenius, the council had not represented the Church because it had acted contrary to the wishes of the secular powers, he insists that the latters' role is merely consultative.[28]

Would it then be true to say that Tudeschi was prepared to defend whatever case he was asked or paid to defend? Certainly, when Eugenius required him to defend him at Basle in 1432-3, he did so; perhaps under some degree of compulsion, Bologna (where he was then lecturing) being pro-papal and on papal territory. But this did not mean that he had no opinions of his own, and I think we may say that he was a conciliarist. The main intellectual influences upon him were Butrio and Zabarella, and his conciliarism may well date from his student days. That he made pro-papal statements in his *Quaestio* of 1426 may only mean that he was shy at that time of expressing his views publicly. This appears to have been the understanding of his contemporaries at the time of his visit to Basle in 1432-3. Piccolomini, who was probably acquainted with Tudeschi from his own student days at Siena and appears to have disliked him, records that on that occasion Tudeschi was 'convicted by his own writings and seemed not to be taken seriously, since he was now stating a case opposed to what he had written; people thought he had written in freedom, but was now speaking at another's wish'.[29] His speech of December 1437 has a genuine ring about it. On the other hand, there is a considerable difference between the scope and emphasis he gives to conciliar authority in the *Commentary*, where we may assume that he was expressing his own opinions, and that which we find in his speeches of 1437 and 1442. In the former he adopts the more pro-conciliar opinions of the Decretists; in the latter he is wholeheartedly Basilean. This may in part be accounted for by the difference between the academic and the publicistic milieu. In an academic commentary on the canon law texts one had to stick to the recognized authorities.

Tudeschi is still, to a certain degree, open to the charge of opportunism. It appears that he was prepared to trim his statements according to the diplomatic requirements of his royal master; this was what members of the council thought in 1438-9.[30] His rejection of Cesarini's policy of reconciliation in 1437, his arguments against deposing Eugenius in 1439, and his continuing support for Basle up to 1442 all reflected the foreign policy of Alfonso. He is not, as a churchman, to be compared with Zabarella; he adopted too readily the role of occasional advocate and diplomat.

Let us now examine the two stages in the development of Tudeschi's conciliar theory, as these are expressed in his *Commentary* and in his speech of 1442. Influenced by Zabarella (whom he refers to as his 'master'), as well as by his own teacher Butrio, Tudeschi was the first post-Constance lawyer, it seems, to take the implications of that council seriously, and the only one to espouse and develop – though not in his *Commentary* – Zabarella's teaching on the corporate structure of the universal Church. Other leading canonists who were writing and teaching in the early fifteenth century, such as Dominicus de Sancto Geminiano[31] and Johannes ab Imola[32] – whom Piccolomini describes as 'deeply ignorant of affairs of the world',[33] – wrote with an academic disregard for the events of the great schism and of the councils of Pisa and Constance. They had little to offer as a solution to the crisis for which their role as constitutional lawyers ought to have equipped them. They adhered rigidly to the monarchical tradition established by the Decretalists, and were unwilling to draw on the wider tradition which the *Decretum* held open to them. As Italians, indeed, they had something to lose by invoking the authority of councils and of the emperor.

Tudeschi provides a refreshing contrast. The power of his work lies in the combination of massive erudition with occasional thrusts of genuinely original thought. He affirms papal sovereignty in a wide variety of contexts,[34] but not in the full treatment he gives to the constitutional relationship between pope and council when commenting on *Decretals* 1.6.4 (which stated that 'all councils are made and received their power through the authority of the Roman Church, and in their decrees an exception is clearly made of the authority of the Roman pontiff'). Tudeschi's teacher Butrio, writing during the schism, had softened the meaning of this text by saying: 'understand this outwith articles of faith . . . in articles of faith the council prevails'.[35] Tudeschi went a good deal further; employing the distinction, which Butrio emphasised throughout his work, between positive and divine law,[36] he said that the pope is above the council in the sphere of positive law, but in the sphere of divine law things are not so simple. He goes on: 'In matters concerning faith, the council is above the pope, whence the pope cannot dispose contrary to a disposition made by a council . . . Hence it is that a council may condemn a pope for heresy . . . Also say that in matters concerning the universal estate of the Church, the pope cannot dispose against the statutes of a council, if by so doing the estate of the said Church would be spoiled . . . Add the singular gloss on d.40,c.6, that if a pope is notoriously in mortal sin and scandalises others, and is not willing to be corrected . . . he can be punished as a heretic . . . And note that gloss always; it is held by everybody'.[37] He also observed that this gloss 'was often cited in the council of Constance on the matter of the schism'.[38] Thus, he followed Huguccio and many others in adding mortal sin and offences against the 'estate of the Church' to heresy as crimes which provided exceptions to the rule of papal immunity.[39] And he followed Teutonicus in saying that the pope was not deposed *ipso facto* or *ipso iure* for such crimes, but was actually to be judged and deposed by a council.[40] He returns, therefore, to the less rigidly papalist thinking of the Decretists;[41] and from within their teaching he combines two elements which, taken together, give the council considerable powers against a pope. This contrasts with what he said in his *Quaestio* of 1426. There, he outlined the Decretist opinion that a council might have occasion to judge a pope, but shied away from it, expressing blandly the hope that such an exigency would not arise. He preferred to envisage the possibility that an erring pope would submit to conciliar judgment voluntarily.[42]

Tudeschi did not, however, here ascribe infallibility to the council, even in matters of faith. On this subject he writes in a way that shows

97

acquaintance with and acceptance of the 'Ockhamist' school of thought.[43] He says that a council, as well as a pope, can err in faith, for it comprises the whole Church not 'truly' but 'representatively'. In matters of faith, 'even the statement of one private person could be preferred to that of the pope, if the former were inspired by better reasons and authorities'. Only the universal Church in the literal sense of all the faithful is incapable of error: 'thus it is possible that the true faith of Christ might remain in one man alone . . . so that it is true to say that the faith does not fail in the Church, just as the right of a corporation may reside in one alone if the others sin'. He juxtaposed Henry of Ghent's example of the Virgin Mary during the crucifixion with Huguccio's *dictum* 'where there are good men, there is the Roman Church'.[44] This was an unusual and original view for a canonist to take, for it removed the whole question of infallibility from the sphere of legal definition.

At many points in his *Commentary*, Tudeschi expounds corporation law with respect to lesser ecclesiastical corporations. Like earlier canonists, he insisted that the concept of legal personality as applied to a 'corporation (*universitas*)' was a mental invention and did not correspond to any real entity. In law a corporation may be 'a kind of fictitious or representative person', but in reality it can never be anything other than the 'individual members'; when we say that bishop and canons 'make up one body', then 'certainly this body is not real but fictitious and representative'.[45] (This implicit contradiction of the holistic corporation theory, found in much Basle conciliarism, disappears in his later works). In discussing the powers of lesser ecclesiastical corporations (chapter, college, monastery, etc.), Tudeschi developed the earlier canonist tradition, which had agreed that a corporation could perform certain acts in certain circumstances in the absence of its head, to say that (in the case of a vacancy) 'those who make up the college are not obliged to elect a ruler for it, but the body itself will have all the power which a ruler is wont to have, and will be able to carry out contentious jurisdiction'.[46] When the ruler is dead or disabled, 'the corporation exercises its own rights through itself.[47] All this he would later apply to the case of council and pope.

Tudeschi is famed for his advocacy of the principle of majority decision-making, which he upholds in a number of areas of Church law where it was in dispute.[48] For instance, what constitutes a *quorum* in a corporation? Everyone agreed that two-thirds make a *quorum*, and that one-third would be aquorate; but what about a simple majority? On this there were contrary opinions. Tudeschi lays down the general rule that a simple majority is a *quorum.*[49] Again, he rejects a gloss that made it relatively easy for a minority, particularly if they were senior members, to override the majority by claiming that they were the 'saner part'. He concludes that, for this to happen, the majority must be guilty of a specific delict: 'although the minority may for a good reason hold up the decree of the majority, nevertheless it cannot decide anything in the name of the whole corporation, unless the majority have been deprived for a delict. Then the power of the whole corporation resides in the non-delinquents'.[50]

In defence of the majority principle he was prepared to cite Bartolus and the contemporary practices of Italian city-states against the canonists. The general opinion of the latter had been that, if everyone were summoned to an election but only a minority turned up, then those absent forfeited their right and the minority could proceed with the election. Tudeschi, however, comments: 'I am amazed that they have not cited the statements of the civilians to the contrary, and that Bartolus did not cite the sayings of the canonists'. For Bartolus expressly said that, when the *magistratus* (magistracy) summoned the whole *universitas* (corporation), the presence of two-thirds of the latter was required for the proceedings to be valid; and, Tudeschi goes on, 'this today is the practice of the corporations of cities in the whole of Tuscany. They never conduct any business in council unless at least two-thirds of the councillors are present. For the council of the city represents the whole people'.[51]

It seems that Tudeschi had been impressed by what he had seen of the workings of city-state constitutions; he had not spent twelve years in Siena for nothing. The remarks just quoted, and his other frequent citations from Bartolus[52] (which we will also find in his later speeches) show that he was eager to cross-fertilize the study of the two laws. He singles Bartolus out for special praise: 'in everyone's judgement he excelled all other writers in equity and truth'.[53] He was also prepared to appeal to contemporary civic practices.

While in his *Commentary* Tudeschi does not yet follow Zabarella in comparing the relationship of Church to pope with the relationship of a corporation to its head, he does already conceive of the general council as belonging to the corporation species. It is 'a kind of corporation (*quaedam universitas*)'.[54] From this he draws two important conclusions. He had argued that the bishops who make up a provincial council act as an *universitas*: they exercise jurisdiction as a body, not as individuals, and — as conciliarists said of the general council during the presidency debate — such a corporation 'received its power in common'.[55] So too, he now says, in a general council, 'those present decide not as individuals (*ut singuli*) but as a corporation (*ut universitas*) . . . Note and hold in mind . . . that a law produced in a council is made in the name of the council itself and not of the pope . . . From this it is inferred that the power of the Church is in the universal council itself, although the pope is there as head of the body itself . . . a constitution of the whole Church is of greater weight than one of the pope alone'.[56] He also ascribes to the general council, much as Bartolus had ascribed to the city-state, 'the rights of sovereign (*iura principis*)'.[57] Secondly, he deduces that the majority principle must operate in a general council: 'For the council represents the universal Church . . . Hence I say that in dispositions of the council one should stand by the judgment of the majority . . . For in the acts of a corporation the opinion of the majority regularly prevails'.[58]

But his doctrine in the *Commentary*, while more pro-conciliar than that of his contemporary fellow-canonists, falls far short of the claims made by the Basle conciliarists for a council. He does not enunciate conciliar sovereignty as a general principle. Even so, in his *Quaestio* of 1426, he had been prepared to say that during a papal vacancy a general council could exercise all the pope's functions; though he had emphasised that it could do so only 'out of necessity' not 'at its own will' (*'erit ergo concilium administrator necessarius, non autem voluntarius'*).[59] This applied to the council a privilege which Hostiensis and others had applied to the college of cardinals;[60] it is reasonable to suppose that Tudeschi here had in mind a situation such as occurred at Constance.

In his speech-treatise of 1442, by way of contrast, Tudeschi employs his juristic learning to defend nearly all the major tenets of Basle conciliarism. He repeatedly employs Zabarella's statement that the pope is 'as head of a corporation, so that power itself is in the corporation itself as in its foundation, and in the pope as in its principal minister'.[61] (Like Zabarella and, in certain contexts, the Decretists,[62] he equates the council with the Church.) He uses this as an argument to validate Eugenius' deposition.[63] He added, as Cesarini and others had said before him,[64] that the canonists' disputes as to the relative superiority of pope and council had been resolved in the latter's favour by *Haec Sancta*.[65] And, remarking that the pope is 'not the true head, but the ministerial or political head' of the Church,[66] he also cited in this context the Venetian constitution. In Bartolist fashion, he regards Venice as a civic corporation, and applies to it the Zabarellan model: 'One can see the same thing in the constitution of the Venetians. For the Doge is the first both in counsels and among individual citizens; but, if he errs, he is resisted by the city, and if necessary deposed; because the foundation of jurisdiction is in the body of the city, and in the Doge as its principal minister'.[67] He also uses Zabarella's *dictum* to disprove the validity of Eugenius' dissolution of Basle in 1431 and his translation of the council in 1437: 'Since therefore in the council representing the universal Church there is fulness of power, the former Eugenius could not, although he was principal minister of the Church ... use the fulness of power against the whole Church, in which is the foundation of fulness of power, because it would then seem that there were two powers in the Church, which would smack of heresy'.[68]

But Tudeschi now, in defending Basle, interprets the council's 'fulness of power' in a far more extensive way than that envisaged by Zabarella himself. For he uses it to mean the *unlimited* juridical supremacy of the council over the pope: 'Although the basis of jurisdiction is in the universal Church, nevertheless, since it is impossible to assemble the universal Church ... *the universal Church itself exercises its jurisdiction through the council representing it*'.[69] To the same end he develops Zabarella's statement that Peter had power 'principally' but not 'totally': while the pope has 'principal' power, 'the general council represents the whole Church (*totam ecclesiam*) with regard to its total power (*quoad totalem sui potestatem*), because the whole (*tota*) ecclesiastical power is in the Church as in its foundation'.[70] What he means by this is that there is nothing which the Church, assembled as council, may not do. Contrary to the whole tradition of canon law and the medieval canonists, he says that the council has power not only to act in certain special circumstances (to define faith, to correct a pope), but can appropriate to itself any aspect of ecclesiastical jurisdiction or administration. Here again he applied to the Church what Bartolus had said of the sovereign city. Those who represent the Church in an assembled council 'have the power of the Church and can makes statutes and precepts and exercise the whole jurisdiction of the Church'.[71] For the exercise of power was collegiately bestowed on the other apostles (as well as on Peter) who then represented the Church.[72] He had already, in December 1437, granted infallibility to the council.[73] He had now gone over completely to the Basle-conciliarist camp. He now views the council as absolutely and unrestrictedly sovereign.

Tudeschi applied the corporation theory which he had expounded in the *Commentary* to prove the continued legitimacy of the council of Basle as against that of Ferrara-Florence, and again he employs both the civic and the diocesan analogies. Just as a cathedral chapter is regarded as automatically representing a diocese, and a city council as automatically representing a people, so too the general council is the solemn assembly (*legitima congregatio*) of the whole Church. This is because the whole Church cannot assemble in any other way, being too numerous, and also because the general council, like the cathedral chapter and the city council, is convoked in accordance with rules that have been laid down in the name of the community for this purpose (i.e. *Frequens*). This explains why Basle and not Florence is the legitimate council. 'Even though the whole clergy of the world were assembled in one place, it would not on that account be said that a council was assembled there, unless they had been assembled legitimately for making a council; as we say of the people of a city that, if the whole people came together to perpetrate a crime, it would not be said that the city had perpetrated the crime, unless the citizens had been legitimately assembled and the matter had been discussed in corporation (*in universitate*)'.[74] He had, in fact, in the Commentary drawn the same civic analogy, but this time with regard to an ordinary ecclesiastical corporation, in order to distinguish between acts which were attributable to the whole body and those which were not.[75] He now drew the conclusion that the acts of individuals are only attributable to the corporation if they have been 'assembled *collegialiter* in the accustomed manner'.[76]

He applied his consistently-held majoritarian principle to prove the legitimacy of the acts of the Basle majority both in 1437 and in 1439, citing the precedents of ecclesiastical and civil corporations, and Bartolus in particular.[77] Of the claim of the minority of 1437 to be the 'saner part' of the council, he says, as he had said in his *Commentary* and in his speech of December 1437, that it is the 'common opinion of doctors and especially modern ones' that the minority cannot override the majority, unless the majority have disqualified themselves by committing a fault specifically referred to in the law — which could not be proved in this case.[78] On the decision to depose Eugenius in 1439 he argued, exactly contrary to what he had said at the time, that those bishops who had not come to the council or who had left before this took place 'made themselves aliens, and total power resided with those that remained'.[79] Since the council constituted the corporate assembly of the entire ecclesiastical corporation, it was itself, like other such bodies, a self-governing corporation: it therefore exercised its power collectively, decisions being taken by a majority of those present.

He also made one reference to the full participation of lower clergy, which, contrary to his speeches at Basle in 1439 (he had avoided the subject in 1437), he defended by again invoking the corporational nature of the council, and making an implicit analogy with the civic assembly as described by Bartolus: 'It is in favour of the action of the council of Basle that, inasmuch as not only bishops but also their inferiors were incorporated into the council, they all together as comprising the council and representing the universal Church have the power of the Church and can make statutes'.[80] This too was a departure from Zabarella, but not one which Tudeschi appears to have espoused with any enthusiasm.

Tudeschi's contribution lay in presenting the Basilean position as a legally tenable case. An interesting feature to emerge from Tudeschi's long-winded, cumbersome and repetitive speech of 1442 (Piccolomini acidly commented that 'only a fool thinks that kings are influenced by tomes and treatises')[81] was the repeated analogy with city-states, and his use of Bartolus. This corresponds with the use made by other Basilean theorists of civic analogies and republican principles. It shows that they had some awareness of, and some admiration for, those contemporary republican institutions which flourished in both Italy and Germany. Tudeschi's use of the analogy with lesser ecclesiastical corporations to support both the general principle of conciliar sovereignty and the specific procedures adopted at Basle is a striking testimony to the validity of Tierney's thesis on this aspect of the 'foundations' of conciliar theory. Combined with his use of civic-republican analogies, derived mainly from Bartolus, it gave rise to a distinctively communal view of Church government.

NOTES

1. *DDC* vi, 1195-1215; Hove, 497; Schweizer: Nörr; Fleury; Lefèbvre; Jacob (1971); Buisson, 121, 191, 235, 248, 267.
2. Above, p. 43.
3. One of the great canonists of the time (d.1408): Hove, 496-7; Schulte (1877), ii, 289ff.
4. Brandmüller (1968), i, 226, 236.
5. *PC* I, 74-5; Brandmüller (1968), i, 245n.
6. Black (1970c), 441.
7. Black (1970c), 442-3.
8. *PC* i, 218-19.
9. Died 1439: *DDC* vii, 22-3.
10. Black (1970c).
11. Piccolomini, *De rebus,* 193.
12. Mansi, xxxiA, 225C.
13. *MC* ii, 1006ff.; Buisson, 212-13.
14 *MC* ii, 1040-1.
15 *MC* ii, 1144-93; cf. *MC* ii, 1122-30.
16 *MC* ii, 1161-5.
17. *MC* ii, 1193.
18 *ASP* 96ff.; Schweizer, 112-30.
19. *Tractatus de auctoritate papae et imperatoris et veritate et institutione sacrorum conciliorum: DDC* vi, 1205.
20. *DRTA* xvi, 438-538; *MC* iii, 1022-1125; Schweizer, 167-70; Vooght (1965), 180-1.
21. *DDC* vi, 1214; *PC* ii, 283.
22. Below, p. 98.
23. *MC* ii, 1169.
24. *MC* ii, 1182-6.
25. *ASP* 98.
26. *DRTA* xvi, 538 (below, p. 102); Nörr, 33, 165ff.
27. *ASP* 174; Nörr, 164.
28. *DRTA* xvi, 536-7; cf. Tierney (1968), 49.
29. Piccolomini, *De rebus,* 179.
30 *ASP* 153; cf. Nörr, 94-5, 155.
31. Died before 1436: Schulte (1877), ii, 294ff.; Hove, 497; Buisson, 14.

32. Died in 1436: Schulte (1877), ii, 297; Hove, 497; Buisson, 12-14, 180-1, 190-1.

33. Ausgewählte, Texte, 410-12.

34. Lefèbvre, passim.

35. Butrio, Comm., vol. i, fol. 97v on 1.6.4; cf. vol. iii, fol. 150v on 3.34.7, and vol. v, fol. 41r on 5.7.4; Buisson, 234-6, 246-8.

36. For example Butrio, Comm, vol. iii, fol. 150v on 3.34.7, and vol. iv, fol. 54r on 4.17.13: 'papa in terminatione sue potestatis si potest debet recurrere ad testamentum novum et vetus, et sic ad legem divinam, non ad suum ius positivum in quo est quandoque "pro ratione voluntas", sed ad ius divinum et impermutabile'. Butrio here endorses the pro-biblical, anti-civilian trend in ecclesiology (above, pp. 61f., below, pp. 128f). For a fourteenth-century example of this, Ullmann (1976), 224. Cf. Tierney (1968), 44.

37. Tudeschi, Comm (1571), vol. i, fols. 140v-2v on 1.6.4. Cf. above, p.10

38. Comm. (1571), i, fol. 142v.

39. Tierney (1968), 59-60, 214.

40. Tierney (1968), 50-1.

41. Cf. Tierney (1968), 47ff.

42. Quaestio I, nos. 20, 22, solutio.

43. Cf. Norr, 132n.; Lagarde (1963), 333.

44. Comm. (1571), i, fols. 140v-2v on 1.6.4.

45. Comm. (1571), vii, fol. 89v on 5.3.30; cf. vi, fol. 85v on 3.10.4, and i, fol. 214r on 1.6.55. Cf. Gierke, DGR iii, 279-85, 425ff.; Fedele; Roberti.

46. Comm. (1571), vi, fol. 35v on 3.5.15.

47. Comm. (1571), ii, fol. 190v on 1.38.15; cf. Tierney (1968), 117ff., 127ff.

48. Gierke (1913).

49. Comm. (1571), i, fol. 160v on 1.6.19; but see vi, fol. 90v on 3.11.1.

50. Comm. (1571), vi, fol. 90v on 3.11.1.

51. Comm. (1571), i, fol. 178v on 1.6.30; cf. Gierke, DGR trans Kolegar, 621b. On Bartolus, Ullmann (1962).

52. For example, Comm. (1571), i, fol. 214r on 1.6.55; vi, fol. 99r on 2.27.23; vii, fol. 197v on 5.36.8.

53. Comm. (1571), vi, fol. 41r; cf. v, fol. 284v on 3.49.4; cf. Woolf.

54. Comm. (1571), ii, fol. 170r on 1.35.1.

55. Comm. (1534), iii, fol. 84v on 2.27.36. Above, p. 55.

56. Comm. (1571), ii, fol. 170r on 1.35.1; cf. vi, fol. 94v on 3.13.3.

57. Comm. (1571), vii, fol. 242r; vi, fol. 99r on 2.27.23; cf. Woolf, 153ff.

58. Comm. (1571), ii, fol. 170r on 1.35.1.

59. Quaestio I, fol. 142v.

60. Cf. Tierney (1968), 230n.

61. DRTA 456, 483, 485, 499, 506, 521, above, p. 20.

62. Tierney (1968), 48.

63. DRTA xvi, 521.

64. Above, pp. 50f.

65. DRTA xvi, 495.

66. DRTA xvi, 521, 523.

67. DRTA xvi, 521.

68. DRTA xvi, 485; cf. 506.

69. DRTA xvi, 499; cf. 504: 'concilium nomine ecclesie exercet iurisdictionem tam excommunicando quam aliter diffiniendo vel statuendo'; and 506: 'ecclesia universalis tamquam maior et comprehendens in se omnem potestatem ecclesiasticum . . .'

70. DRTA xvi, 483; cf. 520-1. Cf. Tierney (1968), 226n.

71. DRTA xvi, 504. Cf. Comm. (1571), vii, fol. 197v on 5.36.8, where he cites Bartolus on the same point. Bartolus had said: 'Quando populus habet omnem jurisdictionem, potest facere statutum': cit. Ullmann (1962), 713.

72. *DRTA* xvi, 503.
73. *MC* ii, 1169.
74. *DRTA* xvi, 513; cf. 499, 504.
75. *Comm.* (1571), i, fol. 214r on 1.6.55.
76. *DRTA* xvi, 468.
77. *DRTA* xvi, 455-73 *passim.*
78. *DRTA* xvi, 457; above, pp. 93, 98f.
79. *DRTA* xvi, 537.
80. *DRTA* xvi, 504; cf. Ullmann (1962), 732-3.
81. Piccolomini, *De rebus*, 203.

CHAPTER 7

FINAL PHASE OF BASLE CONCILIARISM

During the final break with Eugenius and the ensuing schism (1437-1449), there was no need to make new claims on behalf of conciliar authority, since what was happening was that the radical conciliarists, led by Aleman and now also Segovia, were seeking finally to implement, without the restraining hand of the moderates and secular powers within the council, the original programme of 1431-4. During the deposition debate (May 1439)[1] the radical conciliarists, in reponse to the immediate situation, laid special emphasis on ecclesiastical (meaning conciliar) liberty from secular interference, and on the juridical equality of priests and bishops in the council. The only original conciliar theorist now was Segovia. We may first glance at the works of Ragusa and the official university statements; from these we find that conciliarists were now relying more and more on a collectivist notion of the Church.

NOTES
1. *ASP* 1-187; cf. Haller in *CB* i, 12-17. Both sides employed procedural devices, movements of closure and the like; when these failed, they shouted at each other and made threats; the city magistrates had to keep the peace.

Ragusa's use of history

Johannes Stojkovic de Ragusa,[1] a native of the city-state of Dubrovnik-Ragusa, a Dominican who like Torquemada had studied theology at Paris, was a leading member of the Parisian delegation at the council of Siena.[2]

He was one of the first to arrive at Basle, charged, along with Johannes de Palomar, with the official opening on behalf of Cesarini (July 1431).[3] He played a prominent part in the early stages of the council: it was he who first suggested the deputation-system instead of the nation-system (February 1432),[4] and he was a leading Catholic spokesman in the Hussite debates (January-March 1433).[5] He represented Basle on embassies to Constantinople in 1435 and 1437-8.[6] His writings show a special awareness of eastern Christendom: he defines a council as comprising all five patriarchates,[7] and sees the east-west schism as a watershed in the history of the western Church.[8] After 1437 he was a member of the new leadership at Basle, and was entrusted with several important diplomatic missions. In May 1438 he went to Vienna to address the new king of the Romans, Albert II;[9] in October he travelled to Nuremberg, returned to Basle in January 1439, and was one of the council's spokesmen at the Mainz Reichstag from February to April.[10] Back in Basle by 24 April, he argued vigorously in support of the majority position and the 'three truths of faith' in the ensuing debates on Eugenius' deposition.[11] From July to October he was again at Albert II's court, entrusted with the arduous task of persuading him to accept the three truths and the deposition of Eugenius. In January-February 1440 he served as Basle's emissary to the electoral princes meeting at Frankfurt;[12] in April he was sent to Vienna to address Frederick III.[13] The council made him bishop of Ardjisch, Romania (October 1438) and cardinal (October 1440). He left Basle in 1443 and died the same year.

The ecclesiological work for which he has hitherto been best known is his 'treatise on the Church (*Tractatus de ecclesia*)'.[14] Binder argues that this was the outcome of his debates with the Hussites and dates it to 1433.[15] Thils and Krchnak date it later, the latter as late as 1440-1, and think that it also contained material used in controversy with the Greeks.[16] In either case, given his other works and the whole of his career, this tract surprises us with its forthright defence of the monarchical-hierarchical theory of the Church in terms characteristic of fourteenth- and fifteenth-century papalism. It propounds such theses as 'That the ecclesiastical hierarchy is reduced to one supreme hierarch; that the ecclesiastical principate and fulness of power of Peter is demonstrated by many passages in the holy scriptures . . . that the said principate and fulness of power of Peter is handed down to his successors; that Peter and any supreme pontiff is and is called head of the Church during his principate'.[17] This has led some to think that he was a papalist who at some point changed his mind. But, whatever the date of this work, he was simultaneously supporting the views and actions of the conciliarist majority at Basle. Rather, it provides us with an instance of a (to us) amazingly advocatorial, controversialist approach, which we also find in other writers. He supports the traditional claims of the pope-oriented Latin Church in controversy with the Hussites and Greeks, while at the same time advocating conciliar supremacy in the controversy within the Latin Church. This is evident from his behaviour at Siena and throughout the council of Basle, from his ambassadorial speeches, and above all from his 'Treatise on the authority of councils and the method of celebrating them (*Tractatus de auctoritate conciliorum et de modo celebratione eorum*)'. This was begun after October 1438 and was probably unfinished; it survives in a single manuscript, a copy of the original with mistakes and omissions. This little-known work has received hardly any attention.[18] One reason for this is perhaps that Ragusa's conciliar works, like his contributions to the Hussite debates, are for the most part long-winded, repetitive and lacking in originality; they reproduce ideas concocted by others, at some points closely following Segovia's *Presidency* (1434).

His one original contribution is his historical analysis of changing constitutional practices in the Church (he himself wrote three accounts of episodes in the council's history).[19] He defends recent innovations in the convocation, composition and internal decision-making procedure of general councils on the ground that these are all matters of positive law on which variation according to the needs of the time is both legitimate and desirable. He makes this most explicit on the question of convocation: 'According to different times, there has been a different method of assembling general and universal councils. It was done in one way in the primitive Church, not yet spread through the world, in another way after its diffusion, at the time when princes of the world and Roman emperors began to receive the light of faith; in another way at the time when church-men, and especially the Roman pontiff, were held in honour and began to abound in power and wealth, especially after the division of the eastern from the western Church; and in another way now in our time, from the time of the great council of Constance'.[20] Similarly, on the composition of councils, he says that 'although, as the faith developed and the Church became organised, in subsequent councils only the bishops appear to have defined, nevertheless others, priests and doctors, are not for this reason excluded'. If the bishops usually had power to define, this was because they were mostly 'learned men', but nowadays you rarely find doctors of theology among them; they are nearly all doctors of canon law. Since councils deal especially with matters of faith, doctors too, especially those of theology 'of whatever status or religious profession', should have a defining voice.[21] Priests should have the same defining power as bishops because the latters' functions derive 'not from privilege but from *status* and ordinary law'.[22]

Lastly, on the question of procedure, he observes that in the first eight general councils all deliberated together; he then gives details of the practice of voting by nations, adopted at Pisa and Constance; and he finally records the measures taken at Basle to establish the practice of voting by heads in deputations.[23]

Ragusa's explanation, then, of the varying constitutional practices in the Church and his defence of the legitimacy of those adopted by Constance and Basle was that in such matters different practices could properly be adopted at different times. In other words, he had some notion of historical relativity. Historiographical discussions of the Church's constitution in the late Middle Ages and early modern period tended to be either developmental or primitivist. The anti-Hussite Netter, the conciliarist Velde and the pro-papal Torquemada each saw the Church's constitution in terms of a gradual evolution; as with the later theory of Newman, their purpose was to establish the legitimacy of relatively late developments. On the other hand, anticlerical sects of the Middle Ages, the Hussites and also some conciliarists aimed at discrediting aspects of the existing church constitution of which they disapproved, by pointing out that these were recent additions and appealing to an authoritative model of 'the primitive Church'.[24] (Segovia employs both arguments in different contexts).[25] Ragusa, unlike both of these schools of thought, is simply concerned to argue that constitutional practices in the Church may vary from one epoch to another, and that such variations — even those relating to the authoritative nature of the episcopate — are legitimate in their own time.

NOTES

1. Krchnak; *LTK* v, 1074.
2. *PC* i, 55ff.; Brandmüller (1968), i, 49-51, 123-5, 142-4.
3. *MC* ii, 126: above, p. 27.
4. Above, p. 28.
5. Jacob (1949), *passim*.
6. Gill (1959), 63ff., 74ff., 79ff.; *PC* ii, 78ff.
7. *Speech* (1), Bibl. Vat., Reg. lat. 1019, fol. 336r; and *De auctoritate*, fol. 195r-v.
8. *De auctoritate*, fol. 186v.
9. *Speech (1)*. Cf. Lazarus, 329, 340.
10. Krchnak, 43-4; *ASP* 12.
11. *ASP* 21, 26; above, p. 45.
12. *Speech* (2).
13. *Speech* (3).
14. Thils; Binder (1951); Duda.
15. Binder (1951), 37, 40-1, 53.
16. Thils; Krchnak, 59-60.
17. Cit. Thils, 224-5; cf. Binder (1951), 49.
18. Apparently discovered by Krchnak; Binder (1951), p.54, says he had not seen it.
19. *MC* i, 1-131 and 135-286; Mansi xxxiA, 248-77; cf. *CB* i, 18-19.
20. Speech (1), Reg. lat. 1019, fol. 336r. He deals with methods of conciliar

convocation in this speech, fols. 336-40, and in *De auctoritate*, fols. 187-97.
21. *De auctoritate*, fols. 209v-10r; he deals with the composition of councils in *De auctoritate*, fols. 197-211.
22. *De auctoritate*, fols. 209-10r.
23. *De auctoritate*, fols. 212r-14v; he deals with procedure in *De auctoritate*, fols. 212-20.
24. Cf. Leff (1967b), *passim*.
25. Below, p. 132f.

The university consilia *(1440-4)*

While it is true that many universities were pro-conciliar and produced the most ardent supporters of Basle, one must note, à propos the various university statements of the 1440's, that the universities were divided both between and within themselves.[1]

Further, the growing subordination of the Church to secular-territorial overlords during the schism of 1378-1417, and again during the neutrality of 1439-48, greatly affected the universities. By 1440 the compartmentalization of esslesiastical Europe into national Churches had done much to undermine the ideal of the univeristy as a cosmopolitan and autonomous body, a cell of the universal rather than of the local Church. Segovia observed that the suppression of anti-Clementine opinion at Paris in 1383 meant that Paris and other universities became more local in composition, so that their members were more dependent on local princes for the safety of 'their persons, their parents, their temporal goods and their benefices'.[2] In short, the universities lost some of their scope and aptitude for independent teaching and action, and tended to act sometimes as supporters and legitimisers of the local potentate, founder or patron.

The doctrine of conciliar supremacy was prevalent at Paris, Cologne, Cracow, Vienna, Erfurt, Leipzig and St Andrews.[3] In the cases of Cracow and St Andrews, this coincided with local secular policy. In the other cases, a distinction must be drawn between support for conciliarism in principle and support for Basle in the present circumstances, and also between endorsement of the conciliar theory associated with Gerson and Constance, and of the more radical doctrines of Basle. As regards the first, the neutrality decree adopted by France and Germany led to outright suppression of public support for Basle at Paris; while Cologne, Vienna, Erfurt and Leipzig were cautious about the immediate situation, and obeyed the letter of the neutrality decree by refraining from naming Felix V as pope. However, while Cologne appears to have been sincerely uncertain, the tone of the statements put out by Vienna, Erfurt and Leipzig suggest that they would have preferred to support Basle publicly.

In general canon and civil lawyers now tended to be only moderately pro-conciliar or definitely pro-papal, while theologians appear to have been readier to adopt the Basilean views. Bologna, situated on papal territory, supported Eugenius;[4] at Vienna, the law faculty dissented from pro-conciliar statements in 1442 and in 1444.[5] In this context, we may note that Basle and its apologists ascribed a *de iure* role in doctrinal decision-making not only to individual doctors within the council[6] but also to the universities themselves, and especially to the theology faculties. The most explicit assertion of the theologians' claim came in a letter written by the council to the emperor (October 1439), urging him to consult the universities when deciding whom to support: the universities, it argued, contained 'many very expert and studious *doctors and masters in theology, whose proper office by the nature of their profession and studies it is to decide on faith* ... Let not our lords the bishops be indignant with us if we say it pertains to theologians to decide on faith; for judgment on faith belonged to bishops alone, in those times when they alone were masters and doctors of this divine science' (i.e. of the study of scripture) 'but now that the weeds of human laws, to which bishops of modern times give such importance, have grown up, this judgment must belong to others than the bishops alone, that is to masters and doctors in the science of faith'.[7] This was taken up by the rector and university of Vienna, who declared (March 1442) that they were 'called to a share in concern' for the church 'in accordance with the office entrusted to us (*cum autem nos in partem sollicitudinis vocatos gloriemur ... iuxta creditum nobis officium*)'.[8]

Turning now to individual universities, the general mood of Paris in 1440 is clear enough. On 22 December, Sabrevois, one of the Parisian delegates at Basle, addressed the university on the council's behalf, praised its past services to the conciliar cause, and requested it 'in its accustomed manner to exhort the kings and princes of Christendom, and especially the king of France ... and the other princes of the realm, through spokesmen, letters and epistles, to remain always in the true obedience of the same council of Basle'. After a long discussion in the faculties and nations, the rector replied that the university persisted in its allegiance to Basle, and that it would grant Sabrevois' request, '*wishing* to exhort kings and princes, and especially the king of France ... through letters, epistles, etc., always to persist in the true obedience of the same holy council'.[9] It appears quite clear that Paris would have liked to campaign publicly on Basle's behalf. It did what it could without fear of reprisal, issuing a statement which affirmed its 'persistence in the obedience of the council of Basle, in conformity with our Lord and King'; it neither repudiated Basle nor openly adopted neutrality.[10] Thereafter Paris tried in vain to encourage Basle to be more accommodating to suggestions by the secular powers for a new, third council.

Official statements on the dispute were made by Cologne (October 1440),[11] Vienna (August 1440,[12] 1442,[13] 1444),[14] Erfurt (August 1440),[15] Leipzig (1442),[16] and Cracow (two in 1440,[17] one in 1442).[18] All of these were in general terms conciliarist, but they differed considerably in tone and emphasis, and in the advice they offered on the immediate situation. Cologne was clear on principle but ambiguous on the present legitimacy of Basle. Vienna went as far as it could in expressing support for Basle without actually contravening the neutrality decree. All the statements by Vienna explicitly denounced independent action by the princes and said that a new council could only assemble with Basle's consent; but in 1442 and 1444 the law faculty dissented, upholding the right of princes to settle the dispute in their own way.[19] Cologne, Vienna, Erfurt and Leipzig all expressed their opposition to the policy of neutrality.[20] But Cologne and Erfurt expressed no opposition to the princes' project for a new council, and by 1444 Leipzig also supported this scheme.[21]

Cracow alone was entirely unambiguous in its support for Basle, to which it adhered until the bitter end.[22] Its statement of 1442 is perhaps the most complete, certainly the most succinct, defence of Basle conciliarism ever produced outside Basle itself. It may actually have been commissioned by the council, which adopted it as its formal reply to Eugenius' bull *Etsi non dubitemus* of 1441;[23] it is clear that Torquemada had this document before him when he refuted conciliarism point by point in his *Summa de ecclesia*.[24] Cracow, then, was one place where the specifically Basilean version of conciliar theory had struck roots. Issued in the university's name, it was the work of five men,[25] and in particular of the canonist Thomas Strempinski.[26] It drew to a considerable degree on a work ('Determinatio de ecclesia') by Jacob de Jüterbog (za Paradyza), a theologian who soon after became a Carthusian and continued to press the need for a reform council on Nicholas V.[27] It also drew heavily, and at times *verbatim*, on Segovia's *Presidency*.[28]

NOTES

1. Keussen (1929), 247ff.; Jedin (1957) i, 35; *PC* ii, 238n.
2. *MC* iii, 531-2, Cf. above, p.16.
3. Bressler; Keussen (1929); Kaufmann ii, 442-68, esp. 462-4; Jedin (1957) i, 34-6; Burns, 77.
4. *DRTA* xvii, 162.
5. Below, p. 112 at n. 19.
6. Ragusa, *De auctoritate*, fols. 209v-10r.
7. *DRTA* xiv, 410.
8. *DRTA* xvi, 288.
9. *MC* iii, 532-3; *PC* ii, 239n.

10. *PC* ii, 240; cf. *MC* iii, 531; *CB* vii, 309n.
11. *DRTA* xv, 464-7 and *HUP* v, 460-2, Cf. *MC* iii, 534; *PC* ii, 259n.; Kaufmann ii, 465n.
12. *HUP* v, 471-9; cf. *MC* iii, 533-4; *PC* 259n.
13. *DRTA* xvi, 289-92; cf. *MC* iii, 536; *PC* ii, 259n.
14. *DRTA* xvii, 266-8.
15. *DRTA* xv, 439-50 and *HUP* v, 462-71; cf. *MC* iii, 530-1, 534; *PC* ii, 259n.; *DRTA* xvi, 452; Kaufmann ii, 468n.
16. *MC* iii, 536.
17. *MC* iii, 531, 535; cf. *CB* vii, 391; Munich Staatsbibliothek, Clm. 18470, fols. 38r-63v.
18. *HUP* v, 479-517; cf. Lepszy ed,. i, 115-26, 457; *PC* ii, 259-60. See also Bressler, 39-67; Black (1977b) 349-51. Lübeck university also adhered to Basle: *MC* iii, 497.
19. *DRTA* xvi, 292 and xvii, 266-7.
20. *DRTA* xv, 441, 465-6 and xvi 290-2; *MC* iii, 536.
21. Kaufmann ii, 464n.
22. *Cod. dipl. univ. Cracov.* part ii, 73ff.; *Monumenta ... Polonias* part ii, 20; Morawski ii, 87ff.; Bressler, 68ff.; *PC* ii, 326.
23. Cf. *MC* iii, 1153-95.
24. Compare the sequence of book ii of Torquemada's *Summa* with that of the Cracow tract.
25. *HUP* v, 479-80.
26. Fijalek i, esp. 428; on Strempinski, cf. *CB* i, 90 and ii, 505; *MC* iii, 606.
27. *DTC* viii, 297-8; Fijalek; Kellner; Meier; Jedin (1957) i, 44. For the parallels between the two works: Fijalek i, 351ff.
28. Compare *HUP*, v, 489-90, 493 with Segovia below, pp.150-3; cf. *DRTA* xvii, 351.

The realist-organic view of the Church-in-council

We are now in a position to determine the distinguishing features of these and other statements of conciliar theory in its final phase of development. First, there were the specifically Basilean tenets, which were not all shared by all conciliarists writing in this period. These may be summarized as follows: the council is infallible;[1] it possesses fulness of power, which includes judicial and executive power;[2] it is the supreme judicial tribunal in the Church.[3] The new emphasis on the equality of 'doctors and preachers of the divine law and word, and learned priests who have the care of souls'[4] with bishops in a council, and on the independence of the clerical council from the secular powers, received a certain amount of support.[5]

Second, there was the ever-increasing reliance on the holistic argument, that the church is a real whole, body or thing, capable of self-expression and self-determination solely through a general council, which as a consequence wields the unique 'total power' of the whole church. The starting-point was the adage, doubtless learnt in every liberal-arts course and cited by Marsiglio, that 'every whole is greater than its part';[6]

conciliarists now repeatedly spoke of the Church as a 'whole', and applied to it the concepts of potency and act, matter and form.[7] In asserting the unique character and powers of the Church-as-a-whole-in-council, they implicitly rejected the view commonly held by lawyers that 'a whole does not differ in reality from its parts (*totum non differt realiter a suis partibus*)'.[8] This argument often carried overtones of epistemological realism, though these were never again as strongly stated as by Velde. The collectivist argument was often used to support the view that a council held power, not on electoral or episcopalist grounds, but because it was the 'legitimate assembly' of the whole Church: here, it was the philosophical counterpart of Tudeschi's legal arguments.

While this line of thought could readily be used in conjunction with the notion of the council's fulness of power, it was also adopted by some who did not explicitly support all the Basilean claims. We find it not only in Segovia, Ragusa and the Cracow statement of 1442, but also in statements by Cologne, Erfurt and Vienna, and in Jüterbog. Erfurt and Cracow (1442) said, as Menaye had said in 1434, that the organic analogy necessarily implied conciliar sovereignty.[9] Cologne used terms reminiscent of Velde to assert the superiority of the mystical body over the pope, without however equating this with the council.[10] Ragusa and Segovia followed Gerson in equating the dispersed Church with the Church in its 'material' or 'potential' aspect, and the assembled Church with the Church in its 'formal' or 'actual' aspect. The Church is more fully itself when assembled in a council. Assembly and dispersal are spoken of as two 'moments' in the Church's being, each realized at different points in time.[11] It is in the council that the powers of the Church as a whole become activated: 'the dispersed Church does not speak, but only the general council representing it' (anonymous Paris doctor, 1440).[12]

Basilean conciliarists spoke as if ideally the council should comprise literally the whole Church, its limited membership being due to purely practical considerations. The only criterion for the validity of an assembly, for it to be acting as the whole, is that it should have been assembled in the manner laid down in the Church's constitutional law. As Cracow (1442) said: '(The Church cannot) actually be assembled together out of all its members in one place simultaneously ... and so cannot go forth (*exire*) into the activation and execution of its actual jurisdiction, which it possesses authoritatively and *in habitu*, so long as it cannot be assembled. Therefore, in order that it go forth into the executive act of its jurisdiction and power, it is necessary for it from time to time to be assembled in certain elements (in *certis suppositis*) and in its more principal members and others'.[13] This closely followed Jüterbog.[14]

The power thus activated by the council is precisely the power of the whole. Here, organic holism was crucial to the conciliarist argument: there is a power which is peculiar to the Church acting 'as a body'.[15] Thus Cracow (1442) spoke of the 'execution of its actual jurisdiction, which (the Church) possesses authoritatively and *in habitu*', and which the Church can only operate when assembled as council.[16] A university group at the Reichstag of Nuremberg (October 1444) put this in more lyrical form: 'And thus the power (*potestas*) of the universal Church is reduced to act (*reducitur ad actum*) through the existence of a general council; so that such power is in the dispersed Church like seed in grass or wine in a grape, while it is in the general council as in its formal and complete being (*esse formali et completo*)'.[17] While conciliarists did not conceive the dispersed Church as a group with a 'real personality', they conceived the collective Church as just that.

The final flourish of medieval conciliarism, then, was characterised by holism and metaphysical realism. While Cusa and Velde, the outstanding exponents of realist conciliarism in 1432-4, had now changed their position, the alignment of conciliar theory with collectivist realism survived their defection; it probably owed little, in fact, to any particular individual thinker. Cologne was indeed a stronghold of philosophical realism, which Velde had helped to establish there. But Cracow was renowned for its nominalism; and it is surprising that, in an age when nominalism was so prevalent in the universities, a movement in ideas created largely by university men should have been so realist in orientation. Clearly it was no longer the case that realism was the natural ally of papalism, and nominalism of ecclesial populism. There was (as has been argued above)[18] no philosophical necessity in such alignments: the relationships were contingent and individual thinkers could to a large extent manipulate ideas to suit their preferences.

This further suggests that ideas were being used, rather like legal precedents, in an *ad hoc*, advocatorial manner. The evidence warns us always to ask whether a writer had adopted a cause for some personal reason, which he then proceeded to defend by ferreting among the philosophical and theological authorities, rather than using the latter as a means for arriving at more objective conclusions. We have noted how Cusa and Velde could use their neo-Platonism to support different views of the Church's constitution; how Escobar could, just after finishing his *Government of councils*, defend the papal position before the Greeks at Florence; and how Ragusa could defend papal monarchy before the Hussites and Greeks, while attacking it before Latin-Catholic audiences. We have observed the tergiversations of Tudeschi. One wonders just how seriously some of these arguments should be taken.

It should also be noted that at least two German conciliarists, writing during or shortly after Basle but not while themselves at Basle, maintained the strongly *anticlerical* and German-imperialist tone of Marsiglio and Niem. The 'Refutation of papal primacy (*Confutatio primatus papae*)', written in 1440 by Mathias Doering (who was elected general of the pro-Basle Franciscans in 1443), drew heavily on Marsiglio. It bitterly attacked the theory of papal fulness of power but above all the papacy's temporal claims, which are condemned as usurpation by an alien power (P. Albert in *HJ* xi, 1890, 439-90). Similarly, Gregory Heimburg (who attended Basle from 1432 to 1434, occasionally speaking on Sigismund's behalf, left Basle with Sigismund, and later enthusiastically served the Hussite king Podebrady of Bohemia) expressed a vigorously anticlerical nationalism in his *Apologia* and *Invectiva*, both written some years after Basle (E. Joachimsohn, *Gregor Heimburg*, Bamberg, 1891). Such men clearly cannot be called mainstream Basileans according to the criteria adopted here; they belong more precisely to the *Vorreformation*. Neither, in fact, made a particularly original contribution to conciliar theory itself.

From Basle's supporters in this period we sometimes hear the outraged cry of the radical reformer, of the 'ideological revolutionary'. It is in this tone, as much as in the constitutional claims and philosophical theories, that one can find some similarity between Basle conciliarism and later radical movements. The spirit of egalitarianism, however limited in its practical application, appears in Aleman's speeches.[19] Republican themes were more insistently voiced as the council of Basle went on.[20] It was left to Juan de Segovia, a gentle spirit, to draw out the implications of the specifically Basilean form of conciliarism for political theory, and so to link this movement more directly, in principle at least, with movements which may legitimately be regarded as its successors.

The conciliar movement effectively ended with Basle. The attempt to resuscitate it in 1511-12 was an abysmal failure.[21] It would be a long time before another attempt was made to reintegrate the principles of conciliar consensus and Roman primacy. Yet, even though conciliarism had lost practically all its momentum as a practical movement, the doctrine of conciliar supremacy as defined by Constance and expounded by Gerson, though not so much as practised and expounded at Basle, continued to be almost the *sententia communis* of north-European christendom. It was the standard teaching in several universities, especially Paris; secular rulers regarded it as worth exploiting for their own ambitions.[22] The view that a council could in some way dispose of a heretical or schismatic pope, a view that long pre-dated the conciliar movement itself, continued to be held by many Catholic theologians long after the Reformation.[23] Indeed, some of the notions of conciliar authority and synodal government that are held in various branches of Christendom today are often surprisingly similar to those held in the fifteenth century.[24]

NOTES

1. *HUP* v, 489-90, 493, 516; Ragusa in *DRTA* xv, 209; Jüterbog, ed. Fijalek i, 374-5;*MC* iii, 535;*ASP* 36ff., 50, 76-8.
2. *HUP* v, 472-3, 489-90, 497-8; *MC* iii, 533, 535; *DRTA* xv, 445; Jüterbog, ed. Fijalek i, 370, 374-5, 378; Ragusa in *DRTA* xv, 210-11; *ASP* 78 and Piccolomini again in *Briefwechsel*, ed. Wolkan part 1, i, 143.
3. 'Numquam licet christiano homine a sacro concilio legitime congregato appellare' (Vienna, 1440: *MC* iii, 533); 'consistorium summum et irrefragabile tribunal est ecclesia synodaliter congregata' (Cologne, 1440: *MC* iii, 534).
4. *DRTA* xiv, 389-90; *ASP* 72, 76-8. But this was not endorsed by any university.
5. *ASP* 113, 141ff., 185; *MC* iii, 580, 589, 949, 1320 (all by Segovia); Segovia, *Explanatio*, fol. 222v; *Contra neutralitatem*, fols. 147r-v; *Justificatio*, fol. 211r; *MAE* fols. 31v-3r, 172r. Among the universities, only Vienna supported this view.
6. *Defensor pacis* I c. 2, 5, 13.
7. Cf. Gerson above, p. 21.
8. Cit. Gierke, *DGR* iii, 425-6.
9. *DRTA* xv, 448; *HUP* v, 502. Cf. *DRTA* xvi, 290-2; *DRTA* xv, 445; *HUP* v, 489-90; Jüterbog, *Determinatio*, ed. Fijalek, i, 353-4, 357, 366-7.
10. *DRTA* xv, 466.
11. *ASP* 78 and Piccolomini again in *Briefwechsel* I, i, 143; Ragusa in *DRTA* xv, 206-7, 209-10 and *De auctoritate*, fol. 257r; *HUP* v, 483, 489-90. Cf. Wilks (1963), 505.
12. *HUP* v, 451.
13. *HUP* v, 492.
14. *Determinatio*, ed, Fijalek i, 373-4; cf. *ibid.*, 356-7.
15. *DRTA* xvii, 367; cf. Ragusa (citing Gerson without acknowledgement) in *DRTA* xv, 210 and in *De auctoritate*, fol. 257r.
16. *HUP* v, 492.
17. *DRTA* xvii, 367; cf. Gierke, *DGR* iii, 461-2.
18. Above, pp.82f.
19. *ASP* 112ff.
20. *ASP* 33-5, 237, 239; below, pp.172ff.
21. Baümer (1971), 8ff., 22ff., 67ff., 71ff., Brosse, 57ff., 185-330; Jedin (1939) and (1957), 106-12; Klotzner, 195-287; Oakley (1964b) and (1972); Ullmann (1972b).
22. Baümer (1971) *passim;* Jedin (1957), 32ff.
23. Küng, 276-7; Hamilton, 73, 78, 81.
24. Rahner and Ratzinger, 75-9, 95-7; Küng, 12, 31; Anglican-Roman Catholic internat. commission, esp. at p. 18. Cf. below, pp.215ff.

JUAN DE SEGOVIA

CHAPTER 8

LIFE AND WORKS

The following account of Segovia's career[1] is intended to indicate the sort of man he was, the circumstances under which he reflected and wrote, and the way in which events affected and sometimes modified his opinions. Juan Alfonsi Gonzalez de Segovia (1393-1458) was born in Segovia, Castile, attended Salamanca university from 1407, began lecturing there in 1418, and became professor of theology in 1432.[2] He played a prominent part in the public affairs of the university: he went to Rome in 1421 to help obtain confirmation of a new university constitution, and again in 1431 to have this ratified by the new pope, Eugenius IV.[3] In 1426 he took part in a legal tussle with local nobility, and produced his first ecclesiological work, 'On the superiority and excellence of the supreme ecclesiastical and spiritual power vis à vis royal and temporal power (*Repetitio de superioritate et excellentia supremae potestatis ecclesiasticae et spiritualis ad regiam et temporalem*)', finished in July 1426.[4] This was a standard expression of the Thomist version of the hierocratic position: the two powers are distinct in origin and principle, but, since the spiritual is necessary to the perfection of the temporal, it may, in a sinful world, rightly intervene in temporal affairs, for instance in a case of tyranny; and the two powers converge in the pope.[5] Like many of his contemporaries, he uses aristotelian arguments for the monistic and therefore monarchical unity of any system; Christ is head of the Church 'in potency', the pope 'in act', Peter and his successors have fulness of power.[6] He already shows a special interest in political theory. Apart from that, there is little connection between this and his subsequent ecclesiology, except that he would always

118

champion the principle of ecclesiastical autonomy.

In spring 1433, Segovia was sent to Basle: 'I held it a singular honour to have been designated to attend the general synod at Basle as the sole representative of (Salamanca) university'.[7] He was incorporated in his own right in April,[8] but delayed incorporation as university representative until the arrival of an official Castilian embassy (27 August 1434); thereafter, he notes with a touch of pride, he was seated beside the Paris university delegates.[9] He was assigned to the faith committee, and became attached to the household of cardinal Cervantes, where he would have the opportunity of meeting Rokycana, the Utraquist archbishop of Prague.[10]

He must have been active and prominent in the faith committee, and he must have quickly adopted the conciliarist views of the majority; for on 3 March 1434 he was given the job of drawing up the report of the presidency debate for circulation among the council's four committees.[11] It seems probable that he and many university men who had reached maturity in the years of Pisa and Constance were already favourably disposed towards conciliar authority as defined by *Haec Sancta* and as expounded by Gerson and d'Ailly, before they arrived at Basle. In that case, his *Repetitio* must be regarded as a *pièce de circonstance*. Anyway, this report became his first conciliar treatise, 'Presidency (*Tractatus super presidentia*)'; as he says in the preface: 'a report was made in the committees (*deputationibus*) on the preceding discussion, and this is a summary of the report that was made in one committee, with a few additions and alterations'.[12] Characteristically, and in this instance in the nature of the work, he expresses lucidly and powerfully the general opinions of the majority, while adding certain distinctive touches of his own, for example an insistent appeal to church history and experience; and, again characteristically, he records his own role very briefly.[13] This work so impressed his colleagues that he was asked to publish it; numerous manuscript copies survive, and it became an important summary and store-house for subsequent conciliarist argument.[14] Like all his conciliar writings during Basle, it was typically and wholeheartedly Basilean, being the product of corporate discussion, built around ideas, largely of Gersonian origin, that were the common property of the Basle majority. On 16 April, he was elected monthly president of the faith committee, and was also put on a special committee on annates.[15]

In September 1434 he accompanied Cervantes on an embassy to the papal court at Florence, in an attempt to secure papal adherence to the reform-decrees; he would have been present when a Greek embassy came to Florence in early 1435. He accepted an archidiaconate from Eugenius, and returned to Basle in March 1436.[16] He continued to be an active member of the majority faction, and, in May and June, was selected by Aleman to defend the doctrine of the Immaculate Conception in the faith committee against two strongly pro-papal Dominicans, Torquemada and Montenigro; on 16 June, acting as reporter for the faith committee, he addressed the general affairs committee on this subject.[17] He took part in debates with the Hussites[18] and Greek Orthodox, a by-product of which was his 'Concordance of the indeclinable parts or words of the whole Bible (*Concordia partium sive dictionum indeclinabilium totius Biblie*)', his only work to be printed in the renaissance period (Froben, Basle, 1496).[19] He does not seem to have played much part in the discussion of reform, on which little emphasis is placed in his writings; but it must be assumed that he supported the majority's views and the council's decrees on reform.

Though his support for the majority in general is clear,[20] Segovia kept an open mind on the majority-minority division over the Greek question, a division which he deeply lamented.[21] His vote on 5 December 1436 indicates an attempt at reconciliation.[22] In the final split of May 1437 he gave qualified support to the minority (according to Piccolomini), a conscientious stand which enhanced his general reputation.[23] But he accepted the majority decision and stayed at Basle, while continuing to press his own views.[24]

The departure of so many senior clergy in 1437 brought Segovia to the forefront of the council's practical as well as its intellectual leadership. After Eugenius' suspension, he was nominated to a group of twelve set up to administer the papal states.[25] He was by now one of those who thought Eugenius must be deposed; and, whatever importance he may have attached to reunion with the Greeks, for the next fifteen years his whole energy was devoted to the pope-council controversy.

The summer of 1438 found him engaged in the council's diplomatic struggle to gain support from the secular powers. In July he was sent to Vienna to win over Albert II. On his return he and Ragusa were chosen to accompany patriarch Teck to represent Basle at the forthcoming Reichstag at Nuremberg, a commission of crucial importance. (The council's notarial record says that Cardinal Aleman insisted on holding a special meeting of the general assembly to confirm these appointments, and on receiving Segovia's oath of allegiance himself, the implication being that this was not normal practice; the reason may have been that Segovia had voted with the minority in May 1437.)[26] Segovia was at Nuremberg from October till December, when the Reichstag was adjourned. He returned to Basle, and during January 1439 took part in debates on whether to promulgate the 'three truths' relating to conciliar supremacy as dogma, as a preliminary to deposing Eugenius. On 13 January Segovia again acted as reporter for the faith committee in conveying its views to the other committees, 'justifying and declaring the authority of the present and other general councils'.[27] This was probably the origin of his next work on conciliar theory, *Tractatus de conciliorum et ecclesiae auctoritate* (Tract on the authority of councils and of the Church)', although this was not published until April, when discussion on the dogmatic status of the doctrine of conciliar supremacy and on Eugenius's trial was entering its final stage.[28] This second work on conciliar theory, then, like his first, arose directly out of discussions within the faith committee.

In March 1439, Segovia had returned to Germany in order to defend the council's proposed course of action at the Reichstag, which had now re-convened at Mainz. He argued that the council had already shown unusual clemency to Eugenius by waiting seven years for him to recognize and implement the conciliar legislation on doctrine and reform. Further negotiations on the 'three truths' would only cloud the issue.[29] The Basle embassy reported back to the council on 10 April.[30] During the acrimonious debates on the 'three truths' in April and May, we find Segovia seconding Aleman in the leadership of the majority group,[31] but once again retaining the respect of his opponents: 'both the conciliarists (*conciliares*) heard him with eagerness as being one of themselves, and the others even unwillingly respected the man's virtue and great goodness' (Piccolomini).[32] From now on Segovia was Basle's foremost theoretician as well as being active in practical affairs both at Basle and elsewhere. While he was unwavering in his adherence to Aleman and the majority, his interventions were often aimed at moderating their course of action.[33] He was one of three chosen to select the conclave for the election of a new pope (October 1439).[34] During the 1440s he worked beside Aleman to maintain the viability of the council itself, and to fight its rhetorical and diplomatic battles in Europe. With Aleman he tried and failed to cement the relationship between Felix V and the council, and faced murmurings from the council's rank-and-file.[35] He was made a cardinal in October 1440,[36] and was later given some responsibility for Basle's finances.[37]

In the European arena, Segovia made two long speeches at the provincial synod of Mainz (23 August 1439). On their return to Basle, he and Thomas Livingstone were asked to publish a report, so that 'they could give it to anyone who wanted it, and so that the justice and truth of the holy council might shine forth'.[38] This was the origin of two more of Segovia's tracts: 'On neutrality (*Dicta circa materiam neutralitatis principum* or *Contra neutralitatem*)'[39] and 'Justification of the sentence against Gabriel (*Justificatio sacri Basiliensis concilii et sententiae ipsius contra Gabrielem, olim Eugenium papam IV*)'.[40] He also wrote his 'Explanation of the three truths of faith (*Explanatio de tribus veritatibus fidei*)'[41] at about this time.

These three works appear to have been aimed, as circumstances demanded, at a somewhat wider and partly lay audience; they are propaganda pieces of a distinctly lower quality than his other writings. For the most part they consist of partisan apologetic for the recent actions and present policies of Basle. Eugenius, he says, bought and sold bulls like a merchant, reneged on his electoral promises, governed the papal states abominably, and now puts his faith in the secular powers.[42] If he is not deposed the reform-decrees will never be put into effect. The most interesting of these works is *On neutrality* (which Haller, mistakenly I think, called Segovia's best work).[43] Segovia was particularly forthright on the subject of clerical autonomy: he deplored the rulers' influence over the clergy and the clergy's fear of those who 'are great lords with very broad power in spiritual and temporal affairs, owing to the acceptance of persons, greed for gifts, benefices and offices, threat of penalties . . . and the infliction of physical torments'.[44] That princes and laymen have no share in the church's teaching authority was, he said, 'perfectly clear from the Old and New Testaments'.[45]

In summer 1440 he was sent to Bourges,[46] and the following winter to Nuremberg and Mainz; at Mainz, he noted, the citizens received the council's envoys with special honour.[47] His speech at the Reichstag of Mainz (March 1441), though ill-suited to its immediate purpose, was one of his most original works.[48] Mainly theological in content, it was delivered, said Cusa, 'in a trembling voice'.[49] The immediate purpose of the speech was to argue the Basilean case against both Eugenius and the neutral princes. He went through the by now customary ritual of defending his own side's behaviour in the recent conflict. Eugenius had no power to dissolve the council, and his attempt to do so was based on fear lest he might be brought to trial there, rather than on desire to accommodate the Greeks.[50] The council had not been dissolved by its own consent, because the majority which voted against transference was constitutionally empowered – and with good reason – to make final decisions within the council.[51] Eugenius' deposition was justified on the grounds that he was a relapsed heretic, 'pertinacious' in his opinions; this was above all evident in that he had refused to submit to the council to which, as the supreme and infallible authoritative voice of the Church, every Christian owed, in accordance with the very principles of his faith, both obedience and trust.[52] Segovia discoursed at length on the dogmatic validity of *Haec Sancta* as an article of faith; indeed it was a fundamental one, for upon the authority of councils depended the canon of the bible and the validity of all other articles of faith which had been proclaimed by councils.[53] Councils – not kings, universities, chapters or diocesan synods – are the mouth-piece of the church, and their statements comprise the

122

ecclesiastical *traditio*; thus belief in their authority is an 'architectonic' element of the Christian faith.[54]

Turning the argument against adherents of the neutrality, Segovia said that the need to have 'simple faith (*credulitas*)' in the credentials of other people was something without which 'human society could not exist'.[55] This was still more true in the Christian dispensation, which was based upon 'faith in things not seen'.[56] The Christian believes implicitly in the reliability of the Church and of its supreme decision-making body, for the trustworthiness of which he has evidence in the past. The very nature of his faith requires him to submit to the teaching of the Church here and now, not because he knows by evidence or by reason that it is right in each point, nor because he has 'heard it from his father or teacher', but because it is the teaching of the Church which he has learnt by former *experience* to accept as reliable.[57] Therefore, he must submit to the Church rather than to 'any appearances (*apparientiae*) of his own or anybody else's reasoning'.[58]

Segovia attended further Reichstags at Frankfurt (1442)[59] and at Nuremberg (1443, 1444).[60] His last diplomatic encounter was at Geneva in summer 1447, and there is pathos in it. The French report is not sympathetic to the Basle delegates. After Segovia had spoken 'par manière de collacion scholastique', the French embassy 'urged them in God's name to return no more to these disputations'; they had not come for a seminar but for a peace treaty. Segovia again spoke 'bien solennelement et longuement', justifying the council and its deposition of Eugenius, and putting forward 'paroles rigoureuses et malgracieuses'.[61] The French again protested that they were not concerned with the rights and wrongs of the business but had come 'from the kings and princes, their common masters, as good mediators to set in motion the measures recommended by their masters'. They were only interested in knowing whether Felix would settle and on what terms; they wanted no more argument, 'for the business required abbreviation and one could only lose time disputing, replying and repeating matters which could not receive any amendment'.[62] It is clear that the two sides were playing different games.

Segovia's little-known work 'On holy Church (*Liber de sancta ecclesia*)' appears to have been written during the 1440s. In it we find him for the first time saying that the Church has 'a form of monarchical government'.[63] This was in part a tactical point, for the hearing of secular monarchs. Eugenius was likened to Lucifer, who abused his legitimate role as 'supreme minister', and against whom the angelic council under Michael offered just resistance.[64] But Segovia was himself now moving to a somewhat more moderate view of conciliar supremacy.[65] After the final settlement (1449) he was compensated with a minor bishopric and 500 ducats a year; in 1451, after Aleman's death, he became bishop of St Jean de Mourienne, and subsequently titular archbishop of Caesarea *in partibus infidelium*. He lived during this period in Savoy, and in 1453 retired to the small priory of Aiton near Aiguebelle.[66]

Retired from active life, Segovia now displayed anew his intellectual creativity. He wrote the '*De magna auctoritate episcoporum in synodo generali* (On the great authority of bishops in the general synod)', probably finished in 1451;[67] in this he expounded the collegiate authority of the bishops as the basis for conciliar supremacy, a considerable shift from his earlier views.[68] He avoided discussion of open conflict between pope and council.[69] Segovia's most famous work, the 'History of the acts of the general synod of Basle (*Historia actorum generalis synodi Basiliensis*)', was written between 1449 and 1453.[70] He had probably been preparing it for some time before then (in 1441 he had headed a committee at Basle 'for investigating the decrees and acts of the holy and great council of Constance with the purpose that an authentic version may be published under the seal of this holy synod)'.[71] The historical reliability and objectivity of this work have been widely praised: it was designed to acquaint churchmen of the future with the historical experience he had lived through.[72] It abounds in theoretical discussion, including both reports of debates and the author's own insertions.[73] Towards the end of the work, he wrote a massive 'Amplification' of his speech at Mainz (1441), his final word on ecclesiology. This contains a remarkable wealth of ideas, including both repetitions of arguments used in earlier tracts and new passages, which range far into theology and political philosophy.[74] He restates what he had said in the 'Authority of bishops' about the church's form of government being one of aristocratic monarchy;[75] but he barely mentions the notion of collegiate episcopal sovereignty.[76] Otherwise, the views presented here are identical with those he had expressed in 1434 and 1439.

From 1453 onwards Segovia occupied himself with the question of Islam; his treatment of this marked a notable advance on earlier medieval approaches.[77] There should be a theological peace conference rather than a crusade, for 'the first root of wars between the Sarracens and the Christians is the difference in their laws'.[78] The zest with which he took up this new task at the age of sixty is remarkable. He died on 24 May 1458 after an illness lasting some three years.[79]

Segovia has been remembered mainly as a historian and as a Basle activist. But he was also a theologian and a political thinker of remarkable fecundity and occasional originality. His weakness was a certain undisciplined prolixity; and, while his interventions at the council were often effective, he was less suited for diplomacy. He played almost as important

124

a role at Basle after 1439 as Gerson had played at Constance, but he was not quite Gerson's equal either as a thinker or as a statesman.

Perhaps his most notable quality was his tolerance towards opponents. He was strongly committed to the principle of free discussion, holding that 'public disputations on theological truths are necessary ... because in them there appear more clearly many signs of sound doctrine and of its opposite'.[80] He was prepared to change his own mind: he believed that truth and justice would be achieved if educated men resolved their differences by discussion. After 1449 he renewed his acquaintance with former adversaries, such as Nicholas of Cusa, who now congratulated him on his performance during the Basle controversy: 'experience bears witness in certain matters elucidated by you at Basle, in such a way that nothing remained to be added'.[81] He combined a gentle personal charm with devotion to principle: 'there was no hardness in him'.[82]

NOTES

1. I have been unable to consult Montes.
2. Haller in *CB* i, 20; Fromherz, 18-19. For further details of his early life, Diener; for his biography in general, Haller in *CB* i, 20-53; Fromherz, 17ff.; Cabanelas, 27-74; Zimmermann, part 1; cf *DTC* viii, 816-19; *LTK* v, 531.
3. Fromherz, 20-1; Gonzalez, 146.
4. Fromherz, 20.
5. *Repetitio*, fols. 135v, 137r-v, 155v, 161v.
6. *Repetitio*, fol. 156r.
7. Cit. Gonzalez, 147.
8. *CB* iii, 383; *MC* ii, 342.
9. *CB* ii, 189; *MC* ii, 101; Fromherz, 23-4; Gonzalez, 147.
10. Fromherz, 24.
11. Above, pp.54-6.
12. *TP* 31.
13. *MC* ii, 631.
14. Haller in *CB* i, 22n.; Fromherz, 152; extract in *MOCC* vi, 8.
15. *CB* ii, 78; *MC* iii, 77, 98; Lazarus, 309.
16. Haller in *CB* i, 24; Fromherz, 24-6; *CB* vi, 688.
17. *CB* iv, 210; *MC* ii, 896; Fromherz, 26-7. For his 6 works on this subject, Fromherz, 154, to which add *Advisamenta septem de sancta conceptione Mariae Virginis*, Paris, Bibl. nat., lat. 3457, fols. 1-162; and lat. 16415, fols. 1-168; 2 further MSS of his *Liber de sancta conceptione* are in Cracow, Jagiellonian university, MS. BJ 1414, fols. 3-602 and BJ 1762, fols. 3-243. In June 1441 he was asked to help 2 Paris theologians revise the office for the Visitation: *CB* vii, 377, 380.
18. Fromherz, 27-8 and for MSS 153; cf. *MC* ii, 1085-1112.
19. Fromherz, 153-4.
20. *CB* iv, 334, 337, 340.
21. *MC* ii, 965.
22. *CB* iv, 350.
23. Mansi xxxi A, 225D.
24. *CB* vi, 78; Haller in *CB* i, 25; Fromherz, 27-8.
25. Fromherz, 30.
26. *CB* v, 170; vi, 231; Fromherz, 34.

27. *CB* vi, 302-3.
28. For MSS, Haller, *CB* i, 27-8; Fromherz, 152 (*re* MSS in Munich Staatsbibl., this should be corrected to: lat. 6605, fols. 70r-141v; lat. 6606, fols. 36r-130v; lat. 18412, fols. 251r-5v — I am grateful to Dr. Hertrich for this information); extract in *MOCC* vi, 7-8.
29. *DRTA* xiv, 147-51.
30. *CB* vi, 359.
31. Cf. *CB* vi, 402, 427, 429, 475, 486, 493, 546, 549, where he is listed beside Lamy and Courcelles for general congregations of May-June, 1439.
32. *ASP* 141.
33. *ASP* 191-3; *CB* vi, 648, 674; cf. *PC* ii, 180; Fromherz, 31.
34. *ASP* 200-9, 221-3; *CB* vi, 378, 626, 628, 630-1, 627, 678.
35. *CB* vii, 391-2, 414; Pérouse, 391ff.
36. *CB* viii, 262.
37. Fromherz, 33.
38. *CB* vi, 567-8, 576, 583; *MC* iii, 343-9; *DRTA* xiv, 392-4.
39. Haller, *CB* i, 30-6; for MSS, Fromherz, 153 (to which should be added Paris, Bibl. nat., lat. 1442, fols. 272-308; 4225, fols. 135-52 — I am indebted to Denise Bloch for this and other information on Segovia's MSS in the Bibl. nat.); several of his works were copied c.1720 by J.C. Iselin: *Athenae Rauricae*, I (Basle, 1778), 91-5.
40. Haller, *CB* i, 36-40; for MSS, Fromherz, 152-3; extract in *MOCC* vi, 14-16; cf. *DRTA* xiv, 331-8.
41. Haller, *CB* i, 28-30; for MSS, Fromherz, 152.
42. *Justificatio* fols. 209r-10v.
43. *CB* i, 36.
44. *Dicta*, fol. 147r.
45. *DRTA* xiv, 389-90.
46. Fromherz, 33-5.
47. *CB* vii, 308; cf. *CB* vii, 281, 283, 289; *DRTA* xv, 516ff.
48. *MC* iii, 568-687.
49. Cit. Fromherz, 37.
50. *MC* iii, 611ff.
51. *MC* iii, 615ff., 621ff.
52. *MC* iii, 628ff., 639ff., 666ff., 684ff.
53. *MC* iii, 647ff.
54. *MC* iii, 649-50.
55. *MC* iii, 572; below, p.176f.
56. *MC* iii, 572-3.
57. *MC* iii, 639, 642; cf. *MC* iii, 580.
58. *MC* iii, 639.
59. *MC* iii, 1002-17; *DRTA* xvi, 350, 594-604.
60. Fromherz, 39; *DRTA* xvii, 316.
61. *CB* viii, 367.
62. *CB* viii, 371.
63. *Liber*, fol. 53v.
64. *Liber*, fols. 23r, 24r, 25r, 53v-4v.
65. Cf. Haller in *CB* i, 40-3; Fromherz, 39-41.
66. Fromherz, 37-41.
67. Haller in *CB* i, 40-3; for MSS Fromherz, 153.
68. Black (1971).
69. MAE fols. 95r, 182v.
70. Beer; Fromherz, esp. 72ff.; Haller in *CB* i 18-19; for MSS *MC* iv, 17ff.
71. *CB* vii, 363; *MC* iii, 515; Fromherz, 33.
72. Fromherz, 73, 126.

73. E.g. *MC* ii, 128-35, 213-4, 272-4.
74. See. esp. pp. 707-21, 840-6.
75. *MC* iii, 707-14; below, pp.191ff.
76. Cf. *MC* iii, 912-30.
77. Cabanelas; Rodriguez; Southern, 86-9; for MSS Fromherz, 155. For earlier references to Islam: *MAE* fol. 99r; *MC* iii, 849.
78. Southern, 90-1; Cabanelas, ch. 3 and pp. 265-6, 272, 304, 306, 309.
79. Fromherz, 37-41.
80. *MC* iii, 539-40, 843.; below, pp. 155f.
81. Cabanelas, 304-12 at p. 312 and in Cusa, *De pace fidei* . . ., 93f.; cf. Southern, 93; Cabanelas, 349; Haubst (1951). For further details of his correspondence, much of which is in *VL* 2923: Haller in *CB* i, 41n.; Cabanelas, 177ff., 307ff.
82. Said by one of his contemporaries but I cannot trace the reference. For an assessment of his character: Cabanelas, 249-57; cf. *MC* ii, 461.

CHAPTER 9

SOURCES AND METHOD

Segovia's attitude to sources and the kinds of argument he used were in some ways distinctive. The primacy of theology, that is study of scripture, in ecclesiology is asserted time and again, perhaps most emphatically in almost his last words on the pope-council debate: 'it is agreed among all learned men that the matter under discussion, the authority of the Church, is principally in the domain of divine law (sc. scripture). Any learned believer (*doctus fidelis*) can see for himself that the question of the Church's authority, being a truth of divine and not human law, must be studied primarily in the context of the words of scripture'.[1] What he objected to was the use of civil jurisprudence and political theory to determine matters of ecclesiastical principle. The theory of papal sovereignty, he believed, was founded on human rather than divine law; the blame for this lay with the jurists.[2] The question of authority in the Church lies in the domain of divine law (scripture), but 'There is also mention of it in canon law; and the ordinary glosses and doctors expounding them and the texts . . . frequently, indeed very frequently, take more arguments from civil than from canon law; certainly many more, beyond all comparison, than they take from divine law. Professors of canon law are not so knowledgeable about divine law as they are about civil; and ... they think that a statement on the authority of the Church is to be made in the same way as the civil laws talk about the authority of secular princes. For this reason, many tracts on the authority of the Church are to be found which not only differ from but contradict scripture, their authors having as their main concern the avoidance of any clash ... with what is written in

128

the books of civil or canon law, in the careful study of which they have spent their whole lives'.[3]

This view was shared by most Basle conciliarists, most of whom were in fact theologians, and is also found in Gerson.[4] But it is nowhere stated so emphatically as here.

Nor should Aristotle be used as an authority on Church matters. The Church's constitution, like the rest of revealed truth, is the product of special divine providence; the Church as an organization is *sui generis:*[5] its structure cannot be deduced from secular theory or practice. 'The polity of divine philosophy differs greatly from the polity indicated to us by the Philosopher ... (as) can easily be perceived by anyone who reads the books of the Gospel and the *Politics,* understanding both and therefore discerning that, although Aristotle's teaching greatly helps to elucidate the Church's polity, nevertheless the general council is not to be straight-forwardly compared to any of the constitutions discussed by him'.[6] Segovia, then, was appealing to unique principles of faith and revelation, and was rejecting the appeal to 'rational' principles and to analogy with ordinary human affairs, which formed such a large part of scholastic philosophy and of medieval ecclesiology. Occasionally, he says that any Catholic and any reader of the gospels can perceive the truth of the conciliar case,[7] but usually it is the interpretation of the learned theologian who has spent many years in scriptural study which he holds up as authoritative.[8] However, while Segovia was consistent in paying little regard to canon law, he himself often argued and thought in terms of secular political theory and practice.

Segovia, like other conciliarists, relies primarily on *Math.* 18:15-20 as his proof text for conciliar supremacy;[9] he believes that this more than counter-balances the proof-texts for papal supremacy (*Math.* 16:18; *Luke* 22:32; *John* 21: 15-17), principally on the ground that these refer to a supremacy over individuals, but not over the whole Church.[10] In other words, Segovia again has recourse to the collective-distributive distinction, using it here to reconcile conflicting claims arising out of different scriptural texts. He emphasized, in the same way as papalists did in interpreting *Math.* 16:18, the universal and unlimited authority implied by Jesus' commission to all the apostles ('*whatever* you bind on earth shall be considered bound in heaven ...') in *Math.* 18:18.[11] He noted that Jesus's statement that, in the case of a brother who does wrong and refuses correction, the next step is 'report it to the community' (*Math.* 18:17), is immediately followed by his statement that 'where *two or three* meet in my name, I shall be with them' (*Math.* 18:20), which he, like Gerson, takes as meaning that Jesus' presence is promised exclusively to a *group.* He concludes from this textual sequence that the jurisdictional authority indicated by the passage on fraternal correction must belong to a group, not to an individual.[12] Therefore, 'the superiority of the Church with respect to the pope, as appears from this text, is not only in matters of faith but also in judgments (*iudiciis*)':[13] conciliar supremacy, then, applies in the jurisdictional as well as the doctrinal sphere. (The prior of Dijon similarly argued that in *Math.* 18:15-20 'there is established the authority and jurisdiction of the assembled Church, that is of the general council, over every man who claims the name of Christian'.)[14]

The dominical and scriptural ascription of jurisdictional power to the Church as a whole, to 'a plural number', is further justified by Jesus' commission to all the apostles in *John* 20:23, and by the way in which *Acts* frequently describes the apostles as acting in unison (*Acts* 1:15; 6:2-3; 15:22; 23:26); these passages show that there was 'a common authority in all the apostles'.[15] (The same texts have recently been used by Rahner to demonstrate the 'collegiality' of the apostles.)[16] Further powerful evidence from *Acts* was the council of Jerusalem (*Acts* 15), over which James rather than Peter presided, and which announced its decision with the words: 'it has been decided by the Holy Spirit and by ourselves . . .' (*Acts* 15:28).[17]

Segovia, like other conciliarists, used St Paul's analogy between the Christian community and the human body (*Rom.* 12:4-8; *I Cor.* 12:12-14, 18-21; *Eph.* 4:12, 16: *Col.* 2:19) as further proof that power belongs to the whole rather than to any part.[18] St Paul's statement that 'to some, his gift was that they should be apostles; to some, prophets; to some, evangelists; to some, pastors and teachers; so that the saints together make a unity in the work of service, building up the body of Christ' (*Eph.* 4:11-12; *I Cor.* 12:28) was used, by Segovia and others, to justify the inclusion of other clergy, in particular university doctors, in the council on equal terms with the bishops.[19] Lastly, Segovia is particularly fond of citing *Math.* 20:25-8, *Luke* 22:26-7, and *I Peter* 5:3, to indicate that authority in the Church means not, as among 'gentiles', domination but humble service.[20]

In interpreting scripture Segovia used not only the allegorical method usual at the time, but also a simple form of linguistic analysis. In scripture, he says, terms are sometimes used not in their literal or logical sense but in what he calls a 'political manner of speaking (*politicus loquendi modus*)'.[21] For example he defends the assimilation of the council to the Church, by saying that 'the whole people' in the Old Testament does not always mean literally all the people, but only those whom one expects to be included for a particular purpose. When one says 'the whole city has gone out to battle' one is referring to males of military age; so too the council consists of the 'whole Church' in the sense of all those fitted by their position or qualifications to take part. 'Universal terms are often used in a greatly limited sense (*universales denominationes magnam . . . recipiunt limitationem*) in holy scripture'; sometimes a general term should be understood '*politice magis quam logice* (in a political rather than a logical sense)'.[22] Similarly, he cites both ordinary human speech and common scriptural usage in support of the distinction, crucial to much of his and others' conciliar theory, between 'the Church understood collectively' and 'the Church understood distributively'.[23] Aristotle had made the distinction between the way we sometimes say, for example, 'James is stronger than all those ten men', meaning that he is stronger than each of them individually; and the way we say, 'James is not stronger than all those ten men', meaning that he could not beat them all at once: and 'holy scripture clearly demonstrates in many passages these two senses (*significationes*) of the word "Church"'. When St Paul in *Acts* 20:28 said 'Be on guard for yourselves and all the flock (*attendite vobis et universo gregi*)', and again when Christ said of Peter 'on this rock I will build my Church (*ecclesiam*)' (*Math.* 16:18), they were speaking 'distributively', that is of the group as individuals. But when *Acts* said, 'the apostles and elders decided to choose delegates . . . the whole Church concurred with this' (*Acts* 15:22), and again when Christ said (in the case of an erring brother), 'report it to the community and if he will not listen to the community . . .' (*Math.* 18:17), they were referring to the whole Church collectively, as a united whole.[24] He shows an interest, unusual for the time, in the way words are used.[25] But it is already evident that he was using certain assumed criteria to interpret scripture.

Segovia's emphasis on scripture was combined with belief in the authority of an ongoing ecclesiastical *traditio*. This is expressed, above all, by the decrees of general councils which have absolute authority; it may also be deduced from a study of ecclesiastical practice over the ages. He says that the 'teaching of the church' is the 'infallible standard of measurement (*mensura infallibilis*)' of a Christian's faith; the 'Church of the faithful pilgrims on earth' is the 'sole, unique or most principal witness' of the 'divine utterances'.[26] Thus he appeals, alongside scripture, to *Haec Sancta* as a 'truth of the Catholic faith.'[27] Faced with the (supposedly) aristotelian argument that monarchy is the best constitution, he replies simply by saying that he prefers to hold the 'conciliar doctrine (*synodalis doctrina*)' as defined by the council of Constance.[28] The canon of scripture itself was fixed by councils, and truths not explicitly stated in scripture become part of the Catholic faith by conciliar decision; it is from councils that the Church derives its 'tradition'.[29] This juxtaposition of the authority of scripture and of councils is based, first, on his belief that conciliar authority itself is unambiguously taught in the New Testament:

131

'from the gospel teaching it is clear that immediate power was given by Christ to the general synod; the gospel authorities imply (*insinuant auctoritates evangelii*) that the ruling power of the faithful people was expressly assigned to a plural number'.[30] Secondly, it is related to his insistence that theologians (i.e. those expert in 'the divine science') should play a prominent role in doctrinal definitions by councils.[31]

Segovia's belief in the ongoing authority of the teaching Church was closely related to one of the most distinctive aspects of his method: repeated and emphatic appeal to church history as a guide in matters of belief and practice. Himself an outstanding historian, he frequently appealed to 'authentic histories of the time' to prove a point.[32] He appealed both to the 'primitive Church' or 'the practice of the apostles', and to later and indeed contemporary ecclesiastical practices.[33] Thus Segovia lays special emphasis on the practice (*praxis, practica, observatio, gesta*) of the Church. Like others, he uses history to prove conciliar infallibility,[34] papal fallibility,[35] and the authority of a council to depose a pope.[36] He also lays a special emphasis on the argument from practice to *implicit* belief; the practice of the Church, which he also calls *experientia,* is used to indicate the true disposition of authority in the Church. This approach is used mainly to consolidate the case of conciliar supremacy; it is also used, to give a clear though minor instance, to decide whether positive canon laws are of purely human institution – he decides that they are, by referring to the *experientia* of the rules of the papal chancery, according to which they are valid only if re-confirmed by each new pope.[37]

For him, history and experience indicate not only the intrinsic nature of the ecclesiastical constitution; not only do they show what the fathers implicitly believed: they also show what has been tried and tested, and so what has been found to be a satisfactory way of doing things. The true constitution of the Church, then, is a product both of Christ's teaching plus apostolic practice, and of experience over time: one must consider what methods of conciliar organization, for example, have produced the best results. From the recent experience of the councils of Pisa, Constance, Siena and Basle we can learn both the truth of conciliar supremacy and the best way of running councils.[38] His own history of the council of Basle was intended not only to provide a true record but also to remind future generations of a particular phase in the Church's experience. Here, he sanctions historical development or variation, in accordance with the needs of a particular time, on such matters as the composition and structure of a council.[39] He is speaking as an eyewitness: paraphrasing *I John* 1:1-2, he says 'we speak of what we have perceived and bear witness of what we have heard'.[40] The members of Basle, he records, when they were considering how best to organize the council, bore in mind both ancient models and recent experience; they found a diversity of practice, ranging from the council of Nicaea to the council of Siena.[41] Finally, 'having considered all the methods practiced hitherto by general synods in order to make discussion free', they hit upon the idea of intermingling ranks and nationalities on an equal basis in committees devoted to different topics. This was 'a practice never known before, but invented in our own day and specially observed in the holy synod of Basle'. This was no condemnation of earlier methods; rather, Basle's method was suited to its own time. Time, indeed, 'is a discoverer in matters of theory, but also is both an inventor and a good helper in the methods of action in practical matters; for additions are continually being made in rights and laws, just as they are in sciences and arts; the task of every craftsman (*artificis*) is to supply what is missing'.[42] To Segovia, then, the council was indeed 'a work of art'.

For Segovia church history virtually replaces canon law as the next most authoritative source after scripture itself. Thus he closes his *Authority of councils* (1439) by saying that he has proved his case by 'sacred scripture, authentic history-books and most familiar experience (*notissima experientia*)'.[43]

It must be said, on the other hand, that Segovia was not wholly consistent in his method of argument. Despite his insistence on the unique data of revelation, he himself used rational arguments and appealed to secular theory and practice. His impressive library, which he bequeathed to Salamanca univeristy, contained theological works (including biblical commentaries by St Augustine and Nicholas of Lyra, Ockham's *Dialogus*, Pseudo-Denis' *Ecclesiastical hierarchy*, Gerson's ecclesiological works), documents and tracts relating to the fifteenth-century councils (including tracts by Cusa and Torquemada), and also the writings of the canonists Zabarella, Butrio and Tudeschi. He possessed Cicero's *De republica* and *De officiis*, Petrarch's *Solitary life*, and Aristotle's *Metaphysics, Ethics, Politics* and *Economics*.[44] While he doubtless believed that his case rested on the theological sources already discussed, he had no hesitation in supporting it, first in his *Authority of councils* and more extensively in his *Amplification*, with arguments from Aristotle and other secular sources. As he does so, the *caveat* that these cannot really be taken as authoritative in ecclesiology tends to be overlooked.

He demonstrates his originality in this field. His contemporaries, whether we look at Marsiglio or Torquemada, selected certain ideas from Aristotle, sometimes wrenched from their context and distorted, to support their thesis; papalists regularly used Aristotle to prove that monarchy was the best form of government. Segovia read Aristotle more carefully and reproduced his ideas more faithfully. In book III of the

Politics, Aristotle concludes tentatively that, in principle at least, 'aristocracy' is the best form of government; elsewhere, he repeatedly emphasised the practical advantages of a mixed form of government, in particular of a mixture of 'oligarchy' and 'democracy'. Segovia, in *Authority of councils,* properly cites Aristotle in support of an 'aristocratic' regime.[45] In *Authority of bishops* (c. 1450), he gives a somewhat obscure description of some of Aristotle's views on oligarchy and democracy;[46] but, both here and in *Amplification,* he is fairly faithful to Aristotle in using the latter's preference for mixed government, primarily on grounds of stability, to support the case he was then arguing for a 'monarchy inclining towards an aristocracy'.[47] Segovia also appealed to contemporary examples of both secular and ecclesiastical government as another form of *experientia.* He cited a wide variety of contemporary institutions as examples of collegiate life and the corporate exercise of jurisdiction: universities,[48] chapters, monasteries,[49] religious orders (on statutory intervals between meetings of the general chapter),[50] and, with most significant frequency, cities or city-states.[51] He would be familiar with these from his travels in Germany and Italy. He cited national and territorial states as instances of the rule of law, regular consultation, regular meetings of assemblies.[52] Secular and ecclesiastical examples are set side by side. The number and variety of Segovia's references to contemporary institutions is striking.

Perhaps the most interesting feature of Segovia's method was this regular appeal to observation and experience. In this he was certainly closer to the spirit of Aristotle than were most of his contemporaries. He used the term *experimentum* to mean roughly the same as *experientia* or 'the lessons of history': for example, he said that 'by evident experience (*palpabili experimento*)' the Christian people is 'most of all amenable to royal government (*regnabilis*)'.[53] It has sometimes been shown *experimento* that the size of the state depends on the power of the ruler.[54] He evolved a kind of natural law of collective action, illustrated by examples from everyday life.[55] And he was fond of using proverbs.[56]

It is possible that Segovia met some of the Florentine humanists during his stay in Florence (1434-6); indeed, Southern comments on Segovia's proposed translation of the Koran that 'in this program of textual accuracy and criticism we can recognise a symptom of the renaissance'.[57] There is, however, nothing specifically 'humanist' about his thought or style of argument, least of all about his Latin; he used Moerbeke's translation of the *Politics* rather than Bruni's new one. Nor, on the other hand, does Segovia show any special interest in questions of metaphysics or epistemology, though his references show that he had an average acquaintance with these topics. It would be difficult to place him at any particular point on the realist-nominalist spectrum; he used philosophical arguments in an *ad hoc* way, sometimes rather originally. It is certainly implausible to call him 'Ockham redivivus'.[58]

One cannot trace with any precision the origin of Segovia's ecclesiological beliefs. One may surmise that he was influenced, like others, by the experience of the schism and the councils of Pisa and Constance (during which he had reached maturity), by the ecclesiology of men like Niem and Gerson, and by the situation at Basle in 1432-4. His change of mind around 1449 from communal to episcopal conciliarism, and from aristocracy to aristocratic monarchy, would appear to be the result of his experience at the council of Basle during the 1440s, perhaps also of his experience of Reichstags, and his contact with secular governments in the course of diplomacy. We can certainly say that Segovia's conciliarism did not derive from canon law. But in what proportion it derived from his study of scripture and from his absorption of existing, contemporary norms of collegiate government in practice, it is probably impossible to say. He often says that the interpretation of scripture does not require secular learning, and that conclusions can be reached from it without recourse to secular arguments. He himself certainly strove, particularly in the *Amplification*, to study scripture objectively. He says that his 'most constant aim' has always been, and still is, to arrive at a 'sober understanding (*sobria intelligentia*)' of scripture, to 'adhere as closely as possible to the word and sense of scripture'; and he adds that it is only by understanding the whole *corpus* of the Bible that one can give each individual text its due weight and its proper meaning.[59] In other words, he claims to rely solely on the internal coherence of scripture. But, as we have seen, the conclusions he derives from scripture are identical with those he derives from contemporary examples of collegiate government: and he relies extensively on the collective-distributive distinction to determine the relation of papal to conciliar authority. In one of his last ecclesiological statements, he supports the view that authority belongs to the Church as a whole, by saying that it is a '*ratio fidei* (principle of faith?) that, just as matters concerning morals should be the exercise of every faithful Christian ..., (so too the gospel texts) denote an activity belonging to the association (*universitati*), not to its individual members'.[60] The term *ratio fidei* implies a 'common-sense' interpretation of scripture; in fact, in this passage he is implicitly appealing both to the principle 'what touches all must be approved by all' and to corporation theory in general. His conclusion was precisely that which elsewhere he described as 'political and natural reason', as something inherent in 'the nature of the association and its members'.[61] As we all know, 'common sense' can include presuppositions, taken from one's own cultural background, which are held as self-evident. Whether one agrees with Segovia's interpretation of scripture will depend on one's own interpretation.

NOTES

1. *MC* iii, 938; cf. *Repetitio*, fols. 131r, 133v-4v, 165r; *CEA* fols. 192r-v Explanatio, fol. 230v; *DRTA* xiv, 390; *MC* iii, 648-50, 764-5, 792, *845*, 895 934-8.
2. *MC* iii, 649, 666.
3. *MC* iii, 837-8; cf. *MC* iii, 647, 934.
4. Gerson, *OC* vi, 227; cf. above, pp.61f., 104n. 44.
5. *TP* 101; below, p.150f.
6. *MAE* fols. 173v-4r; the next chapter is 'De maxima differentia politie Aristotelis et evangelii': fol. 175v. Cf. *MC* iii, 707, 764-5, 934.
7. *CEA* fol. 215v; *MAE* fols. 173v-4r.
8. *DRTA* xiv, 390; *MC* iii, 642, 938.
9. *TP* 43, 57, 64, 99, 101, 105; *Dicta*, fol. 138r; *MC* iii, 585-6.
10. *TP* 39-40, 43-4, 97-9, 102; below, pp.141f., 148ff.
11. *TP* 44, 113.
12. *TP* 103; *MC* iii, 728-9.
13. *TP* 45.
14. Dijon prior, 18.
15. *TP* 74; cf. citation of *Acts* 20:28 in *TP* 64.
16. Rahner and Ratzinger, 75-9, 95-7.
17. *TP* 64, 103.
18. *TP* 37, 48, 97; below, pp.140ff.; cf. Gerson, *OC* 131; Ragusa speech (1), Reg. lat 1019, fol. 358r, and *DRTA* xv, 210; Jüterbog, *Determinatio*, 358.
19. *MC* ii, 29-30, and iii, 651; *ASP* 143-5; below, p.188. It was also argued that the priests represented the 72 disciples (*Luke* 10:1ff); cf. Congar (1965), 125.
20. *TP* 46-7, 105: *CEA* fol. 225v; *MC* iii, 724, 925; Black (1970a), 38n; below, pp.166ff.
21. *MC* iii, 729.
22. *MC* iii, 833-4, 736.
23. Above, p.21; below, pp.148f.
24. *MC* iii, 729-30.
25. *MC* iii, 766-8 on 'super'; 769ff. on 'mediate' and 'immediate'; 883-5 on 'per'.
26. *MC* iii, 640-1; cf. Leff (1967b), 60, 72; *DLO* 519-22.
27. *MC* iii, 647, 937.
28. *MC* iii, 708.
29. *MC* iii, 649-50.
30. *MC* iii, 895.
31. Above, pp.111ff; below, pp.187f.
32. *TP* 76ff.; *CEA* fols. 224r, 227v; *MAE* fol. 31v; *MC* iii, 575, 695, 824-5.
33. *CEA* fol. 218r; *MAE* fols. 163v, 171v; *MC* ii, 1102-3; cf. Niem in Heimpel (1929), 33ff.; d'Ailly, cit. Oakley (1964a), 153; Finke, *Forschungen*, 292, 303 Compare Leff (1967b), esp. 81.
34. *Dicta*, fol. 138v; *MC* iii, 642.
35. *TP* 51; *CEA* fols. 204r, 212v. Cf. above, p.50 at n.6.
36. *TP* 56; *CEA* fol. 229v.
37. *MC* iii, 649 and 407 (on papal elections).
38. *MC* ii, 213-14, 220.
39. Cf. Velde and Ragusa: above, p. 77 and 108f.
40. *MC* ii, 129.
41. *MC* ii, 129-30.

42. *MC* ii, 135.
43. *CEA* fol. 227v; cf. *TP* 51.
44. Gonzalez, 151-211; cf. Bonmann; Lopez.
45. *CEA* fols. 218v-19v.
46. *MAE* fols. 172v-3v; cf. *MC* ii, 272-3.
47. *MAE* fols. 173v-5v; *MC* iii, 710ff.
48. *MC* ii, 363; below, p.165.
49. *MC* iii, 736, 806; below, p.157.
50. *MAE* fols. 180r, 185v; *MC* ii, 629.
51. *MC* iii, 781, 802-3; below, pp.172ff.
52. *MC* iii, 894, 710ff., 790, 793; *MAE* fols. 176v-91r. Below, pp.191f.
53. *MC* iii, 707.
54. *MC* iii, 787, 710ff.; *Justificatio*, fols. 213r, 215v, 219r; *Liber*, fol. 23r; *MAE* fols. 149r, 176v-91r. For these terms, cf. J. Weisheipl, *Development of physical theory*.
55. Below, pp.156f.
56. Below, p.157.
57. Southern, 90; cf. Cabanelas, ch. 8.
58. Dempf, 554-5; cf. Lagarde (1963), v, 312ff.
59. *MC* iii, 810, 937-8.
60. *MC* iii, 895.
61. *CEA* fol. 225r; below, p.162.

CHAPTER 10

THE CHURCH AS A 'FUNCTIONAL WHOLE (TOTUM POTESTATIVUM)'

In its substantive conclusions Segovia's constitutional theology was the same as that of his fellow-Basileans.[1] Here, we will examine his development of certain aspects of constitutional philosophy (or political theory) and constitutional theology (or ecclesiology), which he undertook partly in support of the Basilean views, and partly as his own exploration of these topics. Ecclesiology and political theory here run for the most part side by side. We will start with his arguments for conciliar sovereignty on the grounds that the Church as a whole is superior to any of its parts; his development of the concept of the Church as a whole (*totum*), body, and legal association (*universitas*); and his distinction between the Church considered collectively and considered dispersively. Here we will find Segovia at once developing Basilean holism (or collectivism) in a special way, and working out certain notions which were to be of special importance for later political theory. We have seen how conciliarists during Basle regarded the Church as an organic whole. In his *Presidency*, drawing on Menaye's speech during the debate, Segovia made the following distinction between different kinds of whole: 'This force (*potestas*) (of self-preservation and self-government) seems to be in the Church, not as in some universal or integral whole (*quodam toto universali aut integrali*), whose essence or virtue is shared by the individual subjective parts; but rather as in some functional whole (*quodam toto potestativo*); and this force is not found integrally (*integre*) in any of its powers (*potentiarum*) or in one principally, in such a way that it is totally communicated by it to the rest, but it is in all the powers together by virtue of the one soul. So we see it to be in the Church'.[2] This was a refinement of the concept of *universitas* (which could signify

138

either a corporation in a technical legal sense, or society in general),[3] and also of the organic analogy.

The term *universitas* had been defined by Hugolinus as 'a bringing-together of many bodies separated from each other, one special name being assigned to them (*universitas est plurium corporum collectio inter se distantium, uno nomine specialiter eis deputato*)'.[4] Hugolinus explained that the term 'collection of many (*plurium collectio*)' was intended to differentiate the *universitas* from the true individual, such as a cow or a man. The term 'separated from each other' was intended to differentiate it from an 'integral whole (*totum integrale*)', such as a box or carriage, in which the component parts were physically connected and had been deliberately designed to fit together. Members of a *universitas*, on the other hand — he seems to have meant — have also an individual existence which is not dependent on their belonging to the *universitas*. Aquinas again had distinguished three kinds of whole. First, there is the 'universal whole (*totum universale*)' which is present in each part 'in its whole essence and force (*secundum totam suam essentiam et virtutem*)'; for example 'animal' applies equally and fully to both 'man' and 'horse'. Secondly, there is the 'integral whole (*totum integrale*)'; by this he means a merely composite whole like a house which is not present in its parts either 'in its whole essence or in its whole force'. (This corresponds to Hugolinus' 'integral whole'). Thirdly, there is the 'functional whole (*totum potestativum* or *potentiale*)', (lit., a power-possessing whole, or 'a whole comprising several distinct powers'), which is present in its parts 'in its full essence, but not in its full force'.[5]

Hugolinus' *universitas* had this in common with the epistemological universal: it referred to a class of objects as distinct from any individual member of that class. But it was distinguished from a universal in that the group to which it referred was legally circumscribed and did not (except in the unique case of 'the association of all men (*universitas hominum*)') refer to *all* members of a particular category, but to a particular grouping of them. Velde, on the other hand, conceived the entire Church as a universal in the epistemological sense; but, being a realist, he ascribed to it the character, not of Aquinas' 'universal whole', but of an entity whose properties were fully realised in no individual part but only in the Church as a whole which was 'prior in being' to any of its individual exemplars.[6] Segovia — who was not a philosophical realist, indeed he cannot be said to have adhered to any particular philosophical school — uses the epistemo-logical analogy strictly as an analogy: employing Aristotelian epistemology, he says that, since 'universals are called prior to their particular (examples) in the realm of thought, but the particulars are prior in the realm of sense', therefore 'priority belongs to the Church or general council in the realm of thought, but to the pope in the realm of sense'.[7]

Aquinas' and Menaye-Segovia's concept of a 'functional whole' must, I think, be understood in terms of the organic analogy; for the term was especially applicable to organic beings. The analogy between society and the human person had been employed by Plato, and had enjoyed a wide usage in Hellenistic and Roman political thought.[8] Throughout the Middle Ages, the term 'body (*corpus*)' was used by jurists and the literate public as a synonym for college (*collegium*), association (*universitas*) and so on, to mean either a legal corporation or society in a general sense,[9] but in either case without any necessarily holistic overtones (much as we today use the term 'member' without such overtones). Its ecclesiological usage derived primarily from St Paul, whose statements were so often cited by Segovia and conciliarists and so influential upon them that they merit quotation: 'Just as a human body, though it is made up of many parts, is a single unit because all of these parts, though many, make one body; so it is with Christ. In the one Spirit we were all baptized . . . Nor is the body to be identified with any one of its many parts . . . the parts are many but the body is one (*1 Cor.* 12:12-14, 18-21) . . . The saints together make a unity in the work of service, building up the body of Christ . . . who is the head by whom the whole body is fitted and joined together, every joint adding its own strength' (*Eph.* 4:12, 16).

This notion of diversity of function within an organic unity had become a commonplace of ecclesiological speculation and controversy. Both the juristic and the theological usages of the term 'body' had been employed in medieval controversies about the location of sovereignty in the Church.[10] They had served to justify the differentiation between clergy and laity and the special authority of the papacy as 'head of the Church'.[11]

A philosophic caution was introduced into the treatment of the organic analogy by Aquinas, who stressed that it was 'a resemblance . . . not an exact correspondence or identity'; the members of Christ's mystical body, unlike those of an organic body, were not united in time or space.[12] The papalist James of Viterbo followed Aquinas when he said that 'the Church cannot be said to be one in the same way that any man is one, that is in a substantial and personal sense (*unitate suppositi et personae*), except perhaps by way of simile . . . The Church is said to be one by aggregation (*collectione*), as many men are one people'.[13] The jurists for the most part rejected the notion of society as possessing a substantial unity: some of them, indeed, argued from the merely fictional character of societal unity to the need for monarchical authority to provide the unity necessary for a coherent pursuit of the public good. According to the 'concession-theory', corporations derive their existence not from nature but from the legislative will of the prince, who 'alone invents what in reality is not'.[14] As the

140

fourteenth century progressed, Ockham's nominalism reinforced the juristic fiction-theory of corporations, and was enthusiastically adopted by Baldus. The connection between nominalism and absolutism was reinforced by Torquemada, who to this end exploited both Aquinas and Baldus. He took Aquinas' depreciation of the organic simile a stage further. Unlike the members of the human body, which constitute 'a certain real whole, one in number, which is subjectively, in itself as a whole, capable of receiving some kind of form or quality or existential influx (*influxus realis*)', the members of the mystical body are separated from each other in time and space, and therefore they do not collectively possess a form or any common properties. Against the conciliarist notion of the church's 'soul' diffused among its members,[15] Torquemada drily quotes Baldus: 'a corporation does not have a soul'.[16]

The conciliarists, on the contrary, *emphasized* the organic simile in order to draw from it holistic conclusions favourable to the theory of ecclesial-conciliar sovereignty. As well as stressing that the pope was but a 'secondary', 'ministerial', 'vicarious' head of the Church, while the 'true head' was (as St Paul said) Christ himself,[17] conciliarists tended also to give a stronger meaning to the church-body analogy in order to emphasize the essential unity of the Church, and to argue that certain essential powers could only be exercised by the whole, never delegated to a part. This tendency was most powerful in Velde, but by no means peculiar to him. Segovia, who employs the definition of the Church as 'the mystical body, animated by the faith of Christ, associated in unity of the Spirit (*corpus mysticum, fide Christi animatum, in unitate Spiritus sociatum*)',[18] uses the organic analogy to support his contention that the Church is not a 'universal whole' nor an 'integral whole', but rather an operational or functional whole; that is, it is an organic whole like the human body, which can act as a whole only with the articulated co-ordination of all its parts, working under the impulse of a single 'soul'.[19]

Segovia was here following Aquinas, who had defined the relationship between soul and body as that of a 'functional whole (*totum potentiale*)' to its parts: it is present in each part 'as to the totality of perfection and essence', but not 'as to the totality of power (*virtutis*)'; for eyes, ears and so on all have different powers.[20] This was the sense in which Menaye and Segovia defined the Church as a functional whole. The power of self-government does not lie in any one part which then communicates it to the rest, but 'it is in all the powers alike by virtue of the one soul'.[21] The argument, therefore, ran as follows: 'There is the greatest difference between calling the pope greater (than others) *within* the Church and (calling him) greater *than* the Church. In the first case, it is a comparison of one part with other parts of the Church; in the second, it is a comparison with the whole body . . . (this is to be rejected) just as the head, though greater than the foot, hand or other individual member (*singulis membris*), is nevertheless not greater than the body'.[22]

Aquinas, however, drew somewhat different conclusions when he himself applied the concept of a 'potential/functional whole' to the 'power of order (*potestas ordinis*)' (that is, sacramental power and in particular the power to confer ordination). He says: 'When we make distinctions within the power of order, it is not like making distinctions in an integral whole with regard to its parts, or in a universal whole, but it is like making distinctions in a functional whole (*totius potestativi*); the nature of which is such that the whole is one entity with regard to its conceptual completeness (*secundum completam rationem*), but others have some participation in it . . . for the whole fulness of this sacrament (sc. of order) is in one order, namely the priesthood; but others have a certain participation in (the sacrament of) order . . .'[23]

His statement that the power of order is in the priesthood 'with regard to its conceptual completeness' conflicts with his other statement that the soul is related to the body as a functional whole to its parts in such a way that the soul is present in *each part* 'as to the totality of perfection and essence'. To be consistent, he should have said that the power of order is in each part of the Church in this respect; he could then still have said, without self-contradiction, that the power of order is in the priesthood 'as to the totality of power (*virtus*)', with others having only 'a certain participation' therein.

In another passage, Aquinas says: 'The division of hierarchy into ranks is (the division of) a functional whole (*totius potestativi*) into its operative parts (*partes potentiales*) . . . the operative whole (*totum potentiale*) is present as to its essence in each part, but as to its complete strength (*virtus*) it is in the supreme part, because the superior power always has in itself more completely those things which belong to the inferior'.[24] Here, he has again departed from his general statement of the soul-body relationship, this time clearly under pseudo-Dionysian influence, to say that the powers of a functional whole belong not to the thing or person as a whole but to their 'supreme part'. In his ecclesiology, then, Aquinas slants the organic analogy and the theory of wholes in favour of the hierarchical theory of systems.

Menaye and Segovia, on the other hand, carry through what Aquinas said of the soul-body relationship in general into their ecclesiology, insisting that 'the totality of power' cannot be located in any part of the body, but belongs exclusively to the whole itself. Another passage from Aquinas indicates that this was a more authentic application to the Church of Aquinas' general notion of society than that made by Aquinas himself.

142

For Aquinas, having defined the unity of society as a 'unity of order', said that 'the whole nevertheless has some function (*operatio*) which is not proper to any part but to the whole, for example the assault of a whole army'.[25]

Segovia refutes the pope's claim to sovereignty by saying that, as in the case of the body, the Church's functions and powers cannot be reduced to or specialised in any one member. By this time the 'hierarchical' (pseudo-Dionysian) interpretation of the organic simile (adumbrated by Aquinas) was being used by papalists to say that the whole power of a system was concentrated in its head, from which it radiated downwards (as it were) into the rest of the body. A few years later, Torquemada, in his reply to the argument for ecclesial-conciliar sovereignty based on the Church's being 'a kind of whole (*quoddam totum*)' of which the pope is but a part — an argument which, he says, 'they esteem their Achilles' — says that the Basilean theory would be true of an integral whole, but is not true of a functional whole (*totum potentiale*). He develops Aquinas' hierarchical argument in a still more unequivocally monarchical direction: in the case of an 'arrangement among powers (*ordo inter potentias*)', whatever power the lower elements have is also possessed by the higher; therefore, 'as regards the proportion of power, (the papal power) has the proportion not of a part but of the whole (*in ratione potestatis . . . non habet rationem partis sed totius*)'. For 'the power of the Church is not to be regarded . . . as some whole composed of particular powers (*totum integratum ex particularibus potestatibus*) . . . but as being like a functional whole (*adinstar totius potestativi*) . . .[26] Sovereignty is a kind of functional whole whose nature is that in its complete apportionment of perfection it is in one alone, *that is in the prince (principatus est quoddam totum potestativum cuius haec est natura, quod secundum completam rationem perfectionis sit in uno solo, sc. in principe)'.*[27]

By exploiting different passages from Aquinas, therefore, Segovia and Torquemada arrived at opposite views of the kind of unity inherent in a society.

Segovia, then, defines the Church as a specific type of whole, namely a whole capable of exercising certain unique powers or functions, in particular those of self-preservation and self-determination. This was his response to the papalist-autocratic use of the organic analogy and of other metaphysical arguments. Functional holism was a foil to the argument that hierarchical monarchy was the natural, legitimate principle of all forms of organized being. Segovia's holism was far more moderate than Velde's: it claimed only that the Church as a whole had certain functions or properties distinct from those of any of its separate parts. Taking up, then, the argu-

ment of d'Ailly, Gerson and others, he said that the Church, like any other
of God's creatures, contains within itself 'virtue and power by which it
may preserve itself in its being and rule itself'. 'Just as God has given to
every creature . . . its own special innate and intrinsic energy (*propriam
virtutem innatam et intrinsecam*), by which to preserve itself in its own
being and to resist destruction by its adversaries — so too he has given to
the Church, which he wished to last until the end of time, energy and
power by which to preserve and govern itself in its own being . . . the
principles of existence and preservation are inherent in every object . . .
the Church's power of self-preservation and self-government resides in the
body itself or all its members taken together; it does not depend on any
one member'.[28]

The purpose of this argument, for Segovia as for d'Ailly, was to show
that the Church could take action to preserve and govern itself, if necessary
without reference to and in defiance of the papacy; by this they meant
that it could assemble itself as a general council, which could in turn act, if
necessary, without reference to the pope. Because he began in this way,
Segovia — like other conciliarists — tended to ascribe to the Church what
we would call 'holistic' properties, that is properties which belong to the
Church only in its entirety and cannot be ascribed to any part of it. Thus,
for instance, he says that the power given by Christ to the Church is
'perpetual and invariable', and must therefore belong to a perpetual and
invariable agency; but all individual members of the Church, including
popes, die, and therefore this power can only be ascribed to the Church as
a whole.[29]

He frequently speaks of the Church as a 'subject (*subiectum*)', and
ascribes ecclesiastical power in its most fundamental sense to the Church
as a whole. Arguing that it is possible for the pope but not for the Church
to be in schism, he says: 'Just as it is impossible for the Church to be
divided, because its formal rationale or intrinsic property (*eius ratione
formali sive intrinseca propietate*) is to be one, so too it is impossible for it
to be separated from any (member), just as it is impossible for fire, whose
rationale or proper condition (*passio*) is to be hot, to become cold'.[30]
The Church has intrinsic properties, and one of these is its essential
unity. Therefore, Segovia argues, 'power dwells in the Church necessarily
and intrinsically . . . but not so in the pope . . .[31] the power of the Church
seems to belong to it as its own proper condition and as a virtue inseparable
from it (*propria conditio et ab ea inseparabilis virtus*)'.[32] Gerson had said
that the same 'supreme ecclesiastical power' could belong in different ways
to pope, council and Church; and Segovia similarly compared ecclesiastical
power to a quality such as 'sharpness' which may be ascribed to different
things, such as a knife, wine and a woman's voice; 'and we do not say that

a sword is sharper than wine or a voice'.[33] But Segovia reinterprets Gerson in the direction of a more unambiguously populist theory of sovereignty: power belongs primarily and inalienably to the Church itself as a single agency or *Rechtssubjekt*.[34] In the Judaic dispensation, power seemed to have belonged 'to the whole society together (*communi societati*)'.[35] The Church, then, is related to papal power as a 'subject' is to 'its own strength (*propria virtus*)'. There is an 'essential relationship (*habitudo essentialis*)' between the Church and the papal office, in that 'the one cannot be understood without the other', but the relationship between the Church and the person of the pope is contingent: he can be deposed, just as he can die, without affecting the Church's essence.[36] This notion of the inalienability of sovereign power from the whole community – a doctrine shared by Gerson,[37] Segovia,[38] and later thinkers, such as Jacques Almain[39] and Jean-Jacques Rousseau,[40] who wished to secure the responsibility of the government to the community – was directly related to functional holism.

Segovia was not an ecclesiological realist in the mould of Velde. His holist arguments are designed to refute papal claims, and are mostly borrowed from other conciliarists. He occasionally refines these arguments, but he shows little inclination to develop them for their own sake; their appearance in Segovia's writings would appear to derive from the case he was arguing rather than from his own predilections. When his argument takes wing, as in his discussion of the process of decision-making within the council, he talks in terms of charity and empirically observed social solidarity rather than in terms of metaphysical holism.[41]

Indeed, Segovia's purpose in using the organic analogy is as much to establish the essential pluralism of the Church as it is to establish its essential unity. St Paul had said not only that the Church was 'a single unit' but that it was 'made up of many parts'. Segovia emphasized this latter aspect of the simile to prove that the whole Church could only be properly represented by an agency that was *a plurality as well as a unity*. Since plurality is an essential feature of the Christian community (the validity of the Eucharist and, according to Mathew 18:19, the full efficacy of prayer being dependent on more than one participant), supreme authority must belong to an entity composed of many members. The 'assembly of the faithful (*congregatio fidelium*)' is 'the whole itself and the body (*ipsum totum et corpus*)';[42] power belongs 'to all the members or the whole body'.[43] The very nature of ecclesiastical power is such that it cannot reside in a single person.[44] This argument was central to the Basilean case, and it led Segovia and others to reflect upon the necessarily collective *locus* of sovereign power.[45] The very term *ecclesia* (Church) signifies a *congregatio* (assembly).[46] Segovia here exploits the dual meaning of *ecclesia*, which had originally been used by the early Christians to signify those who were 'called out', 'set apart', but which was also the normal Greek term for the deliberative assembly of the whole citizenry. Segovia argues that, when authority is commonly ascribed to the *ecclesia* as such, this signifies an assembly, and therefore the council has a better claim than the pope to exercise this ecclesial authority. It is self-contradictory to say that the Church can consist in one person, any more than a city (*civitas*) can;[47] rather, it means 'a great multitude':[48] 'the council can no more exist in the singularity of one (person) than the Church can'.[49]

Segovia also derived the necessarily collegial nature of the *locus* of supreme ecclesiastical power from those New Testament texts in which authority is bestowed upon, or spoken of as belonging to, the apostles as a group (*Mathew* 18:15-20; *Acts* 20:28 and so on).[50] 'All the authorities which speak of the power of the Church or council are in the plural . . .[51] The authoritative texts of the Gospel expressly describe the ruling power of the faithful people in the plural'.[52]

The '*ratio fidei* (principle of faith)' contradicts the notion that authority in moral matters can be exercised by 'any *one* of the faithful'. Rather, these texts 'denote the action of an association (*universitas*), and do not apply to its individual parts (*singulis suppositis*)'.[53]

NOTES

1. Above, pp.49ff, 55f., 106, 113.
2. *TP* 37-8; Menaye in *MC* ii, 615; Cracow University in *HUP* v, 494-5; Gerson in *OC* vi, 220, 222. Above, pp.21, 55, 71.
3. Michaud-Quantin, 11-57, esp. at 15, 21; Schnörr; Gillet.
4. Cit. Gierke, *DGR* trans Kolegar, 613a; Michaud-Quantin, 28.
5. *Summa Theologiae* Ia. 77.1, ad 1 (vol. xi, p.92); cf. Ia. 76.8 (vol. xi, p.84); and Ia IIae. 57.2. ad 2.
6. Above, pp.64f.
7. *MC* iii, 878-9. (probably referring to the legislative-executive distinction).
8. Barker, 314-5, 321; Wulf, 355.
9. Michaud-Quantin, 59-64; cf. Wilks, 21ff. Note the usage of Pillius: 'collegium est personarum plurium in corpus unum quasi coniunctio vel collectio: quod generali sermone universitas appellatur, corpus quoque, vulgariter apud nos consortium vel schola': cit. Gierke *DGR* trans Kolegar, 612b.
10. Gierke, *DGR* iii, 247-52; cf. Lewis (1938); Roberti; Wilks (1963), 21ff.
11. Ullmann (1965), 3, 141-2, 267-8, 415, 439-40.
12. *Summa Theologiae* 3a. 8.1 ad 3: cf. Gilby, 255, 260; Gierke, *DGR* trans. Maitland, 133 n. 81; Eschmann; Lewis (1938), 858-9.
13. *De regimine christiano*, I, c. 3, pp.109-110; cf. John of Paris, ed. Leclerq, 186.
14. Gierke, *DGR* iii, 280-5, 425-36.
15. Above, pp.55, 113f.
16. *Summa*, II, c. 71, fols. 195v-198r; Stockmann, 101-12. Cf. above, pp.82f.
17. Oakley (1964a), 54-9; above, pp.20, 55.
18. *CEA* fol. 194v; *MC* iii, 654; cf. Aquinas, *Theol. texts*, p.340.
19. *TP* 37-8.
20. *Summa Theologiae* Ia. 76.8 (vol. xi, p.84-8) and 3a. 2.1.
21. *TP* 38; cf. Aquinas, *Theol. texts*, p.340.

22. *TP* 101; cf. TP 47-8; Cracow university in *HUP* v, 502. For earlier lit., Wilks (1963), 24, 41n.
23. *Comm. in quartum Sent.* d. 24, q. 2, a. 1, ad 2; cf. Black (1970a), 167, 171; Gilby, 251-64.
24. *Comm. in secundum Sent.* d. 9, q. 1, a. 3 ad 1; cf. Black (1970a), 168n.
25. *In X libros Ethicorum*, I, i at p.4; cf. Eschmann, de Wulf, 351ff., E. Lewis (1938), 857. I intend to explore the topic of social wholes in medieval thought in an article, 'Pre-modern notions of society'.
26. *Summa*. II, c. 83, fols. 216r-v.
27. *Summa*, II, c. 53, fol. 169v.
28. *TP* 36-7; cf. Cracow university in *HUP* v, 494.
29. *TP* 94-6; cf. Augustinus Triumphus, cit. Wilks (1963), 505.
30. *TP*, 49.
31. *TP*, 50.
32. *MC* iii, 784-5; cf. below, p.173.
33. *MC* iii, 808.
34. *TP* 57-61; *MC* iii, 786-808; below, pp.173f.
35. *MC* iii, 823-4.
36. *TP* 95-6.
37. *OC* vi, 131-3; cf. Riesenberg, 48ff.
38. Below, pp.172ff; cf. *GC* 267.
39. Below, pp.194f.
40. *Du contrat social*, II, c. 1, pp.124-5.
41. Below, pp.155ff.
42. *TP* 101.
43. *TP* 37-9, 94-6.
44. *TP* 37-9, 94-6.
45. Below, pp.162ff, 189.
46. *TP* 100; cf. Aquinas, *Theol. texts*, p.340; *CC* II, xviii, p.191.
47. *CEA* fol. 206r; *MC* iii, 574-5, 721, 931-2. The opposite view is in Augustinus Triumphus, cit. Wilks (1963), 515.
48. *MC* iii, 641; cf. Jüterbog, *Determinatio*, 364.
49. *MC* iii, 601.
50. *TP* 36; above, p.129f.
51. *CEA* fol. 217r.
52. *MC* iii, 895.
53. *MC* iii, 895, 918.

CHAPTER 11

THE CHURCH CONSIDERED COLLECTIVELY AND DISTRIBUTIVELY

One of the original contributions made by conciliarists to social thought was the elaboration of the distinction between society understood collectively and society understood distributively.[1] The distinction itself derived from Aristotle: observing that 'the word "all" is used in two senses, "all separately" and "all together"', Aristotle defended his theory of the collective wisdom of the many by arguing that 'each individually will be a worse judge than the experts, but when all work together, they are better or at any rate no worse'.[2] This was, of course, exactly the kind of conclusion the conciliarists wished to draw from the distinction. Similarly, they could appreciate Aristotle's saying of the jury or assembly that 'it is not the individual juryman, councillor or assembly member who is in control, but the court, council and people'.[3] This was similar to the distinction customarily made by medieval jurists (beginning with Roffredus in the twelfth century), when they contrasted the powers or rights of 'all as all (*omnes ut universi,* or *ut universitas)*' with those of 'all as individuals (*omnes ut singuli)*', in their analyses of collective legal persons (chapter, city, etc.).[4] The jurists held that a corporation possessed and could exercise certain collective rights and powers, which were denied to its members as individuals. In fact, the Aristotelian term 'taken collectively (*collective sumpti)*',[5] as applied to a corporate group, had become a recognised synonym for 'as corporation', when the association acting as such was indicated.[6]

The doctrine implied here, when these juristic terms were applied to the Church as a whole by Zabarella,[7] constituted the juristic equivalent of the functional holism discussed above: the Church as a whole has powers that cannot be delegated to or specialised in individual members. Gerson was making the same point when he applied the Aristotelian form of this distinction to the whole Church.[8] Segovia appreciated the importance of the juristic distinction, which he expounded thus: 'Although a chapter has jurisdiction, this does not belong to individual canons, for although they can be excommunicated, the chapter cannot; and so one thing is said to apply to the corporation, another to its individual components (*suppositis*) . . . the actions, debts, rights, indults or privileges of corporation and of individual members are different'.[9]

Segovia believed, further, that the distinction between society taken collectively and society taken distributively was to be found not only in civil and canon law and in Aristotle, but also in the Bible and in ordinary everyday political speech;[10] we might almost say he saw it as rooted in human language. He certainly held that the different legal powers ascribed to a corporation as a whole and to its members reflected a real difference between the felt moral powers of the two. As will be seen in more detail later, he thought that members of a society will generally accept their ruler's authority over them as individuals, on the understanding that he is acting for the common good, but will not accept his authority over all members assembled together (partly because their common perception of the common good then overrides his).[11] He appeals, we may say, to a natural political instinct in people; this is the ultimate point to which the collective-distributive distinction is taken by Segovia.

Segovia also restated the argument made at Constance that the pope's legal immunity applied only to the dispersed Church, not to the Church assembled in a council.[12] He dealt with texts which said that the pope or Roman see could be judged 'by nobody' by observing that: 'These distributive terms "nobody" and "no man" are understood of individual persons of this congregation of the faithful, but not of the congregation itself, which is unique and cannot be multiplied. Therefore, a distributive term cannot apply to it, just as one cannot properly say "every god", since there can be but one . . .[13] This doctrine (sc. that the pope is not immune from conciliar judgment) seems to be made manifest both from political or civil science and from canonical or divine science. Such phrases (sc. on papal immunity) refer, according to the type of action, of actor and of thing acted upon (*iuxta conditionem operationis aut subiecti aut appositi*), to individual members of the association, but not to the association itself'.[14] Segovia sees the distinction in question as rooted in linguistic usage and in social reality; though his expressions are somewhat obscure, the tenor of his argument seems to be in tune with Aristotle's thought.

Segovia further developed the collective-distributive distinction in terms of a contrast between the Church considered as 'the mystical body of Christ' and the Church considered as a 'political body'. In his *Presidency*, he elaborated the point made by Beaupère during the preceding debate: 'The Church may be considered in two ways: as the mystical body of Christ, and as a kind of political body. In the first way, it is considered as it is ruled by Christ with the gifts and charisms of graces; and it is one body living always by a spiritual life, by faith and charity' (sc. as a human body lives by its soul) '. . . In the other way, the Church is considered as a political body, in the same way as any other community or political society, which is ruled without the influx of graces and charisms . . . And in this sense, as a natural entity, it is ruled through one person whom they call head, as a king or prince is head of a kingdom or princedom. And in this way it is said by some that it belongs to the pope to be head of the Church, viz, insofar as it is a political body. But insofar as it is the mystical body he is not properly or simply head, but may be called the vicar or minister of the head . . . Moreover, when the Church is considered as assembled in a general council, it exists there as a mystical body rather than as a political body'.[15]

For Christ has promised his presence at such an assembly ('where two or three . . .'), and the assembly asks the special guidance of the Holy Spirit; therefore, it is not guided by human reason alone, as political bodies are. Christ requires no representative at such a council, he is there himself as 'principal agent', as head of the council, directly inspiring the fathers.[16] Just as Rousseau was to say that, when the people assemble, the government ceases to act as their representative, so Segovia says that in the council the pope ceases to represent Christ as head of the Church: 'the actions of the substituted head appear to cease, just as those of a delegate in the presence of him who delegated (the actions)'.[17]

Segovia and Beaupère were evidently here using the concept 'mystical body of Christ' in a somewhat unusual way. The ascription to the Church, from the twelfth century onwards, of the term '*mystical* body of Christ' in place of the earlier appellation '*true* body of Christ'[18] fitted in with the watering-down of the organic analogy by Aquinas and the lawyers, with the possible if not originally-intended implication that the Church was *only* a mystical unity. By the fourteenth century, the term 'mystical body' (on its own) became virtually synonymous with other general terms for social collectivities, secular as well as ecclesiastical,[19] and could be used without any holistic or organic overtones (much as the terms 'moral person', 'moral body' were later so used). One may see a direct contrast (whether deliberate or not) between Segovia and Baldus. The latter had said: 'a *universitas* (corporation) can be considered in two ways: in one way in the abstract (*in abstracto*), and in this case it is not a person nor an

150

animated body, but a kind of intellectual body and a kind of legal name with some sort of symbolic meaning; and in another way in the concrete (*in concreto*), and then it is the appellation of persons and is taken for *the single persons* contained in that corporation'.[20]

Whereas the jurists, then, emphasized the purely fictional character of the whole, Segovia and other conciliarists asserted that the whole, in the case of the Church, corresponds to an ontological reality, and is in a more literal sense a 'body' — 'animated', as was often said, by faith. Once again, one finds a contrast between the nominalism of the jurists and a degree of organic realism among the conciliarists of Constance and Basle. For one point of the above passage was to draw attention to the unique sense in which the Church, unlike other societies, was a unified whole.

Not only do Beaupère and Segovia implicitly retrieve the term 'mystical body' from its secularized usage, by contrasting it with 'political body'. Segovia here also underlines the dissimilarity between the Church and other societies, rejecting in principle the argument from political theory to ecclesiology — for the time an almost revolutionary move. Segovia derives two points from this asymmetry. First, the Church is more deeply united than is any secular society. Here he was not alone. Gerson had said that, whereas the 'coherence (*connexio*)' of a state is based only on 'laws and the gifts of nature', the Church 'as a polity, and an ordered one, has this unity and, over and above this, another supernatural and divine unity'.[21] Torquemada too would soon after be saying that the 'mystical body' (by which he meant here the Church) differs from a 'political body' (by which he meant here a state) because a political body lacks 'one spirit, unifying and ruling all its members'.[22] Secondly, Segovia was, quite clearly, arguing that the uniquely corporate nature of the Church and of the general council derives from divine institution. By this means he intended to refute the application of secular monarchical norms to the Church (which had been a major theme in Torquemada's speech during the presidency debate).[23] He was also implying that the collegiate structure of ecclesiastical government has no bearing on secular polities; this view, we will see, he openly contradicts in other passages.

The most striking point in this passage is the identification made between the Church *qua* mystical body of Christ and the general council itself. A parallel could be found in the current usage of the term 'mystical body of the realm *(corpus mysticum regni)*' as meaning a national parliament — this is found in Gerson himself;[24] and d'Ailly had said the council was 'like *(velut)* a (? the) mystical body'.[25] But Beaupère's and Segovia's idea, that the general council possessed those charismatic qualities which were generally sharply distinguished from the juridical qualities of visible, identifiable ecclesiastical offices, is remarkable, if not a little peculiar.

Segovia elaborated the point in his speech at Mainz in 1441: 'According to the teaching of many great doctors the Church is considered in two ways: as a political and as a mystical body; to speak more openly, as a community under one president which is governed by a hierarchical principate clearly known to its members, by the judgment of human reason; or as it is governed by Christ under the direction of the Holy Spirit. This distinction is commonly made with regard to the known and unknown method (of governing), and according to mediated and unmediated rule . . . The Church is said to be ruled as a mystical body, when it is directed concerning what is to be done immediately by Christ by a certain special influence, Christ infusing his *carismata*, gifts of graces and hidden inspirations to persons. It is governed by the ministry of these gifts *either as a whole in one place or as particular persons in different places*, as occurred with the apostles whether they were acting together or separately . . .'[26]

It seems that Segovia was seeking to establish a particular conception of the relationship between the invisible and the visible church, between the charismatic community and the juridical structure. Juristic theology had separated the official hierarchy from the charismatic aspect of the Church; tenure of office and ecclesiastical authority itself were held to be unrelated to charisma which might be found in unspecified, unspecifiable persons — hence, for instance, the possibility of self-declared *prophetae*. Aquinas, applying the organic analogy in yet another context to the Church, distinguished between 'the interior *influx* of grace' which comes from Christ, who is alone, therefore, head of the Church in this sense; and 'the *influx* into members of the Church as regards their external government', which 'can belong to others, and in this way some others can be called heads of the Church, for example popes during their pontificate'.[27] Conciliarists had made use of this distinction to argue that the council, as the immediate recipient of Christ's power, could claim the authority of the supreme head, Christ, in its dealings with the derivative head, the pope. Segovia here took this further, to say that the council possesses the internal graces as well as the power of external government. To this Torquemada would later reply by interpreting Aquinas in such a way as to show that the pope could, in line with the tradition of juristic theology, possess fulness of governmental power without possessing fulness of spiritual qualities.[28]

Segovia, then, argues that the governmental and spiritual aspects of the Church do coincide at one point, in the council. Elsewhere, he says that the council includes all the categories which St Paul defined as the constituent parts of the body of Christ, 'prophets' and 'evangelists' as well as 'apostles' and 'teachers'.[29] In virtue of Christ's promise 'where two or three are gathered in my name, there am I in the midst of them', the council enjoys 'the internal (*intranea*) influence of graces'.[30] What is peculiar to Segovia and some of his colleagues is the overlaying of juridical conceptions of conciliar sovereignty with a spiritual meaning. Segovia is thus poles apart from Ockham's quasi-individualist notion of the Church as a mere 'aggregate of the faithful (*collectio fidelium*)'. The juridical structure remains, but when the council sits it has a superior: the council is the Church not only as a whole but also as a spiritual communion. As he once said when episcopal and princely authority was invoked against the conciliar majority: 'why await prelates and princes when the divine majesty is present?'[31]

The significance of the collective-distributive distinction for the development of political thought will be discussed later.[32] Its importance for the conciliarist argument is attested by the attention given to it by opponents. Denis Rickel 'the Carthusian' (himself a moderate conciliarist in the mould of the late d'Ailly)[33] refuted it with care, about the time of the end of the council of Basle.[34] And Torquemada met Segovia's linguistic argument with a similar counter-argument: 'it is contrary to the nature of a collective noun to be taken distributively and not collectively'.[35] The passage in Segovia's *Presidency* on the mystical and political aspects of the Church was reiterated by Escobar,[36] by Thomas Strempinski,[37] by the Basle delegation at the Nuremberg Reichstag of 1444 (which included Segovia himself),[38] and it was included, beside Aquinas' passage on internal and external influence, in the famous Cracow university treatise of 1442.[39] Rickel too quoted the passage, and countered it by saying that the Church was nothing if not Christ's mystical body endowed with 'charisms of graces': the mystical-political distinction, therefore, has no force, and the pope is head of the Church in both senses.[40]

One legitimate point which Segovia deduced from this rather far-fetched idea was that the Church's supreme decision-making body must reflect the spiritual values of the Christian community, as set out in the New Testament and in theological tradition: among these are communal unity and fraternal love. The council is thus presented as a non-hierarchical body (though no such conclusion is drawn for the Church at large). This reflected Segovia's new and elevated view of the council as postulating in tangible form, at the very *locus* of ecclesiastical sovereignty, the behaviour-pattern of the Christian ethic. Christian thought was, in its first principles, deeply imbued with the idea of a group of persons, ideally all human beings, as forming a single spiritual entity, bound together by mutual love and their pursuit of the knowledge of God. The most important novelty in Segovia was to apply this ideal to the governing body of the universal Church, from which it could hardly, if one were to be consistent, remain for ever excluded.

NOTES

1. Cf. above, pp.21, 65ff.
2. *Politics*, II c. 3, p.58; III, c. 11, pp.125-6.
3. *Politics*, III, c. 13, p.131.
4. Gierke. *DGR* iii. 391, 432-49; *DGR* trans. Maitland, 63, 72; *DGR* trans. Kolegar, 616a.
5. Cf. Aquinas, *Comm. in II Polit.*, lect. 2, p.145
6. Gierke, *DGR* iii, 432.
7. Above, pp.20, 100f., Gierke, *DGR* iii, 253-61.
8. Above, p.21.
9. *MC* iii, 736.
10. *MC* iii, 735-6. Above, p.130f.
11. *MC* iii, 720-1; below, pp.162ff.
12. Anon., *Impugnatio*, 293-4; *TEP* 956; cf. Tierney (1968), 57n.
13. *TP* 101-2; *MC* iii, 735.
14. *MC* iii, 736.
15. *TP* 63-4; Beaupère, fols. 174r-v; cf. above, p.55. Cf. *MC* ii, 609; and Velde in *EP* fol. 185r: above, p.70f.; and Black (1977a), 288-9.
16. *TP* 64-5. For the whole passage, cf. *CEA* fol. 214v and Cracow university in *HUP* v, 489-90, 493, 513.
17. *TP* 66. Cf. Rousseau, *Du contrat social*, III, c. 14.
18. Lubac, esp. 130ff.; Gillet, 56-60.
19. Gierke, *DGR* iii, 247-52; *DGR* trans. Maitland, 131n. 75; Kantorowicz, 201, 208, 210 (including examples from Gerson). Cf. Tierney (1968), 132ff.; Wilks (1963), 22-3.
20. Cit. Gierke, *DGR* iii, 432. Cf. Zabarella and Corneus: cit Gierke, *DGR* iii, 433.
21. *OC* vi, 131-2, 247-8. Cf. above, pp.50, 129.
22. Mansi, xxx, 1032; cf. Stockmann, 183-96.
23. *MC* ii, 614.
24. Kantorowicz, 220; Oakley (1964a), 59.
25. *TEP* 953.
26. *MC* iii, 603; cf. *MC* iii, 857.
27. *Summa Theologiae* IIIa. 8.6. resp. princ. Cf. Gerson, *OC* vi, 128, 131.
28. *Summa*, II, c. 23, fol. 136v.
29. Below, p.187f.
30. *TP* 48.
31. *ASP* 147.
32. Below, pp.202-4.
33. *DHGE* xvi, 256ff.; Mougel; Mulder.
34. Rickel, 565-6, 576-7, 639, 673.
35. *Summa*, II, c. 25, fol. 139r.
36. *GC* 305.
37. Fijalek, i, 428.
38. *DRTA* xvii, 351.
39. *HUP* v, 489-90.
40. Rickel, 565-6, 673-4.

CHAPTER 12

THE NATURAL LAW OF 'ASSEMBLY (*CONGREGATIO*)'

The dialectic between the universal Church and the small group, between the norms of the anonymous 'civil society' or *Gesellschaft* and of the communal association or *Gemeinschaft*,[1] operated at many points in conciliar thought: and it reaches a climax in Segovia's reflections on the internal functioning of the council. For the norms of apostolic comradeship and of corporation theory – in a word, collegiality – are applied to the sovereign body of the Church. This had both constitutional and spiritual implications. It means that there must be freedom of speech, full discussion and equality of voting power; the deputation-system was designed, said Segovia, so as to 'arrive freely at the common consent of the fathers'.[2]

In councils there must be 'freedom of speech (*libertas dicendi*) . . . so that everyone may state his opinion'.[3] There must be freedom from censure or punishment for views expressed. Segovia favourably compared the practice of the council of Basle, where even Hussites were given freedom of speech, with that of the Roman *curia* where, he alleged, there was no such freedom.[4] Furthermore, he argued that the general council (*concilium generale*) had the same advantage as the university (*studium generale*), in that debate was not being conducted on the territory of the members' own ruler or lord. Thus, 'anyone can easily perceive the pre-eminence of a synodal judgement, when from every part of Christendom prelates and wise, learned men of the greatest virtue come together, and are supported with the utmost freedom of a safe-conduct, and are free from all fear of affliction for their parents or friends, or of loss of their

155

benefices or temporal goods, these being far away from the dominion of the place in which they are residing'.[5]

One advantage of the deputation-system over the nation-system is that, if the council is divided into nations, 'subjects are deliberating in the presence of their lords'.[6] On the other hand, Segovia was well aware of the danger of protracted discussion. It is difficult, he said, to get decisions out of a large body of learned men, who tend to want plenty of time to think and, when their turn comes to speak, either dry up or can't stop talking — 'this is the plain lesson of experience'; it is therefore best to have treatises circulated beforehand. They should try to agree on matters of principle before debate begins, but secret collusions should not be allowed (as Rousseau also said).[7]

Segovia argued for the superiority of collective decisions by appealing to illustrations and principles drawn both from inanimate nature and human experience. First, 'An example known to all is burning logs, which do not glow so brightly in themselves or light up their surroundings so clearly, or give off so intense a heat when separated as when they are stacked together; for they are stimulated by attachment to one another (*aggregatione mutua*)'.[8]

The same is true of human labour: 'When many combine on a single task, each labourer finds his own strength not only kept intact but increased by the common effort (*ex concursu communi*)[9] . . . Most evident experience shows everyone that, whatever strength men have, they can do some things by themselves, but other things only with the help of others'.[10] The same principle operates within the individual person: each separate moral or mental power (*virtus*) is increased when the effort of the whole person is applied to it ('*secundum totum conatum aut posse suum*'): 'Just as memory is increased by a most strenuous effort to recall, knowledge grows by ardent study, so do justice, liberality . . . when they operate at full strength on great matters; as occurs in any vital operations, through the constitution of nature (*nature conditione*), which gives strength to any vital power through its proper exercise . . .[11] This suggests, once again, the unique 'total power' of the Church assembled as a whole.[12]

Segovia particularly emphasized the force of this argument in the case of intellectual activity. He argues that knowledge is increased and better decisions are taken when many minds have worked together in shared debate and mutual discussion ('*communi disceptatione et collatione*').[13] Joint effort, once again, produces generically better results (as Homer said, when two go together, now one now the other is the first to notice something).[14] Segovia expressed this in proverbial form, drawing (it would appear) on contemporary lore as well as on the Hebrew wisdom literature:

'Two eyes see more than one . . .'[15] There is safety in many counsels, and a judgment confirmed by the opinions of many is sound . . . Wisdom declares that she dwells in counsel, and attends upon learned cogitations . . . Radiant wisdom does not despise advice but listens to it . . . Steel is sharpened upon steel, the wise man who listens is made the wiser. And when many with much knowledge confer together, they make a better decision on what is just or expedient'.[16]

Lastly, the superiority of collective action is a political law: 'So it is with a kingdom, which is better able to resist enemies when adequately assembled in armed soldiery; so it is with a city, when it gives just laws to its inhabitants; with a multitude of wise men, when they give more learned advice; and with an enclosed convent, when it gives correction to its monks'.[17]

Segovia, then, explicitly presented this principle of collective action as a general 'law' to be found throughout nature, governing all forms of life; though not, to be sure, as an empirical law in the modern scientific sense, since he conceived it *a priori*, and referred to examples and experience only by way of illustration. Sometimes he expressed the principle in language that seems deliberately designed to cover both natural and human phenomena: 'A united force is greater than a divided force (*virtus unita seipsa divisa fortior*)[18] . . . An assembled whole (*congregatum totum*) is said to be stronger (sc. than a whole not assembled) even if it receives no accretion of force (*incrementum virtutis*); for the parts become more vigorous in their actions by reason of their shared fomentation (*ex mutuo confomento*)'.[19]

That parts 'assembled together' enjoy an increase rather than a loss of energy is a 'general law' inherent in 'the nature of assembly'.[20] The conclusion to be drawn is that 'in the assembly (*congregatio*) of the general council, everyone's energy (*virtus*) is preserved, naye increased'.[21] Such arguments, incidentally, provided an appropriate counter to the naturalistic-metaphysical arguments often adduced for papal monarchy — that it corresponded to a cosmic law of nature, was the most efficient form of decision-making, and so on. It is the council, rather than the pope, that possesses 'fulness of knowledge, maturity of circumspection and appropriate sollicitude'.[22]

The increase of energy or power by combination or assembly, then, is a general law of life, exemplified in the council. Out of the physical act of assembling together and the psychological process of communal discussion and dialogue, decisions emerge which are generically superior to those attainable by scattered parts of the community. Virtue and wisdom are both intensified by people meeting together.[23] Velde, similarly, suggested that the theological virtues were 'transformed' to a higher pitch in the conciliar assembly.[24] For Segovia, this is not because some additional energy is created *de novo*, but rather because of the intensification of the existing energy of each component through its interaction with others. Assembly enhances the moral and intellectual qualities of individuals.

All this reminds one in certain ways of Rousseau's concept of the 'general will (*volonté général*)'. As in Rousseau, the unity of the group is given an ethical value insofar as it is related to the common good. But, above all, the very act of coming together in an assembly is seen as a prerequisite for the emergence of this (as it were) collective conscience. This point, which is almost the very heart of Rousseau's political theory, is clearly stated by Segovia: for the Church to arrive at a wise conclusion, 'it must meet in one place; in order that those considering a course of action may agree on a single decision (*unum iudicium*), each must *hear the other and his deliberation*'. This cannot be done by messengers, because people might change their mind or not know exactly what is meant. 'But when they are actually present in one place . . . and when it is most clearly true that all who are standing in the place have agreed on the same proposal, all have as it were one heart and one mind (*anima*) in respect of what is being defined; then truly it can be said that the Church is of one lip and the same speech, with one unconfused tongue, when each hears the voice of whoever is next to him saying the same thing as himself'.[25] Could one have a clearer statement of the general will as the product of face-to-face collaboration in decision-making?

It is not only that deliberation produces the best results; it also has an inherent moral value. The deputation-system is to be commended 'not only on account of the agreement that was reached after deliberation, but on account of the very nature of their being joined together (*ex ipsa coniunctionis natura*) . . . Such joining-together gave an increase of *duty and desire* both to superiors and to inferiors, that their judgments should be of one mind'.[26]

Segovia is saying — once again, like Rousseau — that collective discussion makes men less self-interested, and makes them love the common good and each other.

Lastly, this theory of concerted conciliar action was related to a constitutional principle laid down by Bartolus for corporate civic action — as also, indirectly, was Rousseau's cognate theory of the general will. Bartolus had said that, in order to obtain 'the consent of all (*consensus omnium*)', 'it is not sufficient if all the people express consent separately in their houses'.[27] Similarly, Segovia declared that a ruler's decisions could be 'believed by all to proceed from the intention of all (*de intentione omnium*), so long as they live separately in different places'; but that when they assemble together, this is no longer the case.[28] Thus, like Bartolus, he could say that 'even if all and each from a city, or its greater part, do something, their action is not imputed to the city, unless it is preceded by common counsel or common consent, tacit or express'.[29]

Segovia expounded these communal ideas in the specific context of Basle's deputation-system, and with an added theological dimension. The deputation-system, he said, was intended to remove differences of both status and nationality within the council. By deliberating together, men of different ranks will be enabled to arrive at a common outlook and judgment 'through the intervention of the temper of-desire'. So closely can superiors and inferiors become associated by being mingled together in the committees that 'out of these two extreme *status* there comes into being one intermediate *status*, each of the extremes preserving its own being and affectionately joining the other for the common task'.[30] (One is reminded here of Rousseau's definition of the citizen as one who is at once a subject and a member of the sovereign people;[31] but the meaning and context are somewhat different.)

The same unity of mind, arising out of a love that is developed through acquaintance and collaboration, can lead to the breaking-down of national differences, and the emergence of an attitude appropriate to the universality of the Church. Again, the face-to-face milieu of the general council is central to Segovia's thought. In a fine statement of international idealism, Segovia suggests that the crookedness (*curvitas*) implanted by the Fall, which makes men love those physically close to them at the expense of those far away, can be overcome by the communal nature of the council: 'The more that (assemblies) partake in the nature of one shared association or meeting of all (*naturam unius communis omnium societatis aut conventionis*), the more justly constituted do they seem to be . . . setting aside crookedness . . . Those who have been incorporated into the general synod are made members of the universal Church . . . Nor can one say to another, "You are not from Italy, Spain, France or Germany". . .[32] As the body is one and its members, though many, are one, so is Christ in the general synod . . . as members of one body they have to suffer together, rejoice together, work together and look to the one common good of all . . . Therefore, out of the intermingled multitude, almost daily forced into each other's company, there is born true love for persons of all nationalities . . . so that, coming together with a certain delight, they explore more wisely the true and common good'.[33]

For the general council has as its aim the 'common good' of the whole Church. Paraphrasing Aristotle, he says that 'in proportion as any good is more common, it is more divine'.[34] So he advocates a comparative method for assessing the common good of the whole church: 'by understanding the various customs of diverse nations, perfect knowledge of the Catholic

159

Church's common good can be obtained by comparing them'. By learning about other nations, people 'perceive new and hidden things and are made more wise'.[35] The spiritual unity of the Church is to be expressed at its top organisational level in the actual sharing of problems and ideas among members of the council.

The theological dimension arises out of the long-standing, indeed scriptural, principle of fraternal 'oneness of mind', which gave rise, in *Acts* and in early and subsequent church tradition, to the notion that unanimity is a sign of the holy Spirit. The principle that the Spirit works through a *group* united in love and purpose was invoked, by Segovia and many others, alongside corporation theory, in support of the view that ultimate authority resides collectively in the council as a whole, and is not dependent upon the consent of the pope or his legates. This produced statements of the communal nature of conciliar, and indeed of all ecclesiastical, authority: 'In councils . . . judgments proceed from all at once . . . all are said to act at once . . . the actions of those who celebrate councils are common (*communes*), and participants have a common authority (*communis auctoritas*) . . .'[36] The Church's power is not peculiar to one person but common to many . . .'.[37]

It was also invoked in support of equality of voting rights for theologians and priests: 'the Saviour wished the Church to be governed by them in common'.[38] Segovia implies that it is the free and communal procedure which enables the holy Spirit to operate: '(matters) are put before all in common . . . God himself concurs together with the fathers of a synod in those things which proceed from the council'.[39]

Segovia, like others at Basle, developed the doctrine of *Haec Sancta*, that a council is assembled 'in the holy Spirit' and has power 'immediately from Christ', to say that Christ is the 'principal actor (*principale agens*)' in the council, that he operates therein 'through himself and immediately', and that 'conciliar actions are said to be from the holy Spirit as their *principale agens*'.[40]

Segovia expressed this particular aspect of the conciliar ideal more ardently and emphatically than any other conciliarist. He sometimes sounds sentimental. What he said was obviously not generally true of the council of Basle and its committees, but it probably reflected Segovia's and others' actual experience on some occasions. Nor is it generally true of meetings and collective action; but it is not generally false either. Characteristically, Segovia expressed the ideal of collaborative, fraternal decision-making — 'government by sense of the meeting' — in the form of a law of nature.

Whereas organic holism as applied to the Church as a whole was a metaphysical theory, Segovia, when writing of the council itself, understands group unity as an experienced unity of mind achieved by working together under certain constitutional procedures; indeed, as an empirically observable phenomenon.

NOTES

1. The contrast is Tönnies', between a 'community' (*Gemeinschaft*) having a 'real and organic life' and a 'society' (*Gesellschaft*) with an 'imaginary and mechanical structure' (Tönnies, 21ff., 37ff.).
2. *MC* ii, 130.
3. *MC* iii, 605; *TP* 65; *CEA* fol. 214v; *Dicta*, fol. 149v; *MC* ii, 214; *MC* iii, 603.
4. *CEA* fol. 214v; *MC* iii, 603.
5. *MC* iii, 531-2; cf. above, p.110.
6. *MC* ii, 131-2.
7. *MC* ii, 131.
8. *MAE* fol. 179r; cf. *MC* iii, 713.
9. *MAE* fol. 179r; cf. *MC* iii, 713.
10. *MAE* fol. 181r; of Aquinas, *Commentum in III Sent.*, xviii, 1 ad 5, and *Contra Gentiles*, IV, 7: cit. Eschmann, 41-2.
11. *MC* iii, 713.
12. Cf. above, p.101.
13. *CEA* fols. 212v, 227r, 231r.
14. *Iliad*, X, 224.
15. *MAE* fol. 176v; *CEA* fol. 218v; *MC* iii, 711.
16. *MC* iii, 710-11 (also in Black, 1970a, 146-7); cf. *TP* 63; *CEA* fol. 218v; *MAE* fols. 179r-v. Cf. *Wisdom*, 6:26; *Proverbs*, 13:10, 20 and 24:6; and also Waley, 65.
17. *MC* iii, 806.
18. *MAE* fol. 87v; also in Langenstein, 48, and Viterbo, 118.
19. *CEA* fol. 226r-7r.
20. *MAE* fol. 191r; 'lege communi illud competit nature congregationis quod partibus invicem congregatis nulla deperit virtus, quinimmo congregationis auxilio earum quelibet in sua fortificatur et augetur virtute'.
21. *MC* iii, 714.
22. *MAE* fols. 172r, 182v; *MC* iii, 601.
23. Cf. Aristotle, *Politics*, III, c. 11, p.126.
24. Above, p.71.
25. *MC* iii, 727-8; cf. *Acts*, 2:4.
26. *MC* ii, 272-4. Cf. above, pp.88f.
27. Cit. Congar (1965), 113n.; cf. Ullmann (1966), 280ff.
28. *CEA* fol. 224v; cf. below, pp.162ff.
29. *MC* iii, 736.
30. *MC* ii, 274.
31. *Du contrat social*, I, c. 6, p.116.
32. Cf. *1 Cor.* 3:4.
33. *MC* ii, 133-4; cf. *CEA* fol. 194r.
34. *MAE* fol. 87r; *TP* 51; *MC* ii, 993; *MC* iii, 400. Cf. Aristotle, *Nic. ethics*, A6, 1098a.
35. *MC* ii, 134; cf. *MC* ii, 274.
36. *TP* 65, 72-4; cf. *MC* ii, 605ff.; for the presidency debate, above, pp.54-6.
37. *CEA* fol. 217v.
38. *ASP* 144; cf. *CEA* fol. 218r.
39. *CEA* fols. 215r-218r; cf. *MC* ii, 130; *MC* iii, 604-7, 625, 726; Escobar, *GC* 265, 328; Dijon prior, 98.
40. *TP* 63-5; *CEA* fols. 215r, 218r; *MC* iii, 603, 761. Cf. *MC* ii, 605ff.; Black (1966), 33,n.1.

CHAPTER 13

THE COMMUNAL THEORY OF GOVERNMENT

We now come to what may most properly be called Segovia's political thought, that is his ideas about society and government that either did not refer specifically to the Church, or were overt generalisations, or that referred specifically to secular affairs. Segovia's political thought consists partly in an application of Basilean-conciliarist ideas to government in general, partly in the expression of ideas that were peculiarly his. We may start with his exposition of corporation lore regarding the relationship between corporation (*universitas*) and ruler (*rector*) as a general theory of government. Segovia was one of the first representatives of a widespread tendency in late-medieval and early-modern thought to extrapolate norms that had been evolved in small groups and make them into a general political theory. Throughout, we shall meet with anticipations of Rousseau.[1]

NOTE
  1. Cf. A. Black, 'Will and wisdom: the political thought of Juan de Segovia' *(History of Political Thought, forthcoming).*

The 'collegiate' model

Segovia's conversion of corporation theory into a general political doctrine was part of his argument that the pope, while greater than the Church taken distributively, is less than the Church taken collectively. After citing Aristotle's opinion on the appropriate size for a royal bodyguard (big enough to overpower individuals and groups, small enough to be resisted by the whole citizenry),[1] Segovia said that the equivalent Basilean doctrine as to the ruler's constitutional power in general was obvious to anyone who considers 'the nature of association and of individual members (*naturam universitatis et singulorum*)'. He will show that conciliar sovereignty conforms to 'political and natural reason (*politica et naturalis ratio*)':

'If anyone duly considers the nature of society and its members (*universitatis et singulorum*), he will judge what has been said not to be absurd but to be in harmony with nature and reason . . . For he who is in charge of a number of people . . . though he is above the individuals is not above them all (*singulos . . . universos*); that is, when they concur together for the same action. So, while he can overcome one part with the aid of another, if he wants to compare himself with the whole number (*multitudini*), he will certainly be overcome. This is clear in the case of the commander of an army or of the president of any number of people.

'The reason for this is that whoever is in charge of the government of many, if he is going to be properly (*debite*) in charge, ceases to be a private person and becomes a public person, loses in a way his solitary oneness, and puts on the united multitude (*perdit quodammodo solitariam unitatem, et induit unitam multitudinem*); so that he is now said to bear or represent the person not of one but of many. He plays the part of a good ruler (*rectoris*), so long as he aims at the public good of the many; but when he sets aside the public good and studiously seeks his own, then he ceases to be a suitable ruler of such a group (*multitudinis rector*).

'For this reason, namely that he is thought to play the part (lit. bear the person, *gestare personam*) of all suitably, attending to the public good, when he is compared to individual persons or particular assemblies (*congregationes*) of that multitude, because he as president is said to play the role (*habere vices*) of all . . . for this reason it is said that the president is greater. But, if it occurs that the whole of that multitude assembles in one place and asserts or desires something, but the president says the opposite, because truth is preferred to fiction, the multitude itself will rightly overcome. For that this multitude is many persons is the truth; but that the president himself, who is really one person, is said to be many by representation, is a fiction. For, in the case of one who is said to have authority on the grounds that he represents the person of another or of many, on account of the very fact that those represented are present, their authority, not his, is heeded.

'Wherefore, the authority of the president in the presence of the whole multitude, if he sets himself above it, is not deemed to have force as before. The reason for this is that his judgment is presumed (*presumitur*) to conform to the intention of all over whom he presides (*intentioni omnium quibus presidet*), for the republic's utility and their own. This is the highest power conceded to any president, that what seems right to him should be believed to be the intention of all, who at that time exist separately in different places. But when the whole multitude itself is present as principal (*principaliter*) and judges something to be useful for it but the president says differently, it is clearly understood that the reason (*causa*) why one should assent to him rather than them — namely, that his judgment was believed to conform to the intention of all — ceases to exist. Rather, since he himself demonstrates that he supports a contrary opinion (*contrariam sententiam*), it is clearly perceived that his judgment does not conform to the intention of all the others, who at this time put forward explicitly what their judgment is. Therefore it does not seem right in this case to stand by the judgment of him alone, unless perhaps it is thought that he alone can see and all the others are blind. But it has been assumed that the many and the one are alike, and can be compared with one another on equal terms with regard to presidency'.[2]

This general statement of the ruler-ruled relationship is in part a development of the concept of the ruler as 'public person' (the Latin *persona* may be translated, in this context, as 'role' or 'function'):[3] Segovia is considering what is implied in the concept of public office or authority. He starts with the commonplace that the ruler's position is contingent upon his pursuit of the public good. But he immediately develops this to say that someone who 'wears the mask/bears the character/exercises the function (*gerit personam*) of many' is identified with those he governs in the *further* sense that he 'loses in a way his solitary oneness, and *puts on the united multitude*'. This is an amazing evocation of the Pauline notion of 'putting on Christ', an analogy used still more explicityly by Giovanni Antonio Campano (1429-1477), who said the magistrate should 'at once put off himself (*seipsum exuere*) and set aside like a garment all self-interest and greed, and put on the public person (*induere publicam personam*) of the whole city'.[4] What Segovia means is that the ruler must indentify himself with the people, must act as if he were they. The ruler's claim to public office depends not only on his pursuing the public good, but also on his being '*presumed to conform to the intention of all over whom he presides*'. 'The intention of all (*intentio omnium*)' is clearly a democratic notion. Since Segovia assumes that all share a common interest, know what it is and pursue it, we may say that the similarity with Rousseau's 'general will' is more than superficial. The key point in Segovia is indeed that 'all' know the common good, which is assumed to be equivalent to what they think and desire.

From these moral formulae Segovia deduces a constitutional model which bears the clear imprint of corporation theory and of Basilean claims, but is something more as well. The 'presumption' that the ruler pursues the common good in conformity with the will of all works in two ways. First, it means that the people as individuals and 'particular congregations' must obey the ruler. Secondly, it means that a general assembly of the people automatically overrides the ruler: if it disagrees with him, the presumption no longer holds. Both the association's right to spontaneous self-assembly and the sovereignty of the assembled association are assumed without question, probably (in view of the *universitas-rector* terminology) on the basis of collegiate theory and practice.

Next, there is the interesting notion that the ruler's representative status and his authority depend upon a *fiction* (as we shall see, Segovia has a good deal to say on the subject of political fictions),[5] and that this fiction holds good *so long as people believe it*. This is because public authority rests solely on the convention that the ruler 'puts on the united multitude'; when the multitude actually express an opinion 'on account of the very fact that those represented are present, their authority, not his, is heeded'.

Segovia's political reflections, which at this point were obviously inspired by the practice and mood of the medieval corporation or guild,[6] embodied the kind of radical democratic theory which surfaces again and again in Europe, particularly at revolutionary moments, and which is alive and well today. What is significant is that in Segovia these ideas appeared without any overall paradigm of the secular polity; this may possibly account for the fact that they were not very fully worked out and that Segovia on other occasions appears to have forgotten all about them.[7] While John of Paris and Zabarella had applied corporation theory only to the Church, Segovia like Marsiglio uses it as a basis for all government. His ability so to generalize owes much to the flexible meaning of the term *universitas*, which could mean either 'corporation' in the technical legal sense, or 'society' in the general sense.[8] It seems probable that he learnt his corporational ideas from experience and observation rather than from legal text-books, which are not cited in this passage; the phrase 'particular congregations' suggests that university constitutions may have been one source of his thought.[9]

Segovia's political theory — both here and at other points — was to a large degree developed out of the collegiate and communal forms of organization which had germinated in medieval Europe and which were now in their florescence. It was part of the harvest of medieval corporation lore, which would continue to exercise a lasting attraction on radical political theorists, and would form one of the jumping-off points for later democratic thought. It was a model derived not from an idealized past but from the inner principles of existing institutions.[10]

The weakness of Segovia's political theory as a general model — though not when he was speaking of the internal functioning of the council – was that it made no allowance for the difference between a small society capable of literal self-assembly, and a large society. Basle conciliarism revealed the defect of the collectivist notion of democracy outside the milieu of the small community in which, for the most part, it had originated. Rousseau, by contrast, was fully aware of this problem. The virtue of Segovia's theory may be seen to lie in the new meaning he gave to representation. Anticipating our discussion of Segovia's concept of trust in authority, we may already detect, in the passage under discussion here, a distinctive view of representation. He indicates, in broad terms, the degree and quality of free-play belonging to a representative, who is neither plenipotentiary nor mere delegate: he may act on his own initiative in the public interest so long as he retains general credibility. It is a flexible relationship.

NOTES

1. *Politics*, III, c. 15, p.142.
2. *CEA* fols. 224r-v; *MC* iii, 720-1; Black (1970a), 142-4, 148-50; cf. Black (1970a), 25-9.
3. Cf. Cicero, *De officiis*, I, c. 34.
4. Campano (unpag.); St Paul in *Eph.* 4:22-4; *Col.* 3:9-10. Cf. F. di Bernardo, *Un vescovo umanista* (Rome, 1975).
5. Below, pp.168ff.
6. I hope to work out the full implications of the guild-type group for political theory, and its role in the history of ideas, in a future work provisionally called 'Community and its modes: Guild and State in political thought'.
7. Below, pp.184ff, 191ff.
8. Michaud-Quantin, 15, 28ff.
9. Cf. Cobban, 85-6. Above, p.118.
10. Ullmann (1966), 216ff.; Pocock (1972), 233ff.

Ruler and ruled

Segovia developed his distinctive notion of the ruler-ruled relationship in a variety of contexts. He repeatedly invoked the New Testament model expressed in Jesus' saying: 'You know that among the pagans the rulers lord it over them, and their great men make their authority felt. This is not to happen among you. No; anyone who wants to be great among you must be your servant, and anyone who wants to be first among you must be your slave' (*Math.* 20:25-7); and in St Peter's injunction, 'never be a dictator over any group that is put in your charge' (*I Peter* 5:3).[1] Even the monarchical ruler is to imitate Christ who, 'giving consummate perfection to monarchical government, wished that he who is in charge of the faithful people as their superior, as first, as greater, should hold himself as less and as a minister, and that he is the more strongly bound to be the servant and slave of all'.[2] While he applied this by analogy to any ruler of any society, it is particularly the 'form of ruling (*forma regiminis*)' for the Church, which was 'practised by the Roman and other bishops in the times of the early Church'.[3] With this we may compare Erasmus who, also quoting *Math.* 20:25-7, said that 'among Christians sovereignty means administration, not domination (*principatio administratio est, non imperium*)'.[4]

Segovia developed the notion of ruler as servant in his own unique way, stressing above all the conformity of mind — a notion pregnant for the theory of representation — that should exist between ruler and people. The ruler should behave towards his people as 'one of them';[5] he should not 'drag them imperiously' but 'charitably and gently mould them (*non trahendo imperative, sed caritative et suaviter disponendo*)'.[6] The 'good servant of the republic (*minister reipublicae*)' is, he says, 'a common person (*persona communis*)'[7] — a concept again used by Erasmus.[8] He was a forerunner of those later republicans and radical Protestants who would insist that the ruler be on equal terms with his people (for example, Milton, who, also using *Math.* 20:25-7, said: 'what government comes nearer to this precept of Christ than a free commonwealth, wherein they who are greatest are perpetual servants ... are not elevated above their brethren ... may be spoken to freely, familiarly, friendly, and without adoration?').[9] Segovia meant both that the ruler should act in a representative manner and, further, that he is in reality 'of the same kind' (as he put it) as the ruled.[10] There is no generic difference between ruler and ordinary citizen.

Segovia made this point most clearly by employing once again the organic analogy and the holist notion of association. He says (speaking of the ecclesiastical ruler) that he 'is made one body with (the people) itself, and is in (the people) as the form in a composite being (*velut forma intra compositum*);[11] and he is held to act in such a way that his operations conform in unison (*in unum conforment*) with the operations of the whole body, in such a way that they are thought to proceed not as from two mutually conflicting or separate materials (*compositis*), but as from one body and a single (soul)'.[12]

Such a statement could again find an exact echo in Giovanni Campano, who said that the ruler 'should so consider the body that the single members move with concordant assent, that there is nothing that is not done by the whole mass, and nothing that is not carried out spontaneously'.[13]

Legitimacy, and conformity with the common good and the people's mind, may be achieved by the employment of good counsellors: 'The president of any society is thought or believed by his subjects to be playing the part of a good pastor . . . when he gives judgment on hard

167

matters with the mature deliberation and council of wise men; then he is the more believed to be playing the role of good pastor, and *the more he departs from this, the more the condition of good ruler or pastor is presumed to be lacking in him*. But the more he abounds in (counsel), the more the suitability of his government is believed in. Whence, if his judgment arises from a council of all the wise and prudent men of that society, he is said to be of much greater authority . . . The name of head, ruler or pastor is said to belong to him more truly, more really (*existentius*)'.[14]

This theme is developed in Segovia's discussion of parliamentary monarchy, to be considered below: if the ruler uses good counsellors, his decisions are wise and the people have good reason to trust him. As we shall see, Segovia often suggests that the presumption of conformity to the common good can be based on this, without the need for a general popular assembly.

NOTES

1. Cited in *TP* 46-7; *CEA* fol. 225r; *MC* ii, 214; *ASP* 29.
2. *MAE* fol. 106r; cf. *MAE* fol. 176r.
3. *MC* iii, 724; cf. *MC* iii, 710, 925.
4. Erasmus, 574, 577. Cf. Ockham: 'principatus papalis . . . non dominativus, sed ministrativus est digne vocandus': cit. McGrade, 207.
5. *MC* iii, 723, 725.
6. *MC* ii, 273 and iii, 670.
7. *CEA* fol. 230r.
8. Erasmus, 574F: 'Quid rex nisi plurimorum pater? Excellat enim, sed tamen *eiusdem est generis*, homo hominibus, liber liberis imperans'; cf. 579E; Mornay, q. 3, pp. 80ff.
9. Milton, 19-20.
10. *CEA* fol. 230r.
11. Sc. a being composed of form and matter, such as a human person composed of body and soul.
12. *CEA* fol. 225r; cf. *MC* iii, 707, 722; Black (1966), 82-4; Wilks (1963), 21n. Cf. *Acts* 4:32; *Eph.* 4:4.
13. Campano (unpag.)
14. *CEA* fols. 226r-v.

Fictional theory of government and law

Segovia's conception of the fictional nature of governmental authority is further refined in a remarkable analysis of the ontological status of laws and political institutions, which he undertook towards the end of his last work on ecclesiology and political theory.[1] He distinguishes four types of causality: 'natural', 'artificial', 'political', 'hierarchical'. An example of natural causality is the generation of a new member of a species from seed; an example of artificial causality is the painting of a picture from a mental image: in both cases, the cause directly affects the real world: 'cause and effect are said to be not a thing of the reason but a real thing (*ens non rationis sed reale*)'.[2] Political causality (the way a political act takes effect) is — by way of contrast — a purely mental process, stemming from an act of will, and only affects the real world, through its influence on other minds. This discussion, then, may be seen as a development of his fictional theory of political power and also of his fiduciary notion of authority.[3] In politics and law 'all efficacy exists and depends on what went before, on what can be changed by the will of the law-maker'. He goes on:

'For, regardless of the lawgiver's (*ordinator*) action or inaction, knowledge or ignorance, willing or not willing, once he has willed and ordained, the effect follows by necessity, so long as the ordinance remains in effect . . . so that, if the law is that he who runs away from war should on that account be killed, the law is the cause of death, not because it brings about death, but because someone has deserved it through such flight, incurring the guilt on account of his not having fulfilled the conditions of the law; the law is not the instrumental or natural cause of death, but its political or civil cause . . . The guilt too, just like the law, is a factor of the reason (*respectus quidam rationis*), set in motion by will, not by intellect, and it is therefore by so much a greater entity inasmuch as the will is a more powerful cause than the intellect . . . The guilt does not follow by necessity out of the very nature of the act of flight, for if on some occasion it was to the republic's advantage that its army should be defeated, or if victory was attained by the flight, it could have been ordained that those fleeing from the war were to be rewarded. And so flight from war is not made culpable by death by its very nature or from any absolute consideration, but by the ordinance of a will. If the law ordained that anyone who took poison should die, since that would certainly happen without the law being in effect, death would occur in him who took poison not by the ordinance of the law, but by the nature of the act; and just as the poison is the real cause, so the death that results from it comes about by the nature of the thing (*natura rei*). For that reason, the cause of this death would not be political . . . Therefore, just as a political cause is said to be a thing of reason (*ens rationis*), so too is its effect; for not every brigand who steals hangs on a gallows as a result, even though he merits this penalty, nor is that penalty always applied to theft, but (it is applied) according to the variety of laws . . .

'In this *genus* of political cause are nearly all the judicial laws of *Exodus*, civil and municipal laws and the statutes of all principalities; so too are all titles (*gradus*) which are conferred in universities for the study of sciences, and so too are all offices of government in a people. For just as the law or ordinance, according to which they are conferred, is a thing of reason (*ens rationis*), so too the offices, titles or dignities themselves (even ecclesiastical ones that are of positive or customary law) are things of reason, their cause and effect being established not by nature but by the will of the lawgiver. Both cause and effect is said to be a thing not of nature but of reason, caused by the intellect, just as one might invent or imagine golden castles in Africa over the sea or silver ones in Austria beyond the Danube. For the intellect is not a cause that produces anything external, except perhaps speech, which depends rather on the will. But the will itself, although unable to produce anything in the realm of reality or nature (*in esse reale seu nature*), can nevertheless produce (something) in the realm of reason (*in esse rationis*) . . . And so these three things which follow upon one another, namely the dignity of sovereignty (*dignitas principatus*), whether in one man who excels in virtue, or in a few virtuous, or in a multitude of people; and law or the ordinance or statute promulgated by the sovereign; and the effect of law, that is making someone guilty of punishment or deserving of reward — although those to whom they belong are real (*eorum subiecta realia sint*), are themselves things of reason; and through these three entities of reason one arrives at the real entity, namely punishment . . . or reward . . . Therefore, just as a political or civil cause is not a real thing but a thing of reason, so too it produces an effect that is not a real thing but a thing of reason; common linguistic usage distinguishes between civil death and real or natural death; no law can of itself bring about the latter, but it can certainly bring about civil death on many occasions'.[4]

The fourth type of causality is 'ecclesiastical', in which God directly affects the real world by a willed act of intervention, as in miracles and the sacraments. In this case, the cause is an act of will, but since it is the will of God this directly affects the real world: 'Although in civil and hierarchial (things) the method of causation is the same, that is, it occurs through the ordinance of the will of someone using their reason . . ., it differs as to its effect: a civil cause can only cause a thing of reason, but a hierarchical one (can cause a thing) both of reason and real'.[5]

In these passages, Segovia comes fairly close to the nominalist approach taken by the jurists in their discussions of the ontological status of corporations, of which Baldus had said that their 'meaning is determined by the mind (*significatio est inventa per intellectum*)': the *universitas*, taken in any sense other than as its individual members as such, is, according to Baldus, 'a kind of intellectual body and a kind of legal name (*quoddam corpus intellectuale et quoddam nomen iuris*)'.[6] This juristic view of the legal fiction had been used to express the dependence of the corporation for its very existence upon the will of the sovereign, who as lawgiver could determine what groups should have the status of legal persons. Hobbes would apply this nominalist argument to society as a whole, alleging that it is only the sovereign who can create, by representation, 'a real unity of them all, in one and the same person'.[7] But Segovia applies this quasi-nominalist approach to *rulership* rather than to association. It fits in with an exactly opposite interpretation of the ruler-ruled relationship to the one implied by some jurists and Hobbes. It fits in with Segovia's view that the *de facto* as well as the *de iure* power of a ruler depends upon the subjects' *recognition* of its propriety, which in turn depends upon the ruler's being *seen* to aim at the common good. As he had said in the *rector-universitas* context, 'the highest power conceded to any president is that what seems right to him should be *believed* to be the intention of all'.[8]

But it would be wrong to interpret the above passage as in any exact sense 'nominalist'. Segovia is not so much saying that laws and political entities are 'mere names'; in identifying the precise way in which political entities and acts achieve their effects, he evolves a somewhat subtler view. It could perhaps be called voluntarist: effects do not follow from a 'political cause' *ex natura rei*, but because someone has *decided* to make a particular law, and has carried it into effect. Segovia is not, however, implying that will is separable from or contrary to reason. It *should* be the product of reason, but the immediate cause is will, not reason. What is striking is his clear, if implicit, denial that government and rank derive their essence from nature, far less from God.

Here, Segovia is also at one with the positivist view of government and law. One may compare him with Pufendorf, who said (in Gierke's words) that 'the legal world was a world not of physical, but of mental factors — or rather, in view of the fact that it was the moral aspect of these mental factors which was really in question, it was a world of moral factors, or *entia moralia*'.[9] This view has been developed by Kelsen, who argued precisely that the 'state' is not a natural-social reality but a 'political fiction': 'the state as an acting person is not a reality but an auxiliary construction of legal thinking'.[10] This view is also implicit in some social-contract theorists who — as is particularly clear in the case of Suarez[11] — started out by demolishing the idea that political authority is inherent in anyone by nature or divine will, and went on to argue that it was the product of deliberate human invention. Segovia, like Locke, was concerned to diminish the ontological status of political authority, and so to make those who wield it more accessible to rational control.

NOTES
1. *MC* iii, 851-7; Black (1970a), 154-5.
2. *MC* iii, 851-2.
3. Above, pp.163f.; below, pp.176ff.
4. *MC* iii, 852-5.

5. *MC* iii, 855.
6. Cit. Gierke, *DGR* iii, 432; cf. above, pp.67f., 150.
7. *Leviathan*, c. 18, p.112.
8. *CEA* fol. 224v.
9. Gierke, *DGR* trans. Barker, 118.
10. Kelsen, 292.
11. Below, pp.202f.

Civic republicanism

Segovia expressed and developed his political theory by invoking the civic-republican tradition. He defended the Basle-conciliarist notion of authority as necessarily inhering in the Church-as-a-whole by working up the theory of sovereignty within the city-state (*civitas*) in such a way as to provide another alleged precedent for his view. There were numerous points of coincidence between the republicanism of certain autonomous or quasi-autonomous city-states and conciliar theory, and these became increasingly clear in expositions of Basle conciliarism from 1439 onwards.[1] Analogies between the Church and the contemporary city-state are used by Segovia in his earlier works, but they become more frequent and elaborate after 1439.

Segovia was familiar with city government from his native country, his visit to Florence, and from his travels in Germany. Indeed, he had visited Florence at a time when the civic ideology was being championed against 'despotic' Milan by Poggio and others, whom he quite probably met at the papal court. In a manner similar to theirs, Segovia contrasted the 'liberty' of conciliar government with the 'tyranny' of the Eugenian papacy; like them, by liberty he meant both autonomy and a degree of internal democracy.[2] He invoked 'Christian liberty' against the 'servitude' which Eugenius was imposing on the Church.[3] The council is 'self-sufficient (*substantiale sibi*)' and enjoys 'its own freedom of will'.[4] Through *Haec Sancta* 'the liberty of the Catholic Church when it is legitimately assembled has been declared'; by his refusal to recognise that decree, Eugenius reveals his desire 'to reduce the Church to that servitude from which it was liberated by the said definition'.[5] This was characteristically Basilean. Basle itself declared (in Rousseauistic terms): 'we see the Church, which God willed to be free, made into a tributary'.[6]

Segovia's starting-point here was Gerson's ascription of supreme power in differing senses to pope, Church and council; Segovia interpreted Gerson's formula to say that power lies fundamentally and inalienably with the Church, is delegated by it to the council, and by the council to the pope.[7] For such a view, he says, 'there is a convenient example in any great community not recognizing a superior in temporal matters'. *Communitas* was a term commonly used of cities, and this phrase is a clear reference to the self-governing 'communes' or city-states of Italy and perhaps Germany. In the passage that follows, the terms *consulatus, potestas, magistratus* also have a civic reference. At this point in his reflections, we may locate Segovia firmly in the civic-republican tradition; once again, it is possible to take Segovia as an indication of just how far one could go without reference to Pocock's 'Machiavellian' paradigm:[8]

'For (the community's) supreme power of guarding and governing itself and its subjects exists first in the community itself (*primo consistit in ipsa communitate*); then in the rulers and magistrates — or consulate, or senate, or whatever it may be called; and subsequently (*consequenter*) in the executive or *podesta*, dictator or governor (*executore sive potestate, dictatore aut gubernatore*), to which has been entrusted the disposition of all matters when the consulate does not dispose otherwise, and the execution of matters which the consulate has decided ... It is plain that such supreme power exists first in the community, from the fact that it seems to belong to the community as its own passion or innate force, inseparable from it (*tamquam propria passio sive innata virtus, ab ea inseparabilis*); so that it is in the community as in its first, and although not its only, nevertheless its commeasurate and principal subject (*tanquam in primo, et quamvis non solum, sed per se adequato ac principali subiecto*). Given the community, by that very fact power is understood to be in it; but if there were no community, (power) would not remain in it, nor in the magistrates, nor in the governor or executive'.

The magistrates and governor (equivalent to council and pope respectively) — he goes on — 'exercise their functions in the name and power of the community'; but 'the community can exercise the power intrinsically belonging to it through itself, whether defending itself from its enemies, making a judgment about malefactors among its subjects, giving recognition of favour to benefactors, or making laws'. The community can give power to another 'when it perceives that an irreparable loss would result for its subjects ... if it exercized its power through itself in all matters every day and hour': despite such delegation, the community 'never abdicates its power, for the reason that its power is inseparable from it ... such power of guarding itself belongs to it without any possibility of its losing it (*inamissibiliter*)'. There follows a sentence of great significance: 'The reason is that (the community) is the one and only and unmediated agency of that power (*unicum subiectum est ac immediatum potestatis ipsius*); even though it is communicated to consulate or ruler, it is not changed: such communication having the force of a kind of transfusion or extension rather than of a new generation (*potius transfusionis sive*

173

extensionis cuiusdam quam nove generationis)'.[9]

Segovia, then, developed Gerson's theory of the division of power between pope, Church and council into a more thorough-going theory of popular sovereignty. The most important point in this passage is the insistence on the inalienability of sovereignty, and the particular way this is expressed. The inalienability of sovereignty from the people was a common enough theme in medieval writers, but it could mean a variety of things. Segovia here takes it in its strong sense, to mean that the people delegate power for convenience and may revoke it at will; sovereignty as a whole resides in the people, who delegate it only conditionally. So too Althusius would say: 'the rights of sovereignty (*majestas*), just as they originated from the associated body, so they adhere to it undividely (*individue*) and inseparably, and cannot be transferred to another'.[10]

The crucial emphasis in Segovia is that such delegation creates no new power, being a 'transfusion' not a 'new generation'. This may be compared with Rousseau's assertion that 'power may be transmitted, but not will'.[11] Delegation of power to the ruler or senate is merely for convenience. Such popular sovereignty is in the nature of things: 'given the community, by that very fact power is understood to be in it'. The community is, once again, seen as a corporate whole which naturally possesses 'supreme power . . . as its own passion or innate force'.

Here Segovia was not, despite his assertion that 'these things are very well-known to anyone with knowledge of the government of any (civic) communities',[12] merely describing the accepted theory, far less the general practice, of civic institutions. He was 'reading off' the Gersonian-Basilean estimate of the Church-council-pope relationship on the template of the city-state; and in so doing he was re-stating, and to a certain extent developing, the civic-republican tradition itself.

This reinforces our impression of the debt which early-modern theories of popular sovereignty owe to the corporational-collegiate mode of thought. To the medieval jurists the city was a species of the *universitas* (corporation) genus; and Baron has indicated the continuity between the earlier communal tradition and Florentine republicanism in the fifteenth century.[13] In the early-modern period civic republicanism served as an intermediary between the old notion of communal self-government and the modern notion of popular sovereignty. The theory of popular sovereignty as sometimes expounded by Savonarola and other Florentine revolutionaries of the late-fifteenth and early-sixteenth centuries would find its way into the English radical tradition of the seventeenth century, most notably in James Harrington.[14] The notion of the community of believers as the *locus* of ecclesiastical sovereignty was also historically fundamental to the development of the theory of popular sovereignty in Europe: and here too the civic milieu acted as an intermediary. As Troeltsch says of Calvinism: 'the final effect of this interpenetration of a city republic with a national Church was a strong impulse in the direction of democracy'.[15]

NOTES
1. For conciliarist use of civic-republican analogies: Niem, 69, 74-5; Gerson, *OC* vi, 233; Velde, *EP* fol. 182r; Escobar, *GC* 260-1, 328; Piccolomini in Mansi xxxi A, 226E. Cf. above, pp.99ff.
2. *MC* iii, 622, 625, 707; Baron (1966), 20-1, 387ff., 407.
3. *TP* 76; *MC* ii, 579. Cf. Erasmus, 578B.
4. *MAE* fol. 174r.
5. *MC* iii, 282-3.
6. Mansi xxx, 1046C; cf. *MD* viii, 995D (using *II Cor.* 3:17); *MC* iii, 701.
7. *MC* iii, 786-808; cf. Gerson, above, p.23; Gierke, *DGR* trans Maitland, 52-4, 157, Gierke (1966), 146ff.
8. Cf. Pocock (1975), 49ff.
9. *MC* iii, 802-3.
10. Cit. Gierke (1966), 42; cf. *ibid.*, 34, 157; and Riesenberg, *passim;* and above, p.144f.
11. *Du contrat social,* II, c. 1, p.124.
12. *MC* iii, 803.
13. Baron (1966), pp. xxvii, 273ff.
14. Albertini, 126-8, 140-1; Pocock (1975), 361ff., 386ff.
15. Troeltsch, ii, 628; cf. Baron (1939).

CHAPTER 14

TRUST AND AUTHORITY

The idea of conformity of mind between ruler and people was expressed in a somewhat different way by Segovia in his arguments against the neutrality of the princes. He argued that there was an absolute obligation to submit to the general council. He invoked a general social and political analogy: the ruled must trust the ruler even when they are not in a position to know in detail the reasons for his action. This notion of the relationship between ruled and, ruler as one of trust or faith was developed to the point of saying that there is an absolute obligation to trust the ruler; for in this case, Segovia held, the ruler (i.e. the council) was infallibly trustworthy. In the process, Segovia developed the notion of trust in the political sphere. While there were obvious differences between this and other models of authority he used in other contexts, we may perhaps hazard that this was in part a restatement of his general political theory for the large society: he also speaks in a similar way about national monarchy.

The need for trust without certain knowledge is, he argued, a general feature of social and political relationships: 'In every state (*politia*), for men to live . . . peaceably, it is necessary for them to believe firmly (*firmiter credere*) even things of which they can hardly or never possess certain knowledge (*certitudinaliter . . . cognosci*)'. Citing 'the law that fathers must be venerated by sons who have very slight knowledge that they begot them', 'the law on contracts, which . . . would not come into being unless the contractors had faith about each other', and other examples, he sums up: 'So there is complete agreement that no state (*politia*) could exist without men's trust (*credulitas*) in each other about things which

176

they do not see . . . Human society cannot exist unless there is mutual trust (*invicem credulitas*) . . . by a law of nature, no state can exist without faith (*fides*) . . . the common definition of which is "belief in things not seen (*credere quod non vides*)".[1]

Trust, then, in the integrity of persons in matters of which one has no direct knowledge oneself is a necessary condition for any government, and indeed for society itself. Such trust differs, first, from direct knowledge of the ruler's rectitude: it is inferred from aspects of his government which are known to his subjects, and carried over to other aspects of which they have little or no knowledge. It differs, secondly, from mere command or brute force, in that the subjects obey willingly in the light of their limited knowledge, and, most emphatically, in that the ruler has been seen to have consulted many wise counsellors. This notion corresponds to Segovia's view of religious faith, particularly of faith in the authority of religious institutions; but he indicates that a mixture of 'credulity' and knowledge is to be found in ordinary human relationships too.

Looking at the relationship of trust from the ruler's end, Segovia emphasizes the advantages accruing to the secular monarch when he has his people's trust. This, he argued, can only be assured when the monarch uses, and is seen to use, good counsellors: 'It most of all and in every way helps subjects to see that judgments are just, that commands are necessary or expedient, and to obey them, when they have knowledge (*notitiam*) that their president has employed the counsels of wise men . . . The definition or sentence itself, when it conforms to the counsels and deliberation of (wise men) is for that very reason presumed (*presumitur*) to be right and just, and is thereafter more readily put into effect . . . He who presides over a monarchical government has credibility (*creditum*), so that his commands are accepted and put into effect, when his subjects think (*arbitrantur*) that he aims at the common good and not his own. And the more that many men give strong witness on that score, the more easily is he believed (*creditur*) . . . So many (witnesses) help the subjects to recognize (*agnoscant*) that their monarchical ruler is aiming at the common good, not his own . . . The employment of the advice of (wise men) gives singular strength to a monarchical régime, so that any president can proceed to fulfil his task with the utmost confidence (*fiducia*) and to carry out a difficult task, when the assent of the great men of his principality has been given that it should be so . . . no one dares call unjust something that has issued from the counsel of many wise men; and the greater the number of them that have concurred, the greater is the respect (*veneratio*) in which their decision is held'.[2] He supports his argument by reference to Aristotle's opinion that a combination or mixture of different forms of government (in this case, rule by one and rule by the best) makes a régime more stable.[3]

The ability to win the confidence of one's subjects, then, stabilizes and also, he implies, legitimizes a king's authority. He does not, in this context, say what would happen if such legitimation were absent; he confines himself to saying that royal decrees have more 'force and authority' when they issue from wise deliberation.[4]

The term *creditus* (credibility), which was also used on occasion by the council of Basle in the same sense,[5] sums up Segovia's view in these passages. The notion of credibility is also found in Segovia's exposition of the corporation-ruler relationship, where he had made the ruler strictly accountable to the people.[6] The link between these passages goes no further, however. All that can be said of Segovia's views of the ruler-ruled relationship *in general* is that public 'credit' is bestowed on the ruler on the presumption that his acts are in the people's best interests, and that this can be presumed when numerous wise persons have been consulted and given their assent.

The idea that a properly-constituted human society was based upon trust was widespread among the ancients; Cicero in particular saw trust as the right relationship between rulers and ruled. In modern times, trust has been used in a wide variety of senses, to justify a variety of forms of government. Segovia did not employ the concept of trust in its quasi-legal sense, as meaning that the ruler was entrusted with the care of his people's interests – the meaning given to it by Cicero,[7] the medieval papacy,[8] and perhaps Locke.[9] He used it rather in a more general sense, to indicate the spiritual relationship between a good and valid government, in Church or state, and the governed. We find it used in exactly this same sense later by Vico: in describing three kinds of authority which in successive historical periods had formed the basis for government, he called the last (existing in his own day) 'that of credit or reputation for wisdom'.[10]

Segovia's idea of trust is further developed in his discussion of the concept of 'authority (*auctoritas*)',[11] to which he gave a quite specific meaning. This occurs in his last ecclesiological work in the course of his defence of *conciliar* authority; he does not ascribe 'authority' to the pope. Having noted that the term is almost wholly absent from scripture, Segovia bases his discussion on remarks by St Augustine. Authority means, in the first instance, 'clear cognition of truth ... truth made clear ... the manifestation of truth in a doubtful case. For when someone is led to perceive something as true by the testimony of another, he will say: "I now understand this to be true; I have no need of other evidence"'.[12] In other words, the processes of teaching and learning, of preaching and conversion, provide the model of authority in general. Segovia refines and elaborates Augustine's notion by emphasizing that authority, while it is first acquired by someone giving repeated evidence of the reliability of their judgment, is eventually ascribed to him even in cases where such evidence is lacking, because his judgment is now believed to be reliable. In this way, not only truth in general but also particular individuals acquire authority. Segovia sees trust in authority as a special characteristic of the area of revelation: in philosophy one considers what is said, in theology one considers who said it ('in the Christian polity one must pay special attention to the authority of the speaker').[13] But, as in the case of trust, he gives instances of its analogous occurrence outside the specifically religious sphere, in the history of ancient letters, philosophy and science (his examples are from Augustine).[14] 'Authority', he goes on, was ascribed to the 'authors' of the gospels, at first because they were able to show 'by multifarious reasoning and sometimes by the most evident of proofs, that their statements were true'; later, 'even though reasons had not been put forward proving their statements true, assent was given to their statements as being true *on their own authority*'.[15] Thus authority means: 'display of respect for the testimony of one to whom the respect is shown concerning a truth which is either made clear or *can most certainly be made clear* ... the more it is believed that someone is incapable of erring from the truth, the greater is that person's authority, that is, the more respect is shown for what he says ... even though (his sayings) are not understood, on account of the authority of the speaker; one must believe it because one knows or believes that he is unable to lie or deceive'.[16] The notion is primarily a theological one, and is closely paralleled by his notion of faith. God is the only one to whom authority may be ascribed unconditionally. He concludes that the Church (that is the general council!) also has authority on the word of Christ, who can be trusted absolutely.[17] Segovia thus ascribes authority to a specific institution, the general council. Authority is finally defined as 'a dignity of pre-eminence to whose precepts belief is given on the grounds that it (he) is able to prove that they are true or just'.[18]

Next Segovia introduces secular government into the discussion, in order to bring out the distinction between recognized and imposed authority. 'Just as (people) believed philosophers' statements because they perceived that they accorded with reason, so they believed the commandments of kings, *having experienced the prudence of their rule* ... kings were accepted by the people on account of their wisdom and virtue.' In Roman law, for instance, the reasons for a law were given with the law itself. While those who acquired royal power by force alone might claim the same 'authority', this was 'a different imposition of the name', since here acceptance was required 'before it was evident to reason that the commands were true and just'. (He may here have had in mind the history of early Rome, and possibly of some Italian city-states). When in course of time such tyrants were overthrown by aristocratic rebellion, 'then the ancient authority returned, by which reverence and veneration were shown to virtuous men, who ruled through wisdom and just laws, just as it had been shown to kings'. Similarly, in more recent times, he says, there have been princes who claimed absolute authority not by means of reason or evidence, but through arbitrary will and force. Since 'no violence is permanent', this authority could be rejected at will, just as it had been imposed at will, by any who were 'unwilling to recognize their dominion'. (One is reminded here of Bartolus' argument for the *de facto* autonomy of certain city-states). Thus, he concludes, there is a clear difference between authority that rests on '*teaching (doctrina)*', and authority which rests on '*command (imperium)*'. The former is a normal human relationship, the latter mere violent 'subjection'.[19] 'Therefore, the authority of natural and moral philosophers, of poets and of other *auctores* in any sciences has been sustained in the same manner in which it began; people venerate their names not because they have been subjected to their lordship, but on account of the manifestation of the truth of the teaching which they left behind in their writings; and thus too civil (sc. imperial) laws, on matters where they are not contradicted by municipal laws, have a position by reason of their learned teaching. Thus one can plainly see that authority in its primary sense (*ex sui primaria ratione*) means the manifestation of truth'.[20] Legitimate authority resting on willing acceptance by the ruled is thus distinguished from illegitimate rule by force.

It will be noticed that Segovia did not reconcile the various remarks he made on political authority and on the ruler-ruled relationship in general with each other. Certain consistent elements are always present, but emphasis sometimes falls on the ruler's strict accountability, sometimes on a much vaguer kind of legitimation, depending on the context and on which analogy (city-state or nation-state) he was using. He does, however, have a consistent theory of ecclesiastical authority, which he locates unswervingly in the general council; in his discussion of good counsellors in the Church, for example, he strongly implies that their absence disqualifies the ruler.[21]

His various discussions of the nature of church authority add up to an important restatement of the relationship between inherent (or *ex officio*) authority and reason (or the conviction of the individual believer). The general council is authoritative *both* because it is authorized in scripture *and* because its decision-making process can be seen to be reasonable, on the grounds that many wise persons attend, discussion is free, and so on. Thus the council is the mouthpiece of God, yet unlike the ancient prophets needs no miracles to attest the validity of its findings.[22] Segovia's elaboration of the doctrine of conciliar supremacy amounts to a *via tertia* between papal authority and the appeal to the individual conscience.

In conformity with his general views on authority, he does occasionally appeal to the perception of the ordinary Christian; as when he says that 'any Christian can see that Gabriel (sc. Eugenius IV) is not worthy to rule',[23] and 'it is evident to any Catholic that the Church in a general council is related to Christ as his mystical body'.[24] But in general he reconciles the claims of *ex officio* authority with the individual's reason by ascribing supreme ecclesiastical authority to the assembly of the learned.

Segovia's favourite terms for governmental office and authority were *presidens, presidere, presidentia,* which he generally used in preference to *princeps* and *rector.* He employed *presidentia* when speaking of Church and state, of conciliar sovereignty and consultative monarchy. The term itself was not new in any of these contexts,[25] but Segovia's regular use of it was. It suggested the status of *primus inter pares,* the first seat (or, indeed, see — *sedes*), committee chairmanship. At Basle the elective office of president of the council was specially important; Segovia's first conciliar tract was devoted to it, and in the presidency debate the Dijon prior discussed various meanings of *presidentia,* along with *principatus,* as a general term.[26] But Segovia had already started using *presidentia* as his preferred term before Basle.[27] It conveniently summed up his notion of rulership as part of a wider system, as related to consent and to be exercised through discussion.

Let us compare Segovia's notion of authority in Church and state with other possible ones, and locate him in a wider historical spectrum. Wisdom and popular consent have been the focus for conflicting doctrines. On the one hand, a 'sapiential' tradition (which both in the ancient world and in medieval and modern history looked to Plato and the 'wisdom' literature of the Old Testament) saw wisdom or sound judgment as the ultimate basis for authority. This could take the constitutional form either of meritocratic republicanism ('aristocracy') or of absolute monarchy (according to which emperor, pope or prince 'holds all the laws in the casket of his breast'). It was partly on account of the evident lack of 'wisdom' in the multitude that political power was denied to it in the period we are considering. Popular sovereignty, on the other hand, could only become a credible alternative if some displacement occurred in this schema. This was later achieved with the aid of Protestant ideas of scriptural interpretation and of the notion of individuals as capable of rational choice (the 'consumer' model of the polity). A key role must be ascribed to Rousseau's advancing of the claims of ordinary people on the basis of their moral sensibility, if they are uncorrupted; for Rousseau moral authority comes not from knowledge but from feeling: thus, it can be that the people are the truly wise. These 'populist' ideas are today still in tension with the meritocratic tradition as expounded by men such as Madison and Schumpeter.

Their absence does much to explain why the medieval communal tradition never developed into a general theory of the polity.

Segovia may be said to stand at a middle point between the Platonic and the Rousseauistic conceptions. On the one hand, inheriting the Platonic legacy through Augustine, he ascribed sapiential authority in the Church to the holy council, on the grounds that it contained many wise and virtuous persons; in secular society, he ascribed it to wise and virtuous counsellors.[28] On the 'populist' front, Segovia occasionally ascribed political knowledge and power to the 'multitude', here invoking — significantly — the *'intention* of all'. But this *ad hoc* evocation of communal theory did not take him very far; despite his close resemblance to Rousseau on the probability that face-to-face discussion in the assembly will produce heightened moral awareness and better decisions,[29] we have seen that he frequently reverted to a much less populist position. Segovia hardly provides an exception to the proposition that communal theory was hampered by lack of support from prevailing paradigmatic notions of being and mind.

But Segovia did not merely oscillate between sapiential authoritarianism and communal democracy. We have seen that he evolved his own *sui generis* view that *ordinary people, though not themselves specially wise, have enough perception to recognize wisdom in others.* The good ruler is one whom the people, in their actual experience and at least to some extent as a matter of observation, can actually trust.

This position *was* based on a prevailing paradigm of relationships — theological faith. Some medievalists say that faith was by its very nature inimical to popular participation in government.[30] Later history would suggest that this is so only when — putting it crudely — the content of faith is decreed by a contemporary human authority. Faith may of course equally well be based on individual interpretation, on the Spirit present in each believer, or on some combination of all these notions. During the later Middle Ages the development of theology as an academic discipline gave rise to new forms of the sapiential argument: as Basileans themselves said, authority belongs to those expert in 'the science of faith'.[31] We have seen that, though Segovia dropped significant hints pointing towards the 'Protestant' notion of individual authority,[32] his main emphasis was on the authority of the *'learned* believer', the trained theologian, who is to play a central role in the sovereign council.

But that is not quite all: he did not see faith in general, even in the case of non-experts, as mere blind submission, but as confidence that something is true or someone is to be obeyed on the basis of some actual evidence and 'experience'. And it is this notion of faith which leads him to envisage a relationship between ruler and ruled that involves an element of real credibility. It is this which leads him to replace the 'descending' view of the *subditus* with a view not of purely 'ascending' authority but of a relationship which shares the give-and-take of other human relationships.

NOTES

1. *MC* iii, 572 and *DRTA* xv, 652 (cf. *Hebrews* 11:1ff.); cf. *MC* iii, 640; Black (1970a), 30-2. The term *credulitas* is used in a similar way by Ockham: McGrade, 70.
2. *MC* iii, 711 (extracts in Black (1970a), 146-7); cf. *CEA* fol. 219r; *MAE* fols. 173r-v, 176v, 178r, 179r-80v, 183r-v.
3. *MC* iii, 708; cf. *MAE* fols. 172v-3v.
4. *MC* iii, 710-3; cf. *CEA* fols. 218v-9r. Below, p.191.
5. *MC* iii, 133.
6. Above, pp.162ff.
7. *De officiis*, 1.25.28 (cit. Barker, 201), *De republica*, II.23, p.160: the good ruler is 'dignitatis civilis quasi tutor et procurator reipublicae'.
8. Ullmann (1966), 48.
9. Barker in Gierke, *DGR* trans. Barker, 299-300, 348-9 (this interpretation has been much disputed, however).
10. Vico, IV. 8, p.298.
11. 'Quid sit auctoritas generaliter': *MC* iii, 840-6 (extract in Black (1970a), 152-4); cf. Black (1970a), 152n.
12. *MC* iii, 840-3.
13. *MC* iii, 843.
14. *MC* iii, 843-4; cf. Augustine, *De civitate dei*, book xviii.
15. *MC* iii, 843.
16. *MC* iii, 844-6; cf. *TP* 59-60; *MC* iii, 572, 580; *ASP* 88.
17. *MC* iii, 843.
18. *MC* iii, 843.
19. *MC* iii, 844-5; cf. Niem in Heimpel (1929), 32.
20. *MC* iii, 845.
21. Above, p.168.
22. *DRTA* xvi, 393; *MC* iii, 652.
23. *Justificatio*, fol. 210v; cf. *MAE* fols. 173v-4r.
24. *CEA* fols. 215v; *MC* iii, 647. Cf. Black (1966), 87, n. 2.
25. Cf. Niem, cit. Heimpel (1929), 32.
26. *MD* viii, 832; above, p.54.
27. E.g. *Repetitio*, fol. 165r.
28. Below, pp.191f.
29. Above, p.158.
30. Ullmann (1967), 11ff.; cf. Pocock (1975), 40-4, 47-9.
31. Above, p.111. Cf. McGrade's assessment of Ockham's view of the role of experts in correction of an erring pope: Ockham treats 'the process of correction in primarily cognitive terms' (McGrade, 53ff.).
32. Above, p.128 n.7.

CHAPTER 15

REPRESENTATION
AND SOVEREIGNTY

Identification of Church with council

There was one major gap in the thinking of Segovia and the fifteenth-century conciliarists. Their theory of ecclesial-popular sovereignty was not supported by any adequate analysis of the relationship between the council and the Church at large. This was partly glossed over by their promiscuous use of the organic analogy. This hiatus was due to the fact that they were appealing to the ultimate authority of the Church primarily, often solely, in order to bolster conciliar claims against the papacy.[1] This was why they considered the Church as juridically and even, in some of Velde's and Segovia's statements, spiritually identical with the council. Segovia argued this point in scriptural terms: 'for there is no universal council unless those present have been assembled in Christ's name. And since Christ professes himself to be present in the midst of these, it follows that the council is not divided from the Church . . . but is one with it, united and identified with it, in such a way that whatever the council does or suffers, the Church itself may be said to do or suffer. For Christ calls such councils by the name *congregatio*, when he says to Peter, "Tell the community (*ecclesiae*) . . .", and immediately afterwards adds, "For when two or three are gathered in my name (*congregati in nomine meo*), there I am in the midst of them".'[2] Matthew 18:17-20, then, clearly refers to 'the Church legitimately assembled'. This was the conciliarist equivalent to the papal doctrine of Petrine succession: it was a way of appropriating scriptural texts to existing institutions.

Secondly, Segovia characteristically employs a linguistic argument, derived from political speech. Distinguishing again between two senses of 'all', this time to prove the identity between Church and council, he says: 'It is a distinction most conformable to reason that the Church should be understood in two senses, either as it is dispersed throughout the whole world, or as it comes together in one place, as it does in a general council. So too an empire, kingdom, duchy or any great principality is customarily understood in two senses, especially when there is talk of its power or *virtus* . . . That the term "Church" applies to such an assembly is demonstrated first by the political manner of speaking (*politicus loquendi modus*); because not only all the inhabitants but also the consulate with the power of ruling the rest is called "the state (*civitas*)". . . . Moreover the scholastic doctors make most frequent use of this dual meaning (*duplicem significationem*)'.[3] The only significant difference between this notion of representation and the absorptive notion expressed in the *ecclesia-in-papa* (Church-in-pope) argument is that Segovia insisted that the Church, being a community, can only be represented by a communal assembly; he also said that the council is more like the Church than is the pope 'in nature, because all the Church's ranks, powers (*virtutes*) and gifts meet together in it'.[4] This borders on the notion of virtual representation; it also rests the council's claim in part on its containing a cross-section of the clerical community. It may perhaps best be described as a theory of symbolic representation.[5]

Segovia's excessive confidence in the 'identity' in title and power between Church and council stemmed from his view that the Church *dispersive* and the Church *collective* are but two aspects of the same entity. The *congregatio* realizes a power of self-expression, of defining the common mind, that can only be latent in the dispersed community. In applying the technical legal notion of *universitas* to the Church, Segovia and the conciliarists tended to overlook the difference between the large group, which they were calling *universitas*, and the small corporation, which the jurists had usually had in mind. The jurists, because they were dealing for the most part with groups which could literally assemble together, had no cause to develop a theory of representation of the group by the assembly. The conciliarists failed to make good this deficiency. In fact we find that, when Segovia described the pope-council relationship in terms of the *rector-universitas* relationship, he spoke precisely as if the whole Church were literally assembled in the council. This was the most serious weakness in conciliar theory.

Gierke and others have justly criticized the conciliar movement for having failed to enfranchise or attract the educated laity. The papacy could appeal to the political sentiments of kings and princes; the conciliarists, had their theology of the Church been thoroughly worked out — or indeed wholly sincere — could have appealed to the political

185

sentiments of some ordinary clergy and laity. They would perhaps have met with some response from the towns. The only group outside the council to which they granted some kind of real participation was the university doctors, and with them indeed they did form a kind of alliance.[6] To be successful in practice or consistent in theory, they would have had to learn more than they were prepared to learn from Marsiglio, Ockham and the Hussites. Championship of the ordinary faithful was left to others. Conciliarists found themselves in the weak position of one élite challenging another élite which already held power; Basle was thus reduced to a mere mandarin revolt.

Segovia and his friends did not take at all seriously the role of the Church at large in electing or in any way independently legitimizing the council which, they claimed, represented the Church; nor did they conceive any role for it in consenting to the council's conclusions. They claimed that the council was sovereign in itself, and that its decrees were not open to question by others. Partly for this reason, they had little of consequence to say about the Church-council relationship, and in this context they contributed little to the theory of representation.

All this could have been remedied if the suggestions put forward by Cusa and Velde for the genuine election of priests and bishops had been followed up. Sixteenth-century Calvinist Protestantism was to do just that.[7] Since representatives of the third estate were, in secular politics, elected (albeit on a restricted franchise), it cannot even be said that Basle and Segovia were abreast of the secular prototypes they were so fond of invoking. Their appeal to 'the Church' as their constituency had the same emotive force as the appeal to 'the people' by some later revolutionaries. The situation of Basle may thus be compared to that of the representative assembly in France in the years following the Revolution of 1789: after an initial period of genuine popular support, the democratic ideology became more shrill as the basis in public opinion became more uncertain. When the constellation of interests or the mood of the moment changed, such concepts as 'the Church' or 'the people' floated off into the realm of idle abstraction. There is a certain similarity, furthermore, in the ideological stance of council and parliament in that each invoked a theory of popular sovereignty to bolster their own claims against a monarchy, as a convenient weapon in a particular conflict. Indeed, much of the political radicalization that took place in late fifteenth-century Florence and in mid-seventeenth-century England sprang from the attempt of the represented people to realize the status to which they had been assigned; that is, to make the assembly truly representative of and accountable to the people. Possibly something similar could be said of the Reformation vis à vis the conciliar movement.

186

The gulf between assembly and people was one which the communal theory of the *universitas* (association) in its existing form did not, perhaps could not, bridge. The corporation idea had evolved in homogeneous, face-to-face societies, to which both its detailed constitutional structure and its ideology were suited. To adapt them to a nation-state or the universal Church required new constitutional mechanisms and perhaps new philosophical ideas. Direct democracy could only operate at the local level; above that it needed the organs of indirect popular sovereignty. Election was suggested by Marsiglio, Ockham and Cusa, and hints could have been found in the constitutions of the international religious orders. In a community above a certain size, as Rousseau so clearly saw, the idea of fraternal association is stretched to breaking-point, unless articulated, as it was to some extent in Switzerland and in Althusius' theory, by a confederate structure.

NOTES
1. Above, pp.20ff.
2. *TP* 103; *Justificatio*, fols. 207r-v; *MC* iii, 585-6, 685; *ASP* 147.
3. *MC* iii, 728-30, 732.
4. *MC* iii, 601; cf. *MC* iii, 602 (also in *DRTA* xv, 681), 727, 729-30, 732, 832-4, 895,918; *CEA* fol. 225r; *MAE* fol. 11v; Black (1970a), 15-22. Cf. above, p.145f.
5. Cf. Pitkin, 92ff.; *Miscellanea Mediaevalia* viii (1971), esp. 202ff.
6. Above, pp.43ff., 110ff.; though see Black (1966), 87n.
7. Troeltsch ii, 593-602, 628ff., 665; Allen (1960), 224-9.

Absolute collegiate sovereignty

Nevertheless, Segovia's creativity as a political thinker is evident in his discussion of conciliar *sovereignty*. In ascribing teaching authority to the council, he again distinguished between two senses of the word 'Church': 'The Church can be understood in two ways: in one way as the assembly (*congregatio*) of all the faithful' — and in this sense it has never assembled together since the Ascension — 'in another way it is taken in the sense in which it is said to be the teacher (*magistra*) of all the faithful . . . and in this sense "Church" means the official, ministerial, illuminated ecclesiastical body'.[1] This consists not only in the pope and bishops, but in all those categories of persons who, according to St Paul, make up the body of Christ. In his works of 1439-41, when the council of Basle was trying to deny the legitimacy of the princely neutrality, Segovia developed this notion of collegiate sovereignty, emphasizing that it involved unquestionable authority: 'The assembly of bishops, priests, doctors, preachers and pastors of the Christian people is the rule and directorate (*regula et directorium*) of all actions and questions which arise among the faithful;

187

and consequently it is the known supreme tribunal, whose definitive judgment the whole Christian community is bound to obey . . .[2] Christ, when ascending to heaven, instituted an authoritative college (*collegium auctoritativum*) made up of apostles, prophets, evangelists, pastors and doctors, and of their successors . . . which is properly called the general council'.[3] Under the Judaic dispensation authority lay with the 'college of priests and levites'; similarly, under the Christian dispensation, it also lies with the 'college of priests' or 'college of clerics'.[4] 'The college of the disciples can be called the Church in its simple and authoritative sense (*simpliciter et auctoritative*).'[5] but the council, though thus broadened in membership and made perhaps for a time actually more representative of the *clergy*, remained very much an authoritative teacher vis à vis the entire lay population.

In his *Authority of Bishops* (c. 1450), Segovia made one important change in his conciliar doctrine, arguing there that the sovereign authority of the council derived solely from the bishops who, as successors of the apostles, are the sole bearers of teaching authority and jurisdiction, which they receive immediately from God.[6] They are the essence of the council.[7] He distinguishes between the power of an individual bishop, which is operative only within his diocese, and the supreme, universal power of the assembled bishops over the whole Church;[8] he thus retained the collegiate notion of sovereignty, and the notion of the supremacy of the assembled over the dispersed Church. Others may attend a council, but not 'as judges'.[9] Doctors do not share in doctrinal decision-making; it is 'relevant' for them to attend a council because they know the ancient canons, and can therefore be of assistance when 'it is a question of the reformation (*reformatio*) of the Church'.[10]

Segovia argued the case for the ecclesiastical sovereignty of the council in such a way as to produce what we may, I think, call a general theory of sovereignty. In his early work on ecclesiastical and secular power (1426), he had distinguished three types of 'superiority (*praeferre*)': that of nature, as gold is superior to silver; that of 'influence', as the heavenly bodies influence the earthly; and that of 'ordering or directing subordinates in matters of action'. He says (following Aquinas) that before the Fall, while there was no superiority (*praelatio*) for the correction of evil, there was *praelatio* 'as regards the useful and convenient rule of subjects', because man is a social being. But, after the Fall, 'it was necessary that there should be some governors of society who should carefully aim at the common good'.[11] In his works of 1439, he developed this much further. Every human association has 'some common superior (entity) (*aliquod commune superius*) to which it has recourse' in order to resolve disputes. 'It is the same in a city and a kingdom; nor is there or was there ever any organized society of men except there was assigned in it a certain and known tribunal of judgment (*certum et notum tribunal iudicii*), in whose statement (*diffinitioni*) that whole society is bound to acquiesce . . .' (otherwise, there would be divisions in the Church, just as these are) 'contradictory opinions and conflicting actions in nations, and unless they have some common entity (*aliquod commune*), by whose judgment they are bound to stand, each person will try to establish for himself some party (*partem*) in that society agreeable to his opinions.' There must be order in the Church, because it is made by God; and for order 'it is necessary to assign in it some supreme tribunal of judgment'.[12] Since it was a doctrinal dispute that was uppermost in Segovia's mind, he emphasized in particular the need to avoid 'contradictory opinions'. His notion of unquestionable authority could hardly be stronger: 'subjects are bound to believe (*credere*) (their superior's) judgment rather than their own, and in a certain way to enslave their intellects into obeisance (*obsequium*) to their superior'.[13]

He also, in his attack on the princely neutrality, developed the argument for sovereignty as a *general political* norm: 'It is well known to all who understand the principles of moral or political philosophy, that for the ordered government of any society of men there must necessarily be assigned some supreme authority or power in accordance with which, through written or verbal laws, simple men, of whom there is a greater number than of wise, must regulate their actions . . . We see this same need in any city or kingdom. And just as *presidentia* is necessary for the proper government of a society of men, so too subjection to that supreme power is necessary on the part of the subordinates'.[14]

For 'among men there easily arise offences . . . Human society cannot otherwise exist, except there be assigned in a determinate manner a superior authority of judgment'.[15] This was the same notion of sovereignty, and also the same kind of argument for it, as had been expressed by fourteenth-century papalists,[16] was developed by Torquemada,[17] and would later be used by Bodin[18] and other post-renaissance political thinkers down to Austin.[19] But, whereas the papalists and many later royalists expressed sovereignty in monarchical terms, as a quality which could only fully be realized in rule by one, Segovia, since he was arguing for a collegiate sovereign, expressed sovereignty in more general terms, as 'some common superior entity (*aliquod commune superius*)'. In this respect his view is more precisely comparable with that of Bodin or Austin.

Segovia also anticipated Bodin in identifying sovereignty as specifically legislative power (*auctoritas diffiniendi*). This arose out of his endorsement of the general Basilean view – also held by Marsiglio – that legislative power is separable from executive power and superior to it. Ultimate authority in government consists in the power to make law, to which the power to execute law is subordinate.[20] 'Judgment on execution must conform itself to judgment on definition'.[21] The pope as executive is constitutionally dependent upon and responsible to the council as legislature; the council can depose any bad 'minister', including the pope.[22] Though the pope's office is endowed by Christ, 'in its use and execution he is submitted to the judgment of the Church'.[23] The council may execute its own decrees if the pope refuses to.[24] Most clearly of all, 'The giving of laws, by which any state (*politia*) must be regulated, is an unquestionable witness of the superiority existing in the founder of those same laws (*editio legum . . . irrefragabile est testimonium de superioritate sistente in ipsarum legum conditore*)'.[25] As so often, Segovia refined the *ad hoc* views of other conciliarists into a more comprehensive statement of political theory.

On the other hand, in his later writings, he asserts against 'petty scholars' who wish to model papal power on that of 'the rectors of Paris university' that no automatic time-limit can be placed on the tenure of the papacy; the pope is the Church's vicar 'perpetual and for life'.[26] Nor can the power of the papacy be divided, he now says; it is 'indivisible' and (as some modern theorists of sovereignty were to say) is 'either total or nothing at all';[27] he even ascribes to the pope 'fulness of power'.[28] These statements occur in Segovia's late works, when he modified his theory of conciliar supremacy and compared the Church to a monarch with aristocratic elements;[29] what he appears to mean by this is that the pope-in-council is sovereign.

Thus Segovia defended conciliar sovereignty *over the pope* by invoking a political theory of popular sovereignty and governmental accountability; and he defended conciliar sovereignty *over the Church* by invoking a political theory of absolute sovereignty. He used the *universitas-rector* model to explain the relationship between council and pope, the sovereign-subjects model to explain that between council and Church. He made no attempt to reconcile these two models, apart from applying to them both the criterion of trust.[30]

NOTES

1. *CEA* fol. 206v; *TP* 62; *MC* ii, 107 and iii, 684; cf. Gerson, *OC* 133-4.
2. *CEA* fol. 218v. cf. *DRTA* xiv, 389-90.
3. *MC* iii, 651; cf. *CEA* fol. 218r; *Dicta*, fol. 149r; *Justificatio*, fol. 207r; *MC* ii, 29-30 and iii, 730.
4. *CEA* fols. 209v-10r, 192r; *MC* iii, 824; cf. *Decretum* C. 6, c. vii, q. 1 in *Corpus*, i, 568.
5. *CEA* fol. 210r; cf. Sigmund (1963), 146n.; Marschall.

6. *MAE* fols. 18v, 56v, 74v-5r; *MC* iii, 911; cf. Black (1971).
7. *MAE* passim.
8. *MAE* fols. 87r-v, 98r-v, 171r-2v, 192r; *MC* iii, 773; cf. Gerson, above, p.22; Congar (1965), esp. 129.
9. *MAE* fols. 21r-33r.
10. *MAE* fols. 23r, 172r.
11. *Repetitio*, fols. 135v-6r, 138r, 165r.
12. *CEA* fols. 206r-7r; cf. *Repetitio*, fol. 136v.
13. *CEA* fol. 216r; *MC* iii, 639; cf. Jüterbog, *Determinatio*, 361; and above, pp.176ff
14. *DRTA* xiv, 375.
15. *DRTA* xiv, 376.
16. Ullmann (1949), 114ff.; Wilks (1963), 151-4, 288-9.
17. Black (1970a), 73-80.
18. I, c. 8; Mesnard, 480ff.
19. Austin, 194.
20. *CEA* fol. 216r; *MC* iii, 649, 798, 867; cf. above, pp.51, 54ff.
21. *CEA* fol. 219r.
22. *TP* 51-2, 94-6; *CEA* fol. 219v; *Liber*, fols. 24r, 25v-6v, 28r, 54r-v, 56r.
23. *TP* 56.
24. *TP* 53-6, 61; *CEA* fol. 219r.
25. *DRTA* xiv, 385; cf. *CEA* fol. 216r; *MC* iii, 639.
26. *MC* iii, 773, 783.
27. *MAE* fol. 182r.
28. *MAE* fols. 164v, 166v.
29. *MAE* fols. 173v-83v, esp. fol. 175v; *MC* iii, 707-9.
30. Above, pp.180ff.

Parliamentary monarchy

In two late works Segovia, attempting to answer the charge that conciliarism was inimical to monarchy as commonly understood in a secular context, expounded a theory of parliamentary monarchy for the national or territorial state. 'The synodal doctrine' (he says) does not impugn monarchy, but upholds the principles of true monarchy, a régime in which a king rules in accordance with the laws and employs wise counsellors; he obtains, and is seen to obtain, their consent prior to any legislative or executive enactment. Segovia contrasted this with the false monarchy advocated by Eugenius' supporters, who would place the king above the law and give him arbitrary power; this would be neither politic nor just. Conciliar doctrine enhances the monarch's glory, which is greatest when he is attended by his counsellors and magnates;[1] prior consultation gives royal decrees greater 'force and authority (*robur et auctoritatem*)'.[2] Segovia, however, nowhere invokes the divine right of kings in any form — a rather striking omission — and remarks that God alone can be said to rule 'absolutely'.[3]

Segovia claimed that the type of monarchy he was advocating was the normal current practice in states which called themselves monarchical:

'In both secular and ecclesiastical government all princes as a general rule govern with consultation . . .'[4] In every polity which is directed by a royal principate this same thing is observed (*observatur*), that *curiae generales*' (this could mean either select advisers or representative assemblies) 'are often held'.[5] There was more truth in this last statement in Segovia's day than there would be a hundred or even fifty years later; and it is no coincidence that, in Segovia, Spain produced one of the major constitutionalists of the fifteenth century. For the Cortes of Castile, Segovia's homeland, were at the height of their power in the early fifteenth century, and played an important part in political disputes during the 1440s; while in Aragon and Catalonia the estates met regularly during this period and had established the *justicia* to oversee the royal government between their meetings.[6] The Aragonese conquest of Sicily and of southern Italy (the latter completed in 1443) led to the development in those countries of the Aragonese form of parliamentary monarchy.[7] (A petition of the Castilian Cortes in 1445 may even have been influenced by the language of *Haec Sancta* when it said that 'no persons *of whatever rank*, estate or condition, pre-eminence or dignity, *even if they are royal* or of royal stock' can be pardoned for treason against the king.)[8]

Segovia's conception of 'parliamentary monarchy', of the Christian monarch who would govern by law and counsel, was in accord with an emerging pattern of political thought which became popular in the following generations, and which conformed in varying degrees with political practice. It was differentiated from tyranny, from the 'despotism' of the Turks, by its ethical norms, by the supposition that the king would act *as if* formal legality and consultation were the token of legitimate rule, even though no definite sanctions were contemplated. Here there is common ground between Segovia, Erasmus and Bodin:[9] Bodin too would say that, while formal sanctions against the king were repugnant to orderly government, it was both normal and advisable for him to consult the estates general.[10] Exactly like Segovia, he would say that the monarch was most glorious when surrounded by the assembled estates.[11]

Segovia's ideas in 1449-53 clearly lack internal consistency and juridical rigour. There is no indication whether he had actually abandoned the Basilean belief in the full jurisdictional powers of the council and reverted to the notion of the council as intermittent legislature and emergency superior of the pope. While some of his statements on the papacy at this time suggest that he might have done so, the truth probably is that he wanted to reconcile papal and conciliar claims in any way that would enable something of the conciliarist programme to survive. He certainly never thought out his modified position systematically.

He was now propounding side by side two contradictory models, the corporational and the quasi-monarchical. This in itself was not unusual for the period. Many people held that different régimes were appropriate for different states. A city might be governed as a republic verging on a democracy, and yet accept imperial authority. From Aquinas to Machiavelli there was a widespread tradition that princely and popular government each had their proper time or place. There was as yet little cross-fertilization between the political *moeurs* and ideology of corporations and towns, on the one hand, and those of national states or territorial fiefs, on the other.[12] Not till the English revolution, one might almost say, would there be an attempt to re-model the large state on republican principles. But Segovia tried to deploy both these models in discussing the same polity, the Church. No doubt his evocation of parliamentary monarchy was largely tactical, to soothe princely sensibilities. One may say that he used the populist association and the republican city to show what the constitution of the Church really is; and then subsequently explained that the result can look like consultative monarchy. Within the Church itself, after 1449 he sometimes avoided discussion of a pope-council confrontation; possibly he was reverting to the notion of the council as occasional legislator. Yet even in his monarchical passages he places more stringent limits on the pope than on other monarchs; for instance, he says that the pope must consult the cardinals 'not only at his free choice but out of constitutional necessity (*ex regiminis necessitate*)'.[13] Once again, the only connection between his different models is the potentially ambivalent concept of trust.

NOTES;
1. *MC* iii, 710-11.;
2. *MC* iii, 710-13; cf. *CEA* fols. 218v-19r.
3. *MC* iii, 723. Cf. *Vindiciae* and other Huguenot tracts, of which Allen says: 'they all assert vigorously that there exists no absolute sovereignty save that of God': Allen (1960), 315. On Milton to the same effect, Gooch, 155.
4. *MC* iii, 710.
5. *MC* iii, 894; cf. *MC* iii, 803.
6. Cf. Merriman, i, 217ff., 428ff., 460ff., 481.
7. Marongiu, 148ff., 157ff.
8. *Cortes . . . Castilla*, iii, 492; cf. above, p.17.
9. Cf. Erasmus, 571-2, 576; Bodin II, c. 2 at pp.54-6 and c. 3 at p.60.
10. Bodin I, c. 8 at pp.31-2; cf. Machiavelli, *The Prince*, c. 22 at p.124.
11. Bodin I, c. 8 at pp.31-2; cf. *MC* iii, 710-11.
12. Cf. Ullmann (1966), 220, 227.
13. *MC* iii, 710.

CONCLUSION

CHAPTER 16

CONCILIARISM
AND POLITICAL THOUGHT

Two inter-locking aspects of conciliarism *qua* political theory require definition: its place in the history of European political ideas, and its own distinctive character. Mention must first be made of Jacques Almain[1] and John Mair (Major),[2] two Paris doctors who wrote in support of the abortive council of Pisa (1511-12); for these both saw conciliar supremacy as an application to the Church of generally valid political norms. They added little of substance to what earlier conciliarists had said, but they stated their argument with great clarity and consistency; and Oakley has made a strong case for their influence on later parliamentarian thought. Almain developed d'Ailly's and Gerson's argument that conciliar supremacy was based on natural justice: every community, like every organism, has an inalienable right of self-preservation.[3] Coercive power belongs primarily to the community as a whole, and only by delegation to the ruler who is a part of the whole;[4] just as the king holds power by delegation from the community, so the pope holds it by delegation from the Church.[5] The community transmits power to the prince for the sake of its own well-being; thus it always retains within itself a greater power, and always has the right to depose the prince if he acts contrary to the public good.[6] Both Almain and the Scotsman Mair, who reproduced the salient points of Almain's argument, maintained – much as the bishop of Burgos and others had done at Basle[7] – that in a true *politia regalis* (royal polity), the ruler has greater power than any individual member, but less than the whole community. Their conciliarism is Constantian rather than Basilean: they see the council as the emergency ('occasional'), not the normal, juridical

194

superior. As Mair puts it, just as 'the king is above any single person and above the whole kingdom as a rule (*regulariter*), and the kingdom is above him occasionally and in a particular instance (*casualiter et in aliquo eventu*)', so too 'the pope is regularly above any single person and occasionally above all dispersed Christians, but when a universal council is assembled, it is above the Roman pontiff'.[8]

NOTES

1. Oakley (1964b); Brosse, 185-330; Bäumer (1971), 67ff.
2. Oakley (1962), 12ff., and (1964b); Burns, 90-1.
3. *De dominio*, 963-4, 971ff.; *De auctoritate*, 978C, 997C-D, 1009. Cf. above, p.20.
4. *De dominio*, 972; *De auctoritate*, 977D.
5. *De auctoritate*, 991.
6. *De dominio*, 964C, 972; *De auctoritate*, 978C, Cf. above, pp.162ff.
7. *ASP* 28ff.; *MC* iii, 261; cf. Black (1970a), 12n.
8. Mair, 1141B; cf. Mair, 1135D, 1137B; Almain, *De auctoritate*, 979, 996C.

Parliamentarism

Conciliarism has long been recognized as an important phase in European political thought;[1] the two best-known late-medieval political thinkers, Marsiglio and Cusa, were both conciliarists. The conciliar movement has been regarded as the most far-reaching and sophisticated attempt at representative and constitutional government in this period. It is worth recalling the claims made on behalf of the conciliarists by Figgis and Oakley respectively. '(The conciliarists) appear to have discerned more clearly than their predecessors the meaning of the constitutional experiments which the past two centuries had seen in considerable profusion, to have thought out the principles that underlay them, and based them upon reasoning that applied to all political societies ... they raised the constitutionalism of the past three centuries to a higher power, expressed it in a more universal form, and justified it on grounds of reason, policy and scripture.'[2] 'These conciliarists are making claims more universal than many of those advanced later by constitutionalists whose memory has been more widely honoured ... In going one step further (sc. than basing their claims on consent and positive law) and grounding them in natural law itself, these conciliarists are doing nothing less than taking the doctrine of consent that is basic to much of medieval legal and constitutional theory and practice, disengaging it from the particularising elements of regional, national or ecclesiastical custom, and raising it to the level of a political philosophy.'[3] I would not dispute these claims. One may add that, in terms of actual constitutional practices, the decree *Frequens* applied to the universal Church the same principle of frequent and regular assemblies that was already established in Aragon-Catalonia;[4] while the council of Basle went further than any contemporary secular counterpart — apart from the city-states — in subjecting the ruler to the assembly. Its conception and implementation of the legislative sovereignty of the assembly was more developed than any other of its time; its attempted takeover of day-to-day judicial and administrative business[5] was, if not quite unprecedented, revolutionary. In a word, conciliarism attempted to apply to the universal Church practices that would only much later be applied to large states.

The striking development, during the conciliar period, of representative institutions with some constitutional powers in Germany may have owed something to the conciliar movement itself. The most impressive such development took place in Saxony. During the 1430s, owing to a ducal minority, the estates took a greater part in government; at the first full Diet, held at Leipzig in 1438, the estates were given the role of supervising taxation; during the civil war of 1446-51 duke Frederick summoned frequent meetings of the Diet, to which he gave regular accounts of his expenditure.[6] Saxony was particularly well represented at Basle, and Leipzig university was strongly conciliarist.[7] Carsten observes, moreover, that in the ecclesiastical principalities the estates 'were usually dominated by the cathedral chapter of the see'.[8] In the empire itself, the Reichstag met with unprecedented frequency during the neutrality (1439-46); the influence of conciliarism on imperial constitutional thought is evident in the case of Cusa, who recommended regular Reichstags on analogy with church councils.[9] (The *Reformatio Sigismundi*, which contained similar and other, more far-reaching proposals, may have been submitted to the council of Basle in 1439).[10] Poland is an instance of a country which had shown significant support for Basle and which subsequently developed an exceptionally powerful Diet.[11]

Oakley has produced extensive evidence from which he argues that conciliarism was an important influence upon parliamentarian constitutionalism in the sixteenth and seventeenth centuries.[12] He notes that Richer's publication of Gerson, d'Ailly, Almain and Mair made available 'a whole arsenal of conciliar arguments', that there was 'a veritable reception of conciliar arguments in England at this time'; and that one edition of Foxe's *Book of Martyrs* devoted one hundred pages to the activities of Basle.[13] The writings and actions of the conciliar movement were cited in England by bishop Ponet, William Prynne, William Bridge, John White and others.[14] Prynne had read Piccolomini's account of the deposition debate and the events of 1439-40, and cited the secular precedents produced by the bishop of Burgos in support of papal deposition.[15] In support of his view that the king is 'greater than each but less than all (*singulis maior, universis minor*)', Prynne remarks that in the Church 'a council was at last resolved to be above the pope'.[16] Rueger finds a connection between the person-office distinction as used by Gerson and its use by parliamentarians in 1642-4, especially by Rutherford.[17] The most often-cited conciliarists appear to have been d'Ailly, Gerson, Almain and Mair;[18] which suggests that Paris university was the intermediary. Oakley argues that conciliarist influence was particularly strong upon the *Vindiciae* and George Buchanan,[19] whose 'Rights of the crown in Scotland (*De iure regni apud Scotos*)' appeared in 1578.[20] The evidence is indisputable in the case of Buchanan, who was taught by Mair at St Andrews,[21] and who in turn influenced Rutherford.[22] In addition, we may note that Rutherford had probably taken from Cusa his idea (or at least his manner of expressing it) that the royal power is 'in the people . . . radically and virtually, as in the first subject', and comes from the people 'by a virtual emanation'. He supported this with the naturalist argument, as used by d'Ailly, Gerson, Almain and Mair, that 'all living creatures have radically in them a power of self-preservation'; and also with the ('Bartolist') example of cities which 'have power to choose and create inferior magistrates'.[23] In general, the transmission of conciliarist ideas to the parliamentarians may be accounted for by the continued currency of conciliar doctrine at Paris throughout the sixteenth and seventeenth centuries.[24] The chief points on which the parliamentarians cited conciliar theory and practice were the popular origin of political power, the at least occasional supremacy of the representative assembly over the prince, and – above all, I think – the legitimacy of deposing a king.

Conciliarist influence may be detected in other quarters as well. Some of the Spanish neo-scholastics, for example Vitoria (who studied at Paris from 1507 to 1522)[25] and Suarez,[26] might have taken some of their political ideas on these same points from the conciliarists. We have noted the influence of conciliarism at Cracow; and we find a sixteenth-century Polish constitutionalist, Zaborowski, saying that the king is 'not lord . . . but *rector*' and that the 'whole community' is his superior.[27] During the revolt of the Netherlands in 1572 it was siad that 'the legitimate and regular power of the kings, no less than the unity and prosperity of the nation and provinces, resides principally in the assembly of the estates, which occupies the same place in civil society as the councils in the Church'.[28] Finally, à propos themes which have emerged in this study, the distinction between the community taken collectively and taken as individuals was employed by the *Vindiciae*, John Knox[29] and others. The identification of the collective community with the representative assembly, however spurious in reality, was restated by a whole school of parliamentarians who, like the conciliarists, were as often as not concerned to establish not so much the literal sovereignty of the whole community, but

197

rather the sovereignty of the assembly over the prince. They repeatedly invoked the collective sovereignty of the whole, using it almost as a kind of myth which others (such as the Levellers) would wish to turn into a reality. Henry Parker said in 1640 that 'the whole Kingdom is not so properly the author as the essence itself of Parliaments'; parliament is 'the very people itself, artificially congregated . . . indeed (it is) the State itself'.[30] An anonymous writer, following Parker, put the same idea in Cusan language: parliament is 'radically and fundamentally by representation . . . the whole kingdom', and supreme power lies with the people 'though dormant till it be by the Parliament thought fit to be awakened'.[31] This was exactly what Gerson and the Basle conciliarists had been saying à propos the Church.[32]

Yet one must beware of ascribing influence[33] in cases where all that may have been involved was a convergence of ideas and a citation of convenient precedents. Obviously, several local national traditions of representative and constitutional government had evolved prior to and independently of the conciliar movement. It is doubtful, for example, whether the constitutional monarchy of Podebrady in mid-fifteenth century Bohemia[34] owed much, if anything, to conciliarism. Fortescue's ideas on the 'royal polity (*politia regalis*)' (expressed in the 1460s), while in some respects similar to Segovia's ideas on parliamentary monarchy, were derived from English custom and the general Thomist tradition of political thought.[35] To a certain extent one can regard conciliarism and parliamentarism as twin offshoots of a common stock of ideas. English and French constitutionalists were developing earlier secular ideas about the rule of law and quasi-popular parliamentary sovereignty, to which was added a significant influx of Protestant, and especially neo-Calvinist, political ideas, such as the notion of kingship as an ordinary calling or ministry (as we find it, for example, in the *Vindiciae*).[36] It seems to me unnecessary to suppose that conciliarism affected the basic tenor of their thought, except in cases where there is clear evidence of direct influence, as with Buchanan, Vitoria and possibly Rutherford. It is surely no coincidence that secular constitutionalism was generally successful in Protestant communities. However, for religious-minded persons in the sixteenth century, the conciliarist example may have helped remove deep-seated qualms about the legitimacy of deposing a crowned monarch.

NOTES

1. Gierke, *DRG* trans. Maitland, 47-58; Figgis, esp. at p.47; Oakley (1962) and (1969), 385-6; Rueger.
2. Figgis, 47.
3. Oakley (1969), 385-6.
4. Marongiu, 65-76. Cf. above, p.192.

5. Above, pp.30f.
6. Carsten, 196-8, and (for contemporary developments in other German principalities), 264-5, 354.
7. Dickens, 171; above, pp.110ff.
8. Carsten, 423.
9. *CC* III, xxv; cf. *CC* III, xii; cf. Molitor, 140-1, 159, 172-205.
10. Dickens, 10-11.
11. Above, pp.112f.
12. Oakley (1962) and (1969).
13. Oakley (1969), 374-6.
14. Oakley (1962), 3-11.
15. Oakley (1962), 8; *ASP* 28-30, also cited by Buchanan (at p.8).
16. Oakley (1962), 5; cf. Oakley (1969), 376n.
17. Rueger, 474ff.; Rutherford's *'Lex rex* or the law and the prince' appeared in 1640.
18. Oakley (1969), 376n; cf. Rueger, 484.
19. Oakley (1962), 10, 12ff., 20ff.; Oakley (1969), esp. 374-6.
20. Allen (1960), 338.
21. Allen (1960), 336-7; Oakley (1962), 29-30; Burns, 101-4; Rueger, 484.
22. Rueger, 474.
23. Rutherford, 6; cf. above, pp.20, 172ff.
24. Martin (1919), 360ff.; Martimort, 19, 48, 50-4.
25. Villoslada, 163-4, 173-4.
26. Below, pp.202f.; cf. Hamilton. 39-40, 61-3, 69-70.
27. ed. Lepszy, 139ff.
28. Cit. Mesnard, 366.
29. Mornay, q. 3, 85ff. at p.89; Knox cit. Burns, 101-2; Buchanan, 31-2; cf. below, pp.202-4.
30. Cit. Allen (1938), 432.
31. Cit. Allen (1938), 433.
32. Above, pp.20ff., 113ff.
33. Cf. Oakley (1962), 30; for pertinent remarks on the question of influence, Tierney (1975), 253-5.
34. Heymann (1965), 389, 589.
35. Chrimes, 300-44.
36. Troeltsch ii, 561ff., 602ff.

Society as an organic whole

If we ask wherein lay the *originality* of conciliar theorists, we must look to the two lines of thought that have been the focus of this study: organic association and communal decision-making. These notions were more fully and systematically developed by conciliarists than by any other thinkers of their time, partly because they arose directly out of the theological bases of conciliar theory, partly because, in the case of the Basle thinkers, the notions of mixed government and of constitutional restraints were superceded by the ascription of unlimited sovereignty to the council.[1]

First, the theory of the conciliar movement as it developed in the fifteenth century, and especially during Basle, is a classic instance of the reification of the community, of the conception of society as a real organic whole. The notion of the community as an entity with a real corporate existence over and above any of its individual members is a common feature in simple or 'primitive' tribal lore. If European medievalists, most notably Gierke[2] and, more recently, Ullmann,[3] have termed such holist communitarian conceptions 'Germanic', this is largely because medieval Europe was peopled by Germanic tribes; no one would deny that the early Greeks also hypostasized their social bonds, as have Slavic and African peoples. What Gierke believed to be the peculiarly Germanic notion of association was in part a general tribal notion; no wonder he could contrast it with the 'atomist' notions of Roman law, which issued from a far more sophisticated milieu. The idea epitomized in the ancient adage of significantly uncertain origin, *vox populi, vox dei* — consultation of the people being a kind of oracular process — corresponded broadly (as both Gierke and Weber point out) to the 'patriarchal communism (*Hauskommunismus*)'[4] often found in early society. This notion of the people as a homogeneous, hypostasized group was invoked by romantic populists of the nineteenth century, took new life from the Marxist reification of the proletariat (or, in many countries, 'the people' *tout court*), and is to be found in many parts of the modern world.

Organic holism has long been recognized as a salient theme in medieval thought,[5] and Gierke was absolutely right in saying that it was eaten into by the combined forces of Roman-canon law and civic-bourgeois culture. Prior to the ascendancy of nominalism, it received added force from the theological concept of the mystical body of Christ. But its constitutional implications were altogether indeterminate. I do not doubt Wilks' thesis that for a time it was used to underpin papal monarchy[6] (much as Hegel regarded the monarch as expressing the 'subjective' will of the whole community, itself conceived by him as a 'historical individual'). Yet in early societies the more prevalent idea seems to have been that the assembly of notables or the whole adult male population expressed the common mind (as in the *Thing*). This was the path followed by both conciliarists and parliamentarians: the common mind of society finds expression in the representative assembly. In arguing towards this conclusion, Velde developed the organic-holist notion of society further than had any other medieval thinker; his neoplatonic-realist view of the social essence is paralleled by no one but Hegel. This was partly because a mystical approach was invited by the ecclesiastical context in which Velde and others wrote; and partly because they had to find an alternative for the electoral and episcopal theories of conciliar sovereignty, both of which they rejected or avoided. For obvious circumstantial reasons, conciliarists used organic realism to support a collective rather than a monist sovereign.

As regards organic holism, Hegel and Gierke himself might be said to approximate more closely than any other modern European thinkers to Basle-conciliarist ideas. But this is an illusory comparison, insofar as both Hegel and Gierke, especially the latter, gave a stronger meaning to the real personality of the *whole* group as distinct from the representative assembly.[7] Gierke was right when he denied that the thinkers of this period understood group personality in the full sense he gave it; they saw it only in literal, physical terms – as the assembly of all – or in terms of a merely mental association, a 'moral person' as later thinkers such as Pufendorf and Rousseau called it. Gerson, Segovia and the rest saw the whole ecclesial community as a purely spiritual whole, which could only act as a legislative, juridical whole in the general council. Their ascription of sovereignty to the whole Church was a metaphorical argument of convenience; 'the dispersed church' has power in an 'unformed and potential' way and can do nothing except through the council.

Madison defined the unique contribution of Europe to political development as the theory and practice of representative assemblies.[8] The ancient polities of Greece and Rome had not built up representation on anything approaching the regular basis achieved in medieval states; here, the patristic ecumenical councils and the early-medieval provincial synods pointed the way.[9] Through representation the abstract 'mind of the people' was given a tangible organ of self-expression, and the way was paved for indirect democracy in extensive territorial units. In utilizing the realist notion of society to this end, the conciliar movement provides one of the first instances of a political tradition that became one characteristic of the ensuing 'early-modern' epoch. The notion of society as a whole as comprising a superior entity, to which the prince is subject, remained a staple meaning of 'popular sovereignty' and a staple element in parliamentary-constitutionalist ideology down to the eighteenth century. Even after this had been replaced, in Anglo-American and French thought, by an individualist notion of society and of representation, it survived elsewhere. I have argued that the fifteenth-century conciliarists (with the exception of Niem and Cusa) dismissed the electoral theory of representation, and so contributed little new in this sphere. Yet they – and Segovia in particular – did develop a theory of representation by typification: the council must be like the Church, must be a plurality, and must contain a cross section of the clerical personnel.[10]

NOTES

1. Above, pp.28ff., 51, 54ff.
2. Gierke, *DGR* i, 3ff., 14ff., 220ff.; cf. J.D. Lewis, Ch. 3.
3. Ullmann (1966), 22-3; cf. Ullmann (1975), 195, 204.
4. Gierke, *DGR* i, 12ff.; M. Weber (1927), ch. 1.
5. See esp. E. Lewis (1938).

6. Wilks (1963), 36ff., 60-1, 527.
7. J.D. Lewis, *passim.*
8. *The federalist*, no. 14, pp.100-1.
9. Marongiu, 19-20, 30-1.
10. Above, pp.185, 187f.

The collective-distributive distinction: conciliarism and contractarianism

The clearest instance of the conciliar movement's evocation of a line of thought that was to become typical of the early-modern period is the collective-distributive distinction, the significance of which for the development of modern political thought merits some attention. We have seen how this distinction, first clearly stated by Gerson, became common currency for Segovia and the conciliarists of Basle.[1] Thereafter it entered the mainstream of political thought. The *Vindiciae* states that 'as the whole people (*universus populus*) is superior to the king, so too (the officials representing them), while inferior to him as individuals (*singuli*), should as a whole (*universi*) be considered superior to him'.[2] Such a statement could have been derived from the jurists and need owe nothing to the conciliarists. But Suarez, on the other hand, used it in a manner strongly reminiscent of Segovia, whom he may possibly have read – and he used it in the context of an embryonic theory of the social contract. Suarez was countering the view that governmental power comes to a king directly from God. 'The power of being lord or of ruling men politically was not given by God immediately to any particular man'; rather, 'by force of the law of nature alone this power is in the community of men'. He supports this by making a distinction very similar to that used by Segovia: 'It is proved that (governmental power) is in men ... and not in individuals (*singulis*) or in any one person specifically; therefore it is in the collectivity (*collectione*); for the distinction is adequate. In order that this may be better understood, it must be noted that a multitude of men may be considered in two ways: first, as a certain aggregate (*aggregatum*) without any order, without any physical or moral unity, in such a way that they do not make up any one entity (*efficiunt unum quid*) either physically or morally; and therefore they are not one political body (*corpus politicum*) and consequently do not need one head or prince. So in men considered thus there is not yet understood to be this power properly or formally ... A multitude of men may be considered in another way, as when by special will or common consent they assemble together into one political body (*in unum corpus politicum congregantur*) with one bond of partnership, and in order that they may help one another (they are consituted) in an order for one political end, in such a way that they make up one

202

mystical body, which can be called morally one in itself; and this consequently does need one head. In this kind of community, as such, there is this power by the nature of the case (*ex natura rei*), in such a way that it is not in the power of men thus to assemble together and yet to prevent (the emergence of) this power'.[3]

The kind of distinction made here between two modes of human association, and indeed the grammatical structure, suggest that Suarez was drawing on the passage in Segovia's *Presidency* (of which numerous copies survived) where Segovia had distinguished between the church *qua* unified mystical body and *qua* dispersed political body (though the terms mystical and political body are used differently by Suarez, indeed almost synonymously).[4] Suarez' point is that the decision of men to band together necessarily entails the emergence of monarchical power. Whereas Segovia was distinguishing between the Church as a divinely-instituted charismatic union and as an ordinary human organization, Suarez was distinguishing between a society formed for a common purpose and an inchoate aggregate of men. Indeed they draw opposite constitutional conclusions, Segovia saying that the closer union needs no single head, Suarez saying that it does.

After Suarez, of course, theorists of the social contract consistently contrasted the loosely-knit, anarchic nature of human society prior to the contract (whatever form this might take) with its more tightly-knit nature thereafter. For Hobbes it is the existence of sovereign power which gives society a 'real unity'.[5] for Locke it is the consent of the members which produces 'one body politic';[6] while Rousseau gave societal unity the strongest meaning of all, when he said that 'the collective body . . . receives from (the act of association) its unity, its dispersed self, and its will'.[7] While such a distinction, in itself rather obvious and certainly to be found in sources other than the conciliarists, was given special emphasis by both the conciliarists and the contractarians, they of course gave it different meanings. The conciliarists, like Aristotle and the jurists, were distinguishing two ways in which the same society could be regarded; they then went on to equate a society in its collective mode with the assembly. For them, therefore, a society might pass from its dispersed to its collective form, and back again, time after time, depending on whether the council was in session or not. The contractarians, on the other hand, conceived the transition from the dispersed to the collective mode as more deeply rooted in social attitudes and political consensus. Nevertheless, the two schools have at least one point in common: they both thought that society in its collective form possessed radically different, in fact far greater, powers in the legislative and juridical sphere than did society in its dispersed form.

The contractarians were indebted to medieval corporation theory in another way. The late-medieval lawyers, in the course of dealing with conflicts that arose in business partnerships, defined the *societas* (a partnership or voluntary association entered into for specific ends, usually business) as something which was 'entered into by contract (*contractu initur*)'; and they proceeded to discuss the respective rights of the contracting parties (particularly in relation to their input of capital or labour), and the proper decision-making procedures for such a group.[8] Grotius argued that a society (in this specific sense) depended upon the 'will of those entering the society . . . that there should be a certain method (*ratio*) for negotiating business'; *inter alia*, majority decisions must be accepted as binding.[9] We find the same language and the same doctrine of the majority verdict being adopted by the contractarians, just as the conciliarists were wont to borrow the majority principle from corporation procedures. Thus Hobbes said that adoption of the majority principle was one mark of the transformation of a 'multitude' into a 'state (*civitas*)'.[10] And Locke declared that 'when any number of men have so consented to make one community or government, they are thereby presently *incorporated*, and *make one body politic*' — the same language that was used by lawyers when discussing colleges or corporations — 'wherein the majority have a right to act and conclude the rest'.[11] It seems probable that we have here a further instance of the influence of corporation lore on later political theory.

NOTES
1. Above, pp.21, 64ff., 148ff.
2. Mornay, q. 3, pp.86-7, 89; cf. Bodin II, c. 6, p.69. Cf. above, p.197f.
3. Suarez, *De legibus*, vol. ii, book 3, c. 2, p.202; Gough, 67ff.; Hamilton, 33.
4. Above, pp.150ff.
5. Hobbes, c. 18, p.112.
6. Locke, *Second treatise*, ch. 8.
7. *Du contrat social* I, c. 6, pp.115-16.
8. Michaud-Quantin, 64-9; Gierke, *DGR* trans. Barker, 169ff.; Gough, 48. Maine observed that the social contract was 'a theory which, though nursed into importance by political passions, derived all its sap from the speculations of the lawyers'.
9. Gierke, *DGR* trans. Barker, 79-80, 247.
10. Gierke, *DGR* trans. Barker, 247.
11. *Second treatise*, ch. 8, para. 95, p.375.

The idea of the commune

But the crowning achievement of the conciliarists of Basle was surely their development of the idea of communal government, insofar as this was worked out within the context of the council itself. The corporational notion of popular sovereignty, which among the conciliarists was most vigorously expressed by Marsiglio, Zabarella and Segovia, stands in the sharpest possible contrast to the group-mind theory of organic holism; it avoids the pitfalls of the latter's potentially mythological notion of popular sovereignty. It operates with clearly-stated constitutional procedures, and, insofar as it is applied to groups small enough to assemble *in toto*, provides a perfect model of direct democracy such as is advocated by some admittedly rather idealistic political theorists today.

The idea of the commune (*Gemeinschaft, koinonia*) was partly of religious origin; but in the Middle Ages it flowed over into, or at least coincided with, similar phenomena in the secular world, most of all the cities and guilds. The idea of the 'common life (*vita communis*)', meaning the sharing of either material possessions or collegiate jurisdiction or both, was found at many points in what Lagarde has called 'the age of corporations'.[1] One may speculate that one reason why Segovia and Rousseau arrived at such similar ideas in such different circumstances was that both had some experience of assemblies in which the 'general-will' situation had been a reality, and that both had connections with the European tradition of the commune, as exemplified in corporations and towns (though Rousseau had no liking for the former). The city was the only instance of the collegiate idea being applied to a territorial society; apart from that, communes (corporations) were groups which one entered by choice and for a specific purpose, for the practice of a particular kind of religious way of life or of a particular craft or calling. They were voluntary, as opposed to 'birthright' societies. One of the chief marks of the political genius of the European Middle Ages was the elaboration by the canon and civil lawyers of specific rules to govern such associations, rules which have become known as 'corporation theory'. We know that the civic model was of some importance to Marsiglio; and Tierney has shown that the corporational model was crucial to the conciliar theory of John of Paris and Zabarella. This study shows that another major thinker, Segovia, took this communal model as the basis for much of his conceptualization both of church government and all forms of human polity and association. What perhaps distinguishes Segovia is that he emphasized, far more than Marsiglio, the lawyers, and their conciliarist heirs (Zabarella and Tudeschi), the fraternal *ethic* as the sociological rationale underlying the collegiate distribution of political power.[2] The primary importance of Segovia, therefore, lies in his having extrapolated from a certain tradition – the medieval-European corporation – its ethical and political implications. He was not a philosopher who started with carefully worked-out first principles, nor a political scientist who made a deliberate study of known constitutions. But precisely for this reason he reflects more faithfully than the more systematic theorists (such as Marsiglio and Cusa) the norms of the collegiate political sub-culture.

In all of these cases, then, we may say that the process was one of extrapolating a set of constitutional principles from a way of life. This was, in the first instance, the work of the corporational-collegiate lawyers, culminating in Bartolus. What Marsiglio, Zabarella and Segovia did was to take these principles, already laid down as norms governing corporations, and apply them to larger societies; to the whole Church (in the case of Zabarella), to Church and state (in the case of Marsiglio and Segovia). This amounted, particularly I would say in Segovia, to a universal reflection-back or out-pouring of the ideals of the intimate group based on shared pursuits onto all types of human society. *The original model, of guild, university, religious chapter or confraternity, was taken as typical and normative for all kinds of human association.* Segovia's political theory reflects the ethic and constitution of the priestly, monastic or intellectual *collegium*, the social relationships generated by a common religious or intellectual pursuit – and we may see an analogy here with the ideal state of Plato – onto ecclesiastical and political society in general. He reveals the full potential of corporation theory when applied to political entities. What happened to the collegiate principles was that, in order to adapt them for the universal Church and other polities, they were stripped of those aspects which concerned daily life and professional activity and worked up into general principles. The idea of the commune was now applied, not to possessions, work or living arrangements, but to law-making and administration. But, because Segovia retained the fraternal ethic – largely for theological reasons – his conception of the council kept a vital and direct spiritual link with the communal group from which it had been derived.

But the insuperable problem remained of the gulf separating the ordinary corporation from the universal Church or territorial polity, in terms of size, numbers and therefore of actual personal relationships among their members; separating, that is, the *Gemeinschaft* from the *Gesellschaft*.[3]

Segovia's model provided a schema, but to realise this in its new context required, at the very least, the discovery and application of some kind of real bond between council and Church, between the 'representative' commune and the greater association it was to represent. This Segovia signally failed to provide, though the answer lay close at hand in Cusa's electoral system. The success of Segovia's system, consequently, was confined to relationships within the council itself, a topic in which he excelled.

Segovia's corporational model moved a great step beyond the primitive holism of folklore when he indicated that decision-making within the council was not the product of some mysterious corporate will, but rather of such unanimity as can be achieved by common deliberation and mutual sympathy; here, he is close to the Quakers' and New-Englanders' 'sense of the meeting'. But, when he puts his schema in the context of the whole Church, he was only adopting another form of mythology. Rousseau, on the other hand, would seem to have reverted to the earlier and more common-sense view of the jurists, as distinct from the conciliarists, Hobbes and Locke, when he insisted that the power of the whole could only belong to the literal assembly of all members. Rousseau steps back into the jurists' world of face-to-face associations, from which the other theorists had departed, as first Bartolus and then the conciliarists sought to make the concept of 'all as *universitas*' into a general model for all societies. The conciliarists, Hobbes and Locke had recourse to various theories of representation; the strength of *their* position was that it could more readily be applied to the political cosmos of large states.

Segovia's persistent references to city-states[4] suggests that this was the kind of polity which he — like Marsiglio in this respect — saw as best reflecting the communal model. And indeed it was in the city states that republican theory and practice, which together with the technique of parliamentary representation provided the mainspring of many modern democracies, flourished in the late-medieval and early-modern periods. We might say that, in political theory, the city-state mediated between the corporational model and the territorial state. Republican theorists, from Marsiglio to Harrington and on to Rousseau, invoked the civic model.[5]

That conciliarism remained an arrested development was partly due to the difficulty of bridging this gulf between the corporational model and the large-scale society, between voluntary associations and territorial states. Social-contract theory would provide a more convincing solution to this problem. For there is a vast difference between the concept of membership or citizenship in a small unit, especially one based on a common pursuit and capable of actual assembly in one place, and in a large society, which will tend to have less communal feeling and personal participation. Obviously, in the small, vocationally-oriented 'guild-type' association, it is usually much easier to have a high level of real 'self-government' than in a large, anonymous 'civil society'. Thus the relationship between the corporate council and the whole Church remained in some ways little different to that between monarch and subjects. There are, indeed, indications that this might not have been the case had conciliarism been allowed to continue to develop; the council of Basle was intent on applying conciliar government to all levels of the clerical structure.[6] Yet apart from Cusa and to a lesser extent Velde no conciliarist during Basle gave the laity any meaningful role.

None the less Segovia took the significant step, albeit only at an abstract level, of conceiving the relationship between ruler and ruled in every community as one of personal, willing *trust*.[7] This was mainly because he described political relationships as analogous to theological relationships, based on faith. While Cusa made 'voluntary subjection' and consensus the basis for authority, Segovia spoke of trust − a quieter concept, perhaps. He was one of the first to transform the notion of trust from a social axiom ('all society is based on mutual trust'), and from its technical legal meaning (as in Cicero), into a term of general political application. He was saying that, for government to be effective and legitimate, the ruler must be of like mind with his people and they must trust him. In this way we may say that he rightly saw that the polity or *Gesellschaft*, whatever its formal constitutional structure, must have at least some of the qualities of the face-to-face commune or *Gemeinschaft*,[8] since it too is a human association.

In the conciliar movement we see how circumstances led certain thinkers to extract the models of organic association and communal decision-making from the prevailing cultural milieu and to elaborate them as general theories of society and polity. This provides an instance of political ideas being generated by specific events.[9] These two ideas were thrown up as arguments in favour of a specific programme; but, as so often happens, some attempt was made to give them general validity. This attempt was not particularly successful; and, as we have seen, the two ideas were in some respects incompatible. No very strong case can be made for the subsequent influence of the conciliarist formulation of these notions. What is of significance for the historian of political thought is that these same ideas have so often been generated by other specific needs at other times. There is no direct continuity between Velde and Hegel, between Segovia and Rousseau. The similarities can only be explained by the continuity, in philosophy of the neoplatonic tradition of social holism, and in the political sub-culture of the tradition of collegiate decision-making. A variety of circumstances could lead people to fashion out of these prototypes general political theories, which would consequently bear some resemblances to each other.

As stated at the outset, I have so far extracted only the political element out of the whole mass of conciliar thought. One must not forget that most of the thinkers discussed here, including Velde and Segovia, saw themselves as primarily theologians. It may be that their contribution to the theology of the Church was at least at important as their contribution to political thought; I hope at least to have provided the theologian with some data on which to base a judgment.

NOTES
   1. Lagarde (1937).
   2. Above, pp.159ff., 166ff.

3. In Tönnies' sense: Tönnies *passim* and esp. 37-41; cf. Sorokin's introd.
4. Above, pp.172ff.
5. Cf. Pocock (1975), 272ff., 361ff., 386ff.
6. Above, p.41 at n.32.
7. Above, pp.176ff.
8. Above, p.161n.1.
9. Cf. Q. Skinner (1969), and his *The foundations of modern political thought*,
   vol. i: *The Renaissance*, vol. ii: *The age of the Reformation* (Cambridge,
   1978), which came out after this book had gone to press. His 'contextual'
   approach is not, of course, quite as novel as he suggests. He endorses and
   develops Oakley's argument about conciliarist influence on parliamentarism
   (vol. ii, 114-23, 227, 321, 344), which I think both he and Oakley somewhat
   exaggerate: there were other traditions, and *citation does not mean influence*.
   Skinner has an interesting section on conciliarism in general (vol. ii, 114-23),
   particularly on Gerson's 'subjective' theory of rights.

CHAPTER 17

POSTSCRIPT

(a) Early-modern conciliarism

Conciliar theory had attempted to strike a balance between authority and consensus, to re-structure the public organization of the universal Church so as to make it representative of local churches, and to turn the Church into a kind of constitutional monarchy. After the outbreak of the Reformation controversy, such aspirations were pushed into the background, as Protestants rejected, for the most part, the idea of ongoing, institutionalized church authority, and as Catholics rallied round the papacy. Luther and Calvin were almost as far removed from the ecclesiology of Constance and Basle as they were from that of Rome; rejecting the notion of institutionalized teaching authority, they had far more in common with Marsiglio, Ockham and Hus than they had with Gerson, Cusa or Segovia. The martyrdom of Hus was a constant reminder of this gulf. To those who believed in the authority of the individual to interpret Christian doctrine for himself, conciliar infallibility — the keystone, perhaps, of conciliarism — was hardly less objectionable than the infallibility of the Roman church or the pope. Some Protestants applied the communal, caritative, inspirational notions, which the Basileans had worked out for the council itself, to the local congregation, and in so doing they revived early-Christian ideas of the local, face-to-face community of believers.[1] They could thus employ the same ecclesiological texts of the New Testament as the conciliarists, but in a different sense. They spiritually enfranchised the laity, and Calvin removed the distinction between bishop and presbyter, as the Basileans had done within the council. Calvin's church structure, like Basle's, drew something from the civic milieu;[2] the ideology of Congregationalism was a kind of diffusion of the conciliar ideal; Quakers, like the Basileans, believed in government by 'sense of the meeting'. While conciliarism looks pale and wan by comparison with Protestantism in the sphere of ecclesiastical democracy and individual autonomy, Protestantism, on the other hand, effectively abandoned the visible unity of the Church. National independence and state control of the Church, which had contributed to the failure of the conciliar movement, gave many Protestant Churches their structural orientation and their sense of community.

Though Catholics now tended more than ever to see the papacy as their standard-bearer, and acknowledgment of papal supremacy as a touchstone of orthodoxy, the idea of the ultimate teaching authority of the general council was not abandoned. And, practically speaking, a council was required to launch the Counter-reformation. Throughout the sixteenth century, leading Catholic theologians retained the notion of the occasional supremacy of council over pope, when the latter becomes heretical. Even cardinal Cajetan, writing on the eve of the Reformation against the conciliarism of Almain, while he maintained that the Church was a pure monarchy[3] and (reversing a conciliarist mode of argument) accused his opponents of relying on canon law at the expense of scripture,[4] allowed that in a case of heresy or schism a council could be called without the pope, and could depose him. 'For then, since when asked he has refused, the cardinals, the emperor, the prelates can make a universal assembly (*congregatio*), in which there will be not the care of the universal Church, but only the power to depose the pope.'[5] Like the fifteenth-century anti-conciliarist thologians, he denies that conciliar superiority extends beyond the spheres of heresy and schism; that is, he rejects *Haec Sancta* and the council's power to decree reforms without papal consent.[6] On the other hand, like Gerson and the later Torquemada, he also denies that the heretical pope is deposed *ipso facto*.[7] The council's power to depose a heretical pope, however, does not mean that the council is even his 'occasional (*in casu*)' superior, since this 'ministerial power of the universal Church extends to deposition alone'.[8] Citing the usual New Testament texts, he says that divine law, which justified such an exceptional action, prescribes it not as an act of 'subjection' but of 'separation'; 'the Church can separate itself from the pope by a ministerial' — as opposed to a superior — 'power only, since it can elect him'.[9]

The great Spanish neo-scholastics based their view of conciliar authority on the divinely-authorized episcopate, following in this respect Gerson and the late Segovia. Vitoria, who had studied under Almain and Mair at Paris, states his desire not to become involved in 'that odious comparison of pope and council' (here too he could have found a precedent in the late Segovia);[10] and he ascribes the disastrous reluctance of popes to call a council in recent times to 'the new ideas of the doctors'.[11] He is prepared to concede that a council derives its power 'immediately from God, not because it represents the universal Church, but because it is the union of all the princes of the Church'. But he still feels able to say, without fear of contradiction, that 'from whatever source a council derives its power, even if it is from the prelates, it can be maintained that it is greater in the whole council than it is in the pope, just as it is greater in a provincial council than in any prelate of that council'.[12] Soto maintained that a pope who is 'in serious ill-repute for heresy' may be judged by a council and, if found guilty, may be solemnly deposed.[13] Similarly, Melchior Cano held that 'it cannot be denied that the pontiff can be a heretic, of which one or another example might be given', and that in such a case he 'is subject to the judgment of the Church in the external forum, by divine institution'.[14] Thomassinus says that a council may judge a pope for schism or heresy, and adds his own testimony as to the state of contemporary opinion – 'as all Catholic doctors teach'.[15] Suarez and Bellarmine, while upholding substantially the same view, try to safeguard the doctrine of papal immunity by insisting that the heretical pope is first *ipso facto* immediately deposed by Christ' (Suarez) or 'ceases *per se* to be pope' (Bellarmine), and is only then judged by the Church.[16] Thus, while Catholic theologians continued to adhere to the moderate views of Teutonicus and the late d'Ailly, there was some tendency to add, as a further safeguard to the doctrine of papal supremacy, that the pope is deposed automatically and is only thereafter subject to conciliar judgment. But in practice – if such views were ever capable of being put into practice – the result would be the same.

When at last the papacy lent its full support to a genuine council of reform, the council of Trent, other issues dominated the agenda, and serious consideration of the pope-council question was understandably avoided. A closely related aspect of the ecclesiastical constitution – the relation between the pope and the episcopate – was, none the less, hotly debated in 1562-3. The question was whether bishops held not only their sacramental power but also their jurisdictional power direct from God as a divine right (*ius divinum*). Several Spanish and French bishops maintained that they did, on the ground that Christ had given his authority directly to all twelve apostles. No conclusion was reached; a canon of the 23rd session merely recognized the bishops' outstanding position as successors of the apostles.[17]

It is well known how in the seventeenth century conciliarism survived as an integral part of 'Gallicanism', which itself was in part a reaction to the centralizing tendency of post-Tridentine Catholicism. This culminated in the conflict between pope Innocent XI and Louis XIV, and was tarred with the political motives of the French *état royale*. At a general assembly of the French clergy held in 1681-2, the French bishops published, in the name of the French Church, four articles which declared that a council was superior to a pope, that the pope was not infallible, and that *Haec Sancta* and *Frequens* had been and still were valid decrees.[18] In defence of these articles, bishop Bossuet cited and supported Torquemada's cautious statements on the pope-council relationship. Implicitly following Segovia — and, in secular theory, Bodin — he said that the Roman primacy 'was not obscured but illuminated and strengthened' and that the Church's constitution included a consultative aristocracy.[19] Archbishop Fénelon, who dissented both from Bossuet's secular absolutism and from his ecclesiastical constitutionalism, comes close to the late Segovia when he says that the council and the apostolic see should interact and never clash, and also when he says that the divine authority of the bishops belongs to them still more when they are assembled in council.[20] But in principle he thinks a general council superior to the person of the pope, which he takes care to distinguish from the apostolic see, and a council may judge and depose a pope for heresy.[21] He would like to see the Roman see 'restored' to become the genuine theological 'centre' of the Church, where expert theologians would give advice; in this way, it would become 'as it were a perpetual council *(assiduam synodum)*'.[22]

A few Gallican writers went further than this and maintained what was in substance an at least partially Basilean theory of the council's nature and supremacy. The bastion of conciliarism in its stronger form remained the university of Paris, which continued to uphold the legitimacy of the council of Basle and the illegitimacy of Florence;[23] and there Basilean theory found an occasional supporter. Furthermore, Sarpi, though not explicitly a conciliarist, defended Gerson against Bellarmine: he thought the Church had degenerated from aristocracy to 'papismo', and advocated a kind of federal constitution for the Church, which should be governed by 'the common council of the priesthood'. The practices of Constance and Basle, he wrote, were appropriate to an age when the Church had been governed 'in liberta'.[24]

There was, however, no significant development of earlier theory. Richer, in the early seventeenth century, follows the theory of Basle to the effect that 'ecclesiastical jurisdiction belongs primarily and essentially to the Church, and only in a ministerial way to the Roman pontiff or to other bishops'.[25] He defended this by an analogy, reminiscent of Almain, with ordinary civil society.[26] He maintains the Basilean view, which had apparently become the standard teaching at Paris, that priests as well as bishops hold their position by divine right in view of their succession to the seventy-two disciples.[27] In characteristically Basilean style, he says that 'the priests should rule the Church in common with the bishops',[28]

213

and that 'the general council can undertake more fully (*amplius*) all the acts of jurisdiction exercised by the pope'.[29] Infallibility belongs not to the pope or bishops individually, but to 'the sacerdotal Church taken collectively'.[30] That such views were a conscious reminiscence of Basilean doctrine is suggested by the fact that Vigor wrote a commentary on Basle's doctrinal letter *Cogitanti* of 1432.[31]

The last exponent of the specifically European conciliarist tradition prior to the contemporary era was Febronius, whose 'Estate of the Church (*De statu ecclesiae*)' was published at Frankfurt in 1763, and caused a flurry of controversy.[32] Febronius' conception of the Roman see is interesting, and he comes closer than most Latins to the traditional eastern view; its main function is as the *'centrum unionis'*.[33] He reproduced, without development, some of the classic theses of Basle conciliarism, appealed to the authority of Constance and Basle in support of his position, and argued that his views were not incompatible with the decrees of Trent[34] — a plausible statement, since Trent had made no dogmatic statement on the primacy. He ascribes the power of the keys to the 'association (*universitati*) of the Church', to which the pope, though first among the Church's ministers, is subordinate.[35] Infallibility belongs to 'the body of the Church, whether united or dispersed'.[36] This last exponent of traditional conciliarism had an episcopal view of the council's nature; like the late Segovia, he bases conciliar sovereignty on the collective authority of the episcopate.[37]

NOTES

1. See esp. Troeltsch, ii, 590-601, 661ff.
2. Baron (1939); Troeltsch, ii, 628ff.
3. Cajetan, c. 6, p.454. On Cajetan, Brosse, 189ff.; *DTC* ii (2), 1313ff.
4. Cajetan, c. 1, pp.446, 493.
5. Cajetan, c. 16, p.470.
6. Cajetan, c. 16, p.470; above, p.46.
7. Cajetan, c. 20, p.474; above, p.24, and Horst.
8. Cajetan, c. 20, p.475.
9. Cajetan, c. 20, p.475.
10. Hamilton, 73; above, p.124n.69.
11. Hamilton, 78.
12. Hamilton, 73.
13. Hamilton, 81.
14. Cit. Küng (1965), 276.
15. Cit. Küng (1965), 277.
16. Küng (1965), 277; Hamilton, 81; cf. Küng (1972), 39; Martimort, 47.
17. Mansi xxxiii, 139B; cf. *DTC* v, 1702-3; *LTK* ii, 491-4; Vigener, 15-17; *HbK* iv, 482ff.
18. Rops (1963), 220-4.; *DTC* vi (1), 1096ff.; *HbK* v, 64-79.
19. Martimort, 549-63.
20. Fénelon (1790), 22-3; *DTC* v (2), 2137ff. Cf. Fénelon (1848), 48-9:

'Verecundia me libere loqui vetat; neque tamen silentio praetermitti potest, summos pontifices ultimis hisce in seculis neglexisse pristinam morem definiendi una cum fratribus episcopis'.

21. Fénelon (1848), 6, 45.
22. Fénelon, (1848), 49.
23. Martimort, 19, 48.
24. Sarpi, 218, 316, 350; Salvatorelli.
25. Richer, *Vindiciae*, I, c. 1; *Libellus*, c. 1; cf. Martimort, 50-4; Martin (1919), 360ff.
26. Richer, *Apologia*, c.7.
27. Richer, *Apologia*, c. 34; Martimort, 19.
28. Richer, *Apologia*, c. 34; above, pp.79, 113, 160.
29. Richer, *Apologia*, c. 23; above, pp.51, 55f, 101, 113.
30. Richer *Apologia*, c. 18 and *Defensio*, book IV at p.194.
31. Vigor, vol. ii,; cf. Willaert, 385-92.
32. Rops (1970), 230-1.; *LTK* iv, 46-7; *DTC* v (2), 2115ff.
33. Febronius, vol. ii, p.382 and vol. iii, pp.32ff.
34. Febronius, vol. i, pp.357ff.
35. Febronius, vol. i, pp.32ff.; cf. Vigener, 39-41.
36. Febronius, vol. ii, p.382.
37. Febronius, vol. i, pp.357ff., 394; vol. ii, p.383, 458; vol. iv, pp.108ff.

(b) The council today

Anyone reading these pages is liable to feel that in our own day history is reversing itself. A hundred or even twenty years ago, the monarchical-centralist option which the papacy, and with it the Roman Catholic (RC) Church, took in the fifteenth century, appeared to have been final. One could point to a 'development of doctrine' on papal prerogatives, of which the Councils of Lyon (1274),[1] of Florence (1439)[2] and of Vatican I (1870)[3] provided decisive and cumulative official formulations. Yet as I have been writing this depressing saga of the fifteenth century, conciliar ideas and practices appear once more to be gaining the upper hand in the RC Church. 'In front the sun climbs slow, how slowly, But westward, look, the land is bright'. They are also gaining a stronger hold in major Protestant Churches and the World Council of Churches; they have never suffered eclipse in the Orthodox Churches. Conciliar ideas are coming to be seen as a focus for ecclesiological agreement between these branches of Christendom as they strive for reunion,[4] as something each has in common; in varying forms, each branch derives conciliar procedures from the common original stock of the first Christian centuries. We may speak of a general conciliar renaissance.

In its decree *On the church (Lumen gentium)*, the Second Vatican Council (1962-5) made statements on 'the hierarchical structure of the Church' which contain many an echo of fifteenth-century conciliarism, and which taken together go some way towards a synthesis of the rival

215

views of late-medieval papalists and conciliarists.[5] Like most such documents it represents a compromise between conflicting views within the council which issued it, and by the same token leaves some questions suspended in mid air. First, it said that the bishops are successors of the apostles, not delegates of the pope;[6] this accords with the view of the main stream of conciliarists at Constance and Basle and clarifies what Trent stated equivocally. Secondly, it said that Christ formed the apostles 'after the manner of a college or fixed group', and that just as 'St Peter and the other apostles constituted one apostolic college, so in a similar way the Roman Pontiff as the successor of Peter and the bishops as successors of the apostles are joined together'; it proceeded to refer to 'the collegial nature and meaning of the episcopal order'.[7] The notion of the bishops as a unified college, which had very recently been expounded in terms of philosophical jurisprudence by Karl Rahner,[8] was thoroughly in line with our conciliarists; but they would not have given such emphasis to the position of Peter and the pope. The collegiality invoked here is, in very general terms, in line with late-medieval corporation theory and with the holistic-corporate element in Gersonian and Basilean thought. On the specific topic of councils, the document said that 'the collegial nature and meaning of the episcopal order found expression' inter alia in 'conciliar assemblies', and that 'the ecumenical councils held through the centuries clearly attest this collegial aspect'.[9]

The most crucial sections of this chapter of the decree concern the ascription of 'supreme power' (III.22) and 'infallibility' (III.25) to this episcopal college, and the relationship between the pope as head and the other bishops as members of the college (III.22, 25). Both these sections have a similar structure: first, it is denied that supreme power or infallibility belongs to the college unless united with the pope, then it is asserted that the pope on his own possesses supreme power and infallibility, lastly it is asserted that the episcopal college, so long as it is united to the pope, also possesses these qualities, which may be exercised through a general council or in other ways. The pro-collegiate, pro-conciliar passages[10] are not only counter-balanced but contextually overshadowed by restatements of the papal prerogatives. While there are repeated references to the collective character of episcopal authority, to the tenure of power 'in common',[11] and while supreme judicial and teaching authority *are* ascribed to the episcopal college, the role given to the pope is clearly quite different to that envisaged by the fifteenth-century conciliarists.[12] (Contrary to the Basilean view, it is only *episcopal* power which is mentioned here; there is no question of doctors and others sharing in this supreme collegiate or conciliar authority. On the other hand, Vatican II had much to say about the desirability of purely consultative participation by others, and went

216

much further than the mainstream conciliarists in elevating the ecclesiological status of the laity).[13]

However, this is not the main point. What mattered was that this collegiate-conciliar doctrine was enunciated at all. For the first time since the fifteenth century a new chord has been struck in RC ecclesiology. Vatican II promoted conciliar practices in other ways. Saying that it 'earnestly desires that the venerable institution of synods and councils flourish with new vigor', it inaugurated regional episcopal conferences with some juridical powers,[14] and recommended that a central, select 'synod of bishops' should give 'helpful assistance' to the pope.[15] The subsequent development of episcopal conferences is probably the most definite sign that at least at this level the conciliarists' programme, which here accorded with the practice both of the early Church and of later Orthodoxy, has been revived and to a great extent implemented. The central Synod of Bishops has, everyone knows, been much less successful in this or any other respect.

While opinion has moved on, it is still pertinent to ask what exactly collegiality meant in the decree. Did it, as Rahner had recently suggested, refer to an ontological relationship, meaning that the pope and his fellow-bishops are really one in their *episkope*? In this case, the obligation upon the pope to act concordantly with his fellow-bishops might be viewed as moral but not juridical. This appears to be how Rahner had taken it.[16] He had added an eloquent plea that the *'nomos* of the Spirit' rather than precise constitutional formulae should order the Church.[17] Certainly the document defines the relation between the pope and the other bishops on the whole in moral and ontological terms rather than in juridical ones, which one might say is in keeping with the general tone of Vatican II's ecclesiology.

Yet the document states unambiguously at least this juridical norm: the college cannot act as such without the pope, and the pope alone may exercise all the powers ascribed to the college. One must ask, what kind of college is it in which the 'head' can, if it chooses, act independently anyway? If collegiality is meant to refer to the *spirit* in which the Church is governed, and if, with Rahner, we eschew the idea that precise constitutional rules are appropriate to the Church, why is this particular constitutional rule (for I cannot see it as anything short of that) specified and upheld? The conciliarists of Constance and Basle, incidentally, certainly thought that precise constitutional law, though with an opposite content, was what was required.

Since Vatican II the conception of collegiality has been developed and expanded by many theologians in theory and by many episcopal conferences in practice; there has been some diffusion of power, *de facto* if not *de iure*,

217

from Rome to local Churches. But the central government of the Church in Rome still lags behind the spirit of *Lumen gentium*; the doctrine of papal power enshrined in the decree is clearly of more than theoretical significance. The situation is fluid and may well change, sooner or later. In fact the formulations of *Lumen gentium* have been widely regarded in the RC Church as opening up new vistas rather than as closing discussion. Many would like to see collegiality expressed more dynamically in the life of the Church, especially at the 'centre'.

If we look at ecclesiological *theory* in the era of Vatican II and since, we shall find a somewhat greater convergence between late-medieval and contemporary phenomena. There can be little doubt that Hans Küng is, broadly speaking, the most conciliarist of contemporary theologians. Like some of our conciliarists, most particularly Velde, he conceives the council as not only an 'institution' but an 'event';[18] similarly, pope John XXIII had said, in his opening address to Vatican II, that 'Ecumenical Councils . . . are a solemn celebration of the union of Christ and His Church'.[19] Again, Küng, like Gerson and the Basileans, described a council as 'the totality of the consciousness of the Church'.[20] On the other hand Küng, unlike the mainstream conciliarists, will not ascribe infallibility to the general council; like Ockham, he denies that quality to any determinate person or body.[21] Fully aware of the ecclesiological heritage of the Middle Ages, Küng has regarded the decree *Haec Sancta* as a binding dogmatic definition, and sees the whole problem of papal heresy and fallibility, to which the medieval canonists devoted so much discussion, as one with which the modern RC Church has still to come to terms.[22] De Vooght, unlike many other recent RC historians, takes the same view of *Haec Sancta*[23]. Küng concludes that it must be held in tension with the statement of Vatican I: each states one side of a paradox in the mystery of the Church's constitution.[24]

Rahner, in a work written on the eve of Vatican II, states the theory of episcopal collegiality in realist-collectivist terms that immediately recall the formulae of Velde and other Basileans (and which may owe something to his Hegelian background). He conceives 'the college as such to be the prior entity' in relation to all its individual members including the pope: 'A real unity is prior to its parts, not made up out of them as parts . . . Ontologically and juridically, then, the apostolic college with Peter at its head forms one entity'.[25] His formulations again resemble those of Gerson when he speaks of pope and council as 'different forms and modes of activity of this one subject (sc. the college of bishops) of supreme ecclesiastical authority'.[26] He too is well aware of the late-medieval heritage; and, in the same work, he called for a modern decree similar to *Frequens* (establishing regular general councils at specified intervals). Of

Frequens he said that it was 'a bold idea. That it was not put into effect is still no proof that it was false or unrealistic'.[27]

While the RC Church has recently been modifying its monarcho-centralist structure and theory, emphasizing the irreducible status of the local Church[28] and the divinely-ordained precept of collegiality at all levels, Protestant Churches have, since their foundation as (for the most part) autonomous congregations or national Churches, been striving to develop inter-congregational and inter-national structures in accordance with the divinely-ordained precept of unity. This process has culminated in the twentieth century with the foundation of the World Council of Churches. These structures are conciliar in form.[29] The Orthodox Churches never abandoned the synodal structure, based on the canons of the early ecumenical councils.[30]

The convergence between different Christian traditions on ecclesiological questions, and not least on the nature and status of councils, is perhaps closest between the Anglican communion, on the one hand, and the Orthodox and RC Churches, on the other. In the latter case, the recent formulation of Anglican and RC theologians (*ARCIC*) appears even to indicate agreement, *mirabile dictu* , on the question of the Roman primacy.[31] Yet both the differences still remaining between these converging traditions, and the difference between the present state of the conciliar renaissance and the conciliarist programme of the late Middle Ages, must not be underestimated. *ARCIC* has not been warmly received by the Roman curia. The twin questions of the jurisdictional supremacy of the Roman Church and of the doctrinal infallibility of the pope are still a portentous stumbling-block to reunion between the Orthodox and the RC Churches, as they are to that between the Protestant and RC Churches, and, unless the *ARCIC* statement were more generally accepted, to that between the Anglican and RC Churches.[32]

As regards the nature and authority of councils themselves, the current term 'conciliarity'[33] should not be allowed to conceal important differences of outlook. It is a useful term for expressing the collective-consultative spirit and the conciliar methods of decision-making which prevailed in the early Church, and which are today widely advocated and used by all the major branches of Christendom. But, in the RC Church, it is still cramped by the official ascription, in the current code of canon law, of ultimate decision-making power to individual office-holders. One of the major problems posed for the RC Church by its tenacious belief in the absolute ascendancy of Rome is that whatever 'collegiality' remains tends to fall into the hands of cardinals and curial officials rather than of the other bishops. As we have seen, Vatican II ascribed ultimate power to the pope acting alone as well as with the college. The insistence of Rahner that the pope, even when acting 'alone', is acting in the name and on behalf of the episcopal college[34] hardly resolves the question in practical terms.

In the Protestant perspective, meanwhile, councils are still regarded as having something less than the status ascribed to them in the earlier tradition of both western and eastern ecclesiology; this is related to a different estimation of the inherent character of church authority, especially of episcopal authority — and one which has very deep theological roots. The World Council of Churches (WCC) itself, and also the synods of the Anglican Church, explicitly eschew the ascription to themselves of the very concept of *council* in the sense in which that term was understood in the era of the first ecumenical councils. Such bodies have very little authority in the doctrinal field, in the case of the WCC virtually none at all; their scope is primarily in the organisational and administrative field. The WCC is explicitly regarded by its members and in its constitution as a loose confederation.[35]

There is, nevertheless, at least this common ground in all of these differences. The ancient idea of 'reception',[36] whereby conciliar decisions, whether at the regional or the ecumenical level, required confirmation by other major foci of the Church (such as Rome, other major sees, the faithful at large), is accorded a different but equally strong role in Roman Catholicism, Protestantism and Orthodoxy. Decisions made by councils are not regarded as binding unless ratified by someone else: in the RC view by Rome, in the Protestant view by the constituent Churches or congregations, in the Orthodox view by the various regional church synods and in some sense by the faithful.

Indeed, one must not overstate the case against convergence. The present tendency in the RC Church to bypass the question of papal infallibility, the erosion of the 'traditional' doctrine of papal supremacy by numerous RC theologians in favour of a more thorough-going conciliarism, and — probably most important of all — a renewed conciliar *practice* and ethos all suggest that our understanding of the Roman primacy is undergoing a fundamental shift (not for the first time). It is a hopeful sign that so many RC thinkers are revolutionizing their conception of the nature and status of both ecclesiastical jurisdiction and formal doctrinal pronouncement; they give a much reduced scope to both in the total life of the Church. It may eventually be possible to return to, or rather to refurbish, the position that seems to have obtained in the 'great Church' of earlier times, according to which agreement between both council and pope was regarded as necessary. Such a position, which in medieval terms is neither exactly 'papalist' nor exactly 'conciliarist', is clearly suggested by the *ARCIC* when it states that 'primacy and conciliarity are complementary elements of the *episkope* . . . The *koinonia* of the Churches requires that a proper balance be preserved'.[37]

Lastly, as regards the comparison between the contemporary conciliar renaissance and late-medieval conciliarism, we must first note some fundamental differences. Late-medieval conciliarists transferred the 'papalist' notion of sovereignty to the general council: its decrees were absolutely binding on the faithful in general and, in the Basilean version, on the pope too. They still thought very much in governmental and juridical terms. They took over the existing notion that a certain determinate legal agent or public person constituted a final appellate court in judicial proceedings and could make infallible dogmatic pronouncements: for them, this meant a general council, with its membership and meetings prescribed by conciliar decrees like *Frequens*. They thus completely overlooked the question of reception, ignoring the ancient claims not only of the Roman see but of other major patriarchal sees and of the faithful at large. Cusa stands out as one conciliarist, not (as we have seen) of the Basilean main stream, who paid proper attention to earlier tradition in this respect. It may not only have been historical accident that kept the Greeks away from Basle. While there has recently been a renaissance of certain features of the conciliarism examined in this study, in other respects its ecclesiology appears today no less culture-bound than papal absolutism itself.

Yet, despite the reservations already referred to, it does appear that there is a many-sided movement in theological opinion and practice in all the major branches of Christendom today towards a convergence that includes some of the central theses upheld by the late-medieval conciliarists in most difficult circumstances: namely, that the visible structure of the Church is essentially and irreducibly conciliar, that there is an inherent dialectic between the communal nature of the local Church and the conciliar nature of the universal Church, that supreme ecclesiastical authority resides with a collective 'representative' *group* or multiplicity of individual office-holder assembled together, and that the Christian revelation includes at least the specific ecclesiological prescription that decisions should be taken by a fraternal group, with the concomitant promise that the infallible guidance of the Holy Spirit is given not to an individual but to a community.

NOTES

1. Denzinger, 217.
2. Denzinger, 253.
3. Denzinger, 503-4; cf. Vigener, 21-6 and, for a typical view of councils *DTC* s.v. *Concile*.
4. Botte et al.; *World council of Churches studies*, no. 5; ed. Margull; J. Deschner (1976).
5. c. III in *Documents of Vatican II*, 37-56; see the commentary in *LTK* for

221

Vatican II, i, 186-217. Cf. Black (1971).

6. C. III. 18, 20, 27 (*Documents*, 37, 40, 52).
7. c. III. 19, 22 (*Documents*, 38, 42-3).
8. Rahner and Ratzinger (1962) (all references here are to passages by Rahner).
9. c. III. 22 (*Documents*, 42-3).
10. 'Together with its head, the Roman Pontiff, and never without this head, the episcopal order is the subject of supreme and full power over the universal Church. But this power can be exercised only with the consent of the Roman pontiff . . . It is definite, however, that the power of binding and loosing, which was given to Peter (Mt. 16:19), was granted also to the college of apostles, joined with their head (*Mt.* 18:18; 28:16-20) . . . The infallibility promised to the Church resides also in the body of bishops when that body exercises supreme teaching authority with the successor of Peter': c. III. 22, 25 *(Documents,* 43, 49).
11. E.g. c. III, 23 (*Documents* 44-5); cf. above, pp.55, 99.
12. A further attempt to qualify collegiality was made in the *nota praevia explicativa* inserted at Paul VI's request.
13. *Lumen gentium,* c. IV (*Documents*, 56-65).
14. Decree *On the bishops' pastoral office in the church (Christus Dominus),* c. III: *Documents*, 424ff.; cf. Bonet (1965). This closely parallels a Basle decree: above, p.41n. 32.
15. *Christus Dominus,* c.I (*Documents*, 399); cf. *Documents,* 721ff.
16. Rahner and Ratzinger (1962), 23-9, 75-81.
17. Rahner and Ratzinger (1962), 80-1.
18. Küng (1965), 12.
19. *Documents*, 711.
20. Küng (1965), 31.
21. Küng (1972), esp. 129ff.
22. Küng (1965), 276ff.; Küng (1972), 151.
23. Above, p.17f.
24. Küng (1965), 255.
25. Rahner and Ratzinger (1962), 77-9; cf. above, pp.67f.
26. Rahner and Ratzinger (1962), 95; cf. above, p.23.
27. Rahner and Ratzinger (1962), 31.
28. *Lumen gentium,* c. III. 26: 'This Church of Christ is truly present in all legitimate local congregations': *Documents*, 50. Cf. Rahner and Ratzinger (1962), 20-30.
29. McNeill (1964).
30. G. Florovsky (1972), esp. 94-103; Hajjar (1965); Afanassieff (1962).
31. Anglican-Roman Catholic Internat. Comm., p.18.
32. Cf. Tierney (1972), 273-81; Küng (1972), 158ff.
33. The term was first coined by the World Council of Churches study, no. 5, and has been given further currency by the ARCIC report; cf. ed. Küppers (1974), 3-4.
34. Rahner and Ratzinger (1962), 97.
35. Constitution of the WCC in Bettenson, 333-4. At its 4th assembly in Uppsala in 1968 the WCC stated in its report that the common ecumenical goal was 'a genuinely universal council' which could 'once more speak for all Christians': ed. Küppers (1974), cf. Deschner, 23, and Walsh, 35.
36. Küppers (1961); Grillmeier.
37. ARCIC p.18.

BIBLIOGRAPHY

PRIMARY SOURCES

(a) Collections

Acta Concilii Constantiensis, ed H. Finke (4 vols., Münster, 1896-1928).

Annales Ecclesiastici, ed O. Raynaldus, vols. xxviii-xxix (Bar-le-Duc, 1874-6).

Bettenson, H., ed., *Documents of the Christian Church* (Oxford, 2nd ed., 1963).

Codex Diplomaticus Universitatis Cracoviensis, part ii, (Cracow, 1873).

Concilium Basiliense, Studien und Quellen zur Geschichte des Conzils von Basel, edd. J. Haller *et al.* (8 vols., Basle, 1896-1936).

Concilium Florentinum, documenta et scriptores. ed Pontifical institute of oriental studies, vol. iv, fasc. 1 (Rome, 1952).

Cortes de los Antiquos Reinos de Leon y Castilla, vol. iii (Madrid, 1866).

Decretum Gratiani \in\ *Corpus iuris canonici,* ed. A. Freiburg (2 vols., Leipzig, 1879-81).

Denzinger, H. ed., *Enchiridion* (Barcelona, 27th ed., 1951).

Deutsche Reichstagsakten, vols. xiv-xvii, edd. H. Weigel et al. (Stuttgart-Göttingen, 1935-63).

Documents of Vatican II, ed J. Gallagher (London-Dublin, 1966).

Dupin, L., ed., *Gersonii opera* (5 vols., Antwerp, 1706).

Finke, H., ed., *Forschungen und Quellen zur Geschichte des konstanzer Konzils* (Paderborn, 1889).

Goldast, M., ed., *Monarchia,* i-ii (Hanover-Frankfurt, 1611-21).

Historia Universitatis Parisiensis, ed. C. Égasse du Boulay, v (Paris, 1670).

Magnum Oecumenicum Constantiense Concilium, ed H. von der Hardt (6 vols., Frankfurt-Leipzig, 1697-1700).

Mansi, J.D. *et al.,* edd., *Sacrorum conciliorum nova et amplissima collectio,* xxvii-xxxiA (Florence-Venice, 1759-98), xxxiB-xxxii (Paris, 1901), Supplementary vols. iv-v (Lucca, 1750-1).

Monumenta conciliorum generalium seculi XV: concilium Basiliense, Scriptores, edd. F. Palacky *et al.* (4 vols., Vienna-Basle, 1857-1935).

Monumenta medii aevi res gestas Polonias illustrantia, ii (Cracow, 1876).

Parlaments a las Cortes Catalanes, edd. R.A. and J. Gassiot (Barcelona, 1928).

Raccolta dei Concordati, ed. A. Mercati, i (Vatican City, 1954).

Spinka, M., ed., *Advocates of reform from Wyclif to Erasmus* (London, 1953).

Veterum scriptorum amplissima collectio, edd. E. Martène and U. Durand, viii (Paris, 1723).

(b) Individual Authors

AILLY, Pierre de, *Epistola diaboli Leviathan,* ed. I. Raymond in *CH* xxii (1953), 185-91.

    Abbreviatio dialogi Okam, Paris, Bibl. nat., MS lat. 14579, fols. 88v-101v.

    Tractatus de reformatione ecclesiae, trans. Cameron, 'Conciliarism' part 2, 189-225.

    Tractatus de materia concilii generalis, ed. B. Meller, *Freiburger theologische Studien,* 1xvii (1954), 290ff.; and ed. Oakley, *Pierre d'Ailly,* 244-342.

    Propositiones utiles, ed. Oakley, 'The *propositiones utiles';* and in *MD,* vii, 909-11.

    Tractatus de ecclesiastica potestate, Dupin, ii, 925-60.

ALMAIN, Jacob, *De dominio naturali, civili et ecclesiastica,* Dupin, ii, 961-76.

    De auctoritate ecclesiae et conciliorum generalium adversus Thomam de Vio, Dupin, ii, 977-1012.

    Expositio circa decisiones magistri Guillelmi Occam super potestate summi pontificis, Dupin, ii, 1013-1120; and Goldast, ii, 558-647.

ANGLICAN ROMAN CATHOLIC INTERNATIONAL COMMISSION, *Authority in the church: a statement on the question of authority, its nature, exercise and implications* (London, 1977).

ANONYMOUS. *De papae et concilii auctoritate,* ed. H. Finke in *Acta concilii Constantiensis,* ii, 701-3.

    No title. Munich Staatsbibliothek, lat. 6503, fols. 231r-7v.

    Tract by 'a Paris doctor': *HUP* v, 450-60.

AQUINAS, St Thomas. *Summa theologiae,* ed. and trans., general edd. T. Gilby & P. Meagher (London and New York, 1964-).

    Commentum in libros IV sententiarum in *OO* ed. S. Frette, xxx (Paris, 1878).

    In decem libros Ethicorum Aristotelis expositio, ed. R. Spiazzi (Turin, 1964).

224

In libros Politicorum Aristotelis expositio, in *00* ed. S. Fretté, xxvi (Paris, 1875).

Theological texts, trans. T. Gilby (Oxford, 1955).

ARISTOTLE. *The Politics,* trans. T. Sinclair (London, 1962).

AUSTIN, J. *The province of jurisprudence determined,* ed. H. Hart (London, 1954).

BEAUPÈRE, Jean. No title (on the presidency). Codex Trevirensis, Trier, 1205/503, fols. 173r-4v.

BODIN, Jean. *Six books of the commonwealth,* ed. and trans. M. Tooley (Oxford, n.d.).

BONAVENTURE, St, *Collationes in Hexameron,* ed. F. Delorme (Ad claras aquas, 1934).

BONET, H., *Somnium super materiam schismatis,* ed. N. Valois in *Annuaire-bulletin de la soc. d'hist. de France,* xxvii (1890), 193-228.

BUCHANAN, George, *De iure regni apud Scotos* in *00* i (Edinburgh, 1715); trans. C. Arrowwood (as) *The powers of the crown in Scotland* (Austin, 1949); trans. D. MacNeill (as) *The art and science of government among the Scots* (Glasgow, 1964).

BUTRIO, Antonius de, *In V libros decretalium commentaria* (5 vols., Lyons, 1532).

CAJETAN, Thomas de Vio. *De comparatione auctoritatis papae et concilii,* in J. Rocaberti, *Biblioteca maxima pontificia,* xix (Rome, 1599), 466-92; and ed. V. Pollet (Rome, 1936).

CAMPANO, Joannes Antonius, *De magistratu liber unicus* (Louvain, 1548).

CICERO, *De officiis* (London, 1913).

De republica (London, 1959).

COLOGNE UNIVERSITY, *Consilium,* in *DRTA,* xv, 464-7 and *HUP,* v, 460-2.

CRACOW UNIVERSITY, *Diffinitio studii universitatis Cracoviensis super rebus conciliaribus,* Munich, Staatsbibliothek, Clm. 1847, fols. 38r-63v. *Consilium,* in *HUP,* v, 479-517.

CUSA, Nicolaus de. *De concordantia catholica,* ed. G. Kallen in *Nicolai Cusani opera omnia,* xiv (Hamburg, 1959-65)

De auctoritate presidendi in concilio generali, ed. G. Kallen, *Cusanus-Texte* ii, in *SHA,* 1935-6, no. 3 (Heidelberg, 1935), pp.10-35.

De pace fidei cum epistola ad Ioannem de Segobia, edd. R. Klibansky and H. Bascour, in *Medieval and Renaissance studies,* suppl. iii (London, 1956).

DIJON, prior of (anon.), *De auctoritate presidendi,* ed. G. Kallen, *SHA,* 1935-6, no. 3: *Cusanus Texte* ii, (Heidelberg, 1935), 92-103.; and *MD,* viii, 826-33.

DIONYSIUS (surname unknown). *Conclusiones,* Cod. Trevirensis, Trier

1205/503, fols. 160r-162v.

DLUGOSC, J., *Historia polonica*, ii (Leipzig, 1712).

DOERING, Mathias, *Confutatio primatus papae*, Goldast, i, 557-63 (mistakenly ascribed to Heimburg: see Albert, 446-7, 460, 488-9).

EIXIMENIS, Francesc., *Doctrina compendiosa*, ed. P. Marti (Barcelona, 1929).

ERASMUS, Desiderius, *Institutio principis christiani* in *OO* iv (Lyons, 1703), 560-611.

ERFURT UNIVERSITY, *Consilium* in *DRTA* xv, 439-50 and *HUP* v, 462-71.

ESCOBAR, Andreas de, *Gubernaculum conciliorum* in *MOCC* vi, 139-334. *Avisamentum* in *CB* i, 214-33.

De Graecis errantibus, ed. E. Candal in *CF* iv, part 1 (Rome, 1952), pp.5-89.

FEBRONIUS (J.N. von Hontheim). *De statu ecclesi* (4 vols. Bullioni, 1765-75).

FEDERALIST papers, the, by A Hamilton, J. Madison and J. Jay (New York, 1961).

FÉNELON F. *De summi pontificia auctoritate* in Oeuvres complètes, ii (Paris, 1848), 5-55.

Sur les libertés gallicanes (Avignon, 1790).

FERRERI, Zaccaria. *Apologia sacri concilii Pisani moderni*, ed. Goldast, ii, 1653-65.

GELNHAUSEN, Conrad of, *Epistola brevis*, ed. H. Kaiser in *Historische Vierteljahrschrift*, iii, (1900), 379-94.

Epistola concordiae in *MD* ii, 1200-26 and ed. F. Bliemetzrieder, *Literarische Polemik*, 111-40.

GERSON, Jean, *Oeuvres complètes*, ed. M. Glorieux, vi: *l'oeuvre ecclésiologique* (Tournai, 1965).

De auctoritate ecclesiae in *OC*, vi, 114-23; and ed. and trans. Z. Rueger in *RHE* 1iii (1958), 775-95.

De unitate ecclesiae in *OC* vi, 136-45; trans. Cameron, 'Conciliarism', part 2, 93-114.

Propositio facta coram Anglicis in *OC* vi, 128-35.

De auferibilitate papae ab ecclesia, ed. Dupin, ii, 209-24.

De potestate ecclesiastica in *OC*, vi, 210-50; and trans. Cameron, 'Conciliarism', part 2, 115-88.

An liceat in causis fidei a papa appellare in *OC* vi, 283-90.

GRÜNWALDER, Johann, (no title) Munich Staatsbibliothek, lat. 6503, fols. 260r-end.

HEIMBURG, Gregory, *Apologia contra detractationes et blasphemias Theodori Laelii Feltrensis episcopi*, ed. Goldast, ii, 1604-23.

Invectiva in reverendissimum patrem dominum Nicolaum de Cusa, ed. Goldast, ii, 1624-31.

HEGEL, G.W.F., *Philosophy of right,* trans. T. Knox (Oxford, 1942).

HOBBES, Thomas, *Leviathan,* ed. M. Oakeshott (Oxford, n.d.).

IMOLA, Johannes ab., *Super primo-tertio decretalium* (Lyons, 1525).

JÜTERBOG (or Paradyz), Jacob de, *Determinatio de ecclesia,* ed. Fijalek, i, 349-80.

Super decretum conciliorum Constantiensis et Basiliensis, Münster Universitätsbibliothek, Cod. 160, fols. 24r-37v (destroyed).

Disputatio pro utraque parte concilii Basiliensis, British museum, Cod. Cotton. Caligula A.1, fols. 243r-7v.

De reformatione schismatis, Wroclaw university library, Cod. 1. Fol. 321, fols. 255b-68a (? destroyed).

Avisamentum ad papam pro reformatione ecclesiae, ed. E. Klüpfel, *Vetus bibliotheca ecclesiastica,* i (Freiburg-im-Breisgau, 1780), 135-45.

LANGENSTEIN, Henry of, *Consilium pacis de unione ac reformatione ecclesiae in concilio universali quaerenda* in *MOCC,* ii, 2-61; and ed. Dupin, ii, 809-40; and trans. Cameron, 'Conciliarism', part 2, 1-92 (abridged in Spinka, ed., 106-39).

LOCKE, John, *Two treatises of government,* ed. P. Laslett (Cambridge, 1960).

MACHIAVELLI, Niccolo, *The prince,* trans. G. Bull (London, 1961).

MAIR (or Major) John, *Disputatio de auctoritate concilii supra pontificem maximum,* ed. Dupin, ii, 1131-45.

MARSIGLIO de Mainardinis, *Defensor Pacis,* ed. C.W. Previte-Orton (Cambridge, 1928); trans Gewirth, Marsilius, ii.

MAUROUX, Jean, *Tractatus de auctoritate concilii,* Munich Staatsbibliothek, lat. 6503, fols. 215r-30v; and ed. Mansi, xxix, 512-26.

MILIS (or Millis), Joannes de, *Consilium,* ed. Mansi, xxix, 814-22.

MILTON, John, *The ready and easy way to establish a free commonwealth,* in *The works of John Milton,* vi (New York, 1932), 111-49.

MORNAY, Philippe de, *Vindiciae contra tyrannos* (Edinburgh-Basle, 1579).

NIEM, Dietrich von, *De modis uniendi ac reformandi ecclesiam in concilio generali* in *MOCC,* i, 68-141; trans. Cameron, 'Conciliarism', part 2, 226-348 (abridged in Spinka, ed., 149-74).

OCKHAM, William of, *Dialogus,* ed. M. Goldast, *Monarchia,* ii, 394-957.

PARIS, Jean Quidort de, *Tractatus de potestate regia et papali,* ed. J. Leclerq, *Jean de Paris . . .;* trans J.A. Watt, *John of Paris. On royal and papal power* (Toronto, 1971).

PICCOLOMINI, Aeneas Sylvius (Pius II), *Der Briefwechsel des Enea Silvio Piccolomini,* ed. R. Wolkan, part 1, i-ii (*Fontes rerum Austriacarum,* 1xi-1xii). (Vienna, 1909).

De gestis concilii Basiliensis commentariorum libri duo, ed. and trans. D. Hay and W. Smith (Oxford, 1967).

De rebus Basileae gestis, stante vel dissoluto concilio (or *De concilio Basiliensi*), ed. R. Wolkan, *Der Briefwechsel* . . ., part 2 (*Fontes rerum Austriacarum,* lxvii) (Vienna, 1912), 164-228.

Ausgewählte Texte, ed. B. Widmer, *Enea Silvio Piccolomini, Papst Pius II. Ausgewählte Texte aus seinen Schriften.* in *Festgabe Hist.—Antiq. Ges. zum Basel* (Basle-Stuttgart, 1960).

PONTANUS, Ludovius. *Consilia* (Frankfurt, 1577).

RAGUSA, Johannes Stojkovic de. Speeches at council of Siena, ed. Brand-müller, *Das Konzil von Pavia-Siena,* ii, 89-190.

Tractatus de ecclesia, Basle Universitätsbibliothek, A 1 29, fols. 302-432.

De auctoritate conciliorum et de modo celebratione eorum, Basle Universitätsbibliothek, A IV 17, fols. 134-297.

Speeches during Basle: (1) May 1438, Biblioteca Vaticana, Reg. lat. 1019, fols. 335-98; and Paris, Bibl. nat., lat. 1446, fols. 176-379. (2) February 1440, *DRTA* xv, 204-20. (3) April 1440, *DRTA* xv, 348-51.

RICHER, Edmonde, *Apologia pro Joanne Gersonio* (Leyden, 1676).

Libellus de ecclesiastica et politica potestate (Paris, 1611).

Vindiciae doctrinae majorum scholae Parisiensis (Cologne, 1683).

Defensio libelli de ecclesiastica et politica potestate (Paris, 1701).

RICKEL, Denis ('The Carthusian'), *De auctoritate summi pontificis et generalis concilii* in *OO* xxxvi (Tournai, 1908), 525-674.

ROUSSEAU, J.-J., *Du contrat social,* ed. R. Grimsley (Oxford, 1972).

RUTHERFORD, Samuel, *Lex rex, or The law and the prince* (Edinburgh, 1843).

SALVARVILLA, Guillaume de, *Conclusiones,* ed. F. Bliemetzrieder in *RHE* xi (1910), 47-54.

SANCTO GEMINIANO, Dominicus de, *Lectura super sexto libro Decretalium* (Lyons, 1520).

SARPI, Paolo, *Istoria del Concilio Tridentino,* ed. G. Gambarin, i (Bari, 1935).

SEGOVIA, Juan de, *Repetitio de superioritate et excellentia supremae potestatis ecclesiasticae et spiritualis ad regiam et remporalem,* Biblioteca de Santa Cruz de Valladolid, MS. 65, fols. 130-65.

Tractatus super presidentia in concilio Basiliensi (Presidency), ed. P. Ladner (1968), 31-113.

Concordantia partium sive dictionum indeclinabilium totius Bibliae (Froben, Basle, 1496).

Tractatus de conciliorum et ecclesiae auctoritate (or *Tractatus decem avisamentorum ex sacra scriptura de sanctitate ecclesiae et generalis concilii auctoritate,* or *De insuperabili sanctitate et summa auctoritate*

generalium conciliorum),VI 4039,fols. 192-232. (*Authority of councils*)
Dicta circa materiam neutralitatis principum, Munich, Staatsbibliothek,
lat. 6606, fols. 131r-49v; *DRTA*, xiv, 367-90.
Justificatio sacri Basiliensis concilii et sententiae ipsius contra Gabrielem,
Munich, Staatsbibliothek, lat. 6606, fols. 205r-19v; *DRTA*, xiv, 347-67.
Explanatio de tribus veritatibus fidei, Munich Staatsbibliothek, lat.
6606, fols. 220r-92r.
Speech at Mainz, March 1441. *MC* iii, 568-687; *DRTA*, xv, 649-759.
Liber de sancta ecclesia, University of Salamanca, MS. 55, fols. 1-91.
De magna auctoritate episcoporum in synodo generali, Basle, Universitätsbibliothek, B.V. 15. (*Authority of bishops*)
Amplificatio disputationis, MC, iii, 695-946. (*Amplification*).

SUAREZ, Francisco, *Tractatus de legibus ac deo legislatore*, ii (Coimbra,
1612, repr. Madrid, 1967).

TOKE, Heinrich, *Questio disputata*, Munich Staatsbibliothek, lat. 6503,
fols. 124r-189r.
Questio mota, Munich Staatsbibliothek, lat. 6503, fols. 189v-92r.

TORQUEMADA, Juan de, *Summa de ecclesia* (Venice, 1561).

TUDESCHI, Niccolo de (Panormitanus), *Questio* I ('Episcopus et quidam
rector') in *Consilia, tractatus, questiones et practica* (Venice, 1578).
Commentarium in primum-quintum decretalium librum (7 vols.,
Venice, 1571)[1]; and as *Super primo-quinto decretalium* (4 vols., Lyons,
1534) (contains passages not in Venice ed.).
Super decreto, Biblioteca Capitolare Feliniana, Lucca, cod. 160, fols.
250v-63v.
Speeches at Basle, 1437: *MC*, ii, 1006-10, 1122-30, 1144-93.
Speech at Frankfurt, 1442: *MC*, iii, 1022-1125; *DRTA*, xvi, 438-538.

VELDE (or Campo), Heimerich van de, *De incomposito ecclesie statu et de
heresi Bohemorum*, Munich Staatsbibliothek, Clm. 14346, fols. 51r-60v.
De ecclesiastica potestate, Cusanus-Bibliothek, Bernkastel-Kues, Cod.
Cus. 106, fols. 89r-194v.
Speech at Cologne, 1440, *DRTA*, xv, 468-70.
Tractatus de potestate papae et concilii generalis, Biblioteket, Kungliga
Universitetet, Upsala, Cod. C 610, fols. 148r-53v.

VICO, G., *The new science*, abridged transl. of 3rd. ed. (1744) by T. Bergin
and M. Fisch (Ithaca-London, 1970).

VIENNA UNIVERSITY, *Consilium in HUP* v, 471-9.
Consilium of theology faculty, 1442 in *DRTA* xvi, 289-92.

VIGOR, S. *00* (4 vols. in 1, Paris, 1683).

---

1. In the copy in Cambridge university library, vols. v and vi are transposed.

VITERBO, Jacobus de, *De regimine christiano*, ed. H.X. Arquillière, *Le plus ancien traité de l'église* (Paris, 1926).

ZABARELLA, Franciscus, *Super quinque libris decretalium commentaria* (Venice, 1602).

Tractatus de schismate, ed. Schardius, *De iurisdictione* (Basle, 1566), 688-711.

SECONDARY SOURCES

AFANASSIEFF, N., 'Le concile dans la théologie orthodoxe russe' in *Irenikon*, xxxv (1962), 316-39.

ALBERTINI, R. von, *Das florentinische Staatsbewusstsein im Übergang von der Republik zum Prinzipat* (Berne, 1955).

ALLEN, J., *English political thought 1603-1660* (London, 1938).

A history of political thought in the sixteenth century (London, 1960).

ANDRES HERNANSANS, T. de, 'A proposito del pretendido Conciliarismo de G. de Ockham' in *Sal Terrae*, 1xi (1973), 714-30.

ANGEMEIER, H., 'Das Reich und der Konziliarismus' in *HZ*, cxcii (1961), 529-83.

ARQUILLIÈRE, H.X., 'L'origine des théories conciliaires' in *Séances et travaux de l'Acad. d. sciences morales et politiques*, clxxv (1911a), 573-86.

'L'appel au concile sous Philippe le Bel et la genèse des théories conciliaires' in *Revue des questions historiques*, xlv (1911b), 23-55.

BACHMANN, A., *Die deutsche Könige und die kurfürstliche Neutralität, 1438-1447* (Vienna, 1889).

BANSA, H., 'Konrad von Weisberg als Protektor des Konzils von Basel 1438-1440' in *AHC* iv (1972), 46-82.

BARBAINI, P., 'Per una storia integrale delle dottrine conciliari' in *La scuola cattolica*, lxxxix (1961), 186-204, 243-66.

BARKER, E., *From Alexander to Constantine* (Oxford, 1956).

BARON, H., 'Calvinist republicanism and its historical roots' in *CH* viii (1939), 30-42.

The crisis of the early Italian renaissance: civic humanism and republican liberty in an age of classicism and tyranny (Princeton, rev. ed., 1966).

BÄUMER, R., 'Eugen IV und der Plan eines "drittes Konzil" zur Beilegung des Basler Schismas' in *Reformata reformanda: Festschrift für H. Jedin*, edd. E. Iserloh and K. Repgen (Münster, 1965), 87ff.

'Die Interpretation und Verbindlichkeit der konstanzer Dekrete' in *Theologisch-praktische Quartalschrift*, cxvi (1968), 44-53.

Nachwirkungen des konziliaren Gedankens in der Theologie und Kanonistik des frühen 16. Jahrhunderts (Münster, 1971).

ed., *Von Konstanz nach Trient: Beiträge zur Geschichte der Kirche von der Reformkonzilien bis zum Trient:* Festgabe für A. Franzen (Munich, 1972).

ed., *Die Entwicklung des Konziliarismus: Werden und Nachwirken der konziliaren Idee* (Darmstadt, 1976).

BAXTER, J., 'Four "new" medieval Scottish authors' in *Scottish historical review*, xxv (1928), 90-7.

BERTRAMS, W., *Der neuzeitliche Staatsgedanke und die Konkordate des ausgehenden Mittelalters*, in *Analecta gregoriana*, xxx, ser. fac. iuris canon., B (ii) (Rome, 1950).

BIANCO, F.J., *Die alte Universität Köln*, i (Cologne, 1855).

BILDERBACK, D.L., 'The membership of the council of Basel' (Seattle, diss., 1966).

'Eugene IV and the first dissolution of the Council of Basel' in *CH* xxxvi (1967), 1-14.

'Proctorial representation and conciliar support at the Council of Basel' in *AHC*, i (1969), 140-52.

BINDER, K., 'Der "Tractatus de ecclesia" Johanns von Ragusa und die Verhandlungen des Konzils von Basel mit den Hussiten' in *Angelicum*, xxviii (1951), 32-54.

BLACK, A., 'The political ideas of conciliarism and papalism, 1430-1450' in *JEH* xx (1969), 45-65.

Monarchy and community: political ideas in the later conciliar controversy 1430-1450 (Cambridge, 1970a).

'Heimericus de Campo: the council and history' in *AHC* ii (1970b), 78-86.

'Panormitanus on the *Decretum*' in *Traditio* xxvi (1970c), 440-4.

'The council of Basle and the second Vatican council' in *SCH* vii, edd. G. Cuming and D. Baker (Cambridge, 1971), 229-34.

'The universities and the council of Basle: ecclesiology and tactics' in *AHC*, vi (1974), 341-51.

'The realist ecclesiology of Heimerich van de Velde' in *Facultas S. Theologiae Lovaniensis 1432-1797*, ed. J. van Eijl (Louvain, 1977a), 273-91.

'The universities and the council of Basle: *collegium* and *concilium*' in *Les universités à la fin du moyen âge*, edd. J. Pacquet and J.Ijsewijn (Louvain, 1977b).

BLIEMETZRIEDER, F., *Das Generalkonzil im grossen abendländischen Schismas* (Paderborn, 1904).

Literarische Polemik zur Beginnung der grossen abendländischen Schismas (Vienna, 1909).

BONET, M., 'The episcopal conference' in *Concilium* viii (1965), no. 1, pp.26-9.

BONMANN, O., 'De testamento librorum Joannis de Segovia. Num Segoviensis ex ordine minorum fuerit?' in *Antonianum* xxix (1954), 209-16.

BOTTE, B., *et al., Le concile et les conciles* (Chevetogne, 1961).

BOULARAND, F., 'La primauté du pape au concile de Florence' in *Bulletin de literature ecclésiastique,* lxi (1960), 161-203.

BRANDMÜLLER, W., 'Besitzt das Dekret "Haec Sancta" dogmatischer Verbindlichkeit?' in *RQ* lxii (1967), 1-17.

Das Konzil von Pavia-Siena 1423-4, (2 vols., Münster, 1968).

BRESSLER, H., *Die Stellung der deutschen Universitäten zum Basler Konzil, zum Schisma und zur deutschen Neutralität* (Leipzig, 1885).

BROSSE, O. de la, *Le pape et le concile, la comparaison de leurs pouvoirs à la veille de la Réforme* (Paris, 1965).

BUISSON, L., *Potestas und caritas: die päpstliche Gewalt im Spätmittelalter* (Cologne-Graz, 1958).

BURNS, J. *Scottish churchmen and the Council of Basle* (Glasgow, 1962).

CABANELAS RODRIGUEZ, D., *Juan de Segovia y el problema islamico* (Madrid, 1952).

CAM, H. *et al.,* 'Recent work and present views on the origins and development of representative assemblies' in *Relazioni del X Congresso internazionale di Scienze storiche,* i (Florence, 1955), 3-101.

CAMERON, J.K., 'Conciliarism in theory and practice, from the outbreak of the Schism till the end of the Council of Constance' (Hartford, diss., 1952).

CAMBRIDGE MEDIEVAL HISTORY, viii: *The close of the Middle Ages,* edd. C. Previté-Orton and Z.N. Brooke (Cambridge, 1936).

CARSTEN, F.L. *Princes and parliaments in Germany from the fifteenth to the eighteenth centuries* (Oxford, 1959).

CASSIRER, E. *The individual and the cosmos in renaissance philosophy,* trans. M. Domandi (Oxford, 1963).

CHAMPION, P. *Procès de condemnation de Jeanne d'Arc* (2 vols, Paris, 1920-1).

CHEVALIER, U., *Répertoire des sources historiques du moyen âge. Bio-bibliographie* (2 vols., Paris, new ed., 1905-7).

CHRIMES, S., *English constitutional ideas in the fifteenth century* (Cambridge, 1936).

CHURCH, W., *Constitutional theory in sixteenth-century France; a study in the evolution of ideas* (Cambridge, Mass., 1941).

CLARKE, M., *The medieval city-state* (Cambridge–New York, 1926).

COBBAN, A., *The medieval universities: their development and organization* (London, 1975).

COGNASSO, F., *Amedeo VIII, 1385-1451* (2 vols., Turin, 1930).

COLOMER, E., *Nikolaus von Kues und Raimund Lull* (Berlin, 1960).

CONGAR, Y. and DUPONT, J., *La collegialité episcopale. Histoire et théologie* (Paris, 1965).

L'ecclésiologie du haut moyen âge (Paris, 1968).

CONNOLLY, J. *John Gerson, reformer and mystic* (Louvain, 1928).

CROWDER, C., *Unity, heresy and reform: the conciliar response to the great schism* (London, 1977).

DELARUELLE, E., LABANDE, E. R., OURLIAC, P., *L'église au temps du grand schisme et de la crise conciliaire (1378-1449)* (2 vols., Paris, 1962-4).

DELUMEAU, J., *Catholicism between Luther and Voltaire: a new view of the counter-Reformation*, trans. J. Moiser (London, 1977).

DEPHOFF, J., *Zum Urkunden und Kanzleiwesen des Konzils von Basel* (Hildersheim, 1930).

DESCHNER, J., 'Visible unity as conciliar fellowship' in *Ecumenical review* xxviii (1976), 22-7.

DICKENS, A.G., *The German nation and Martin Luther* (London, 1974).

DICTIONNAIRE DE DROIT CANONIQUE ed. A. Villien *et al.*, (Paris, 1924-).

DICTIONNAIRE D'HISTOIRE ET DE GÉOGRAPHIE ECCLÉSIASTIQUE, edd. A. Baudrillart *et al.*, (Paris, 1912-).

DICTIONNAIRE DE THÉOLOGIE CATHOLIQUE, edd. A. Vacant *et al.*, (15 vols., Paris, 1915-50).

DIENER, H., 'Zur Persönlichkeit des Johannes de Segovia: ein Beitrag zur Methode der Auswertung päpstlichen Register des späten Mittelalters' in *Quellen und Forschungen aus italienischen Archiven und Bibliotheken.* xliv (1964), 278ff.

DÖLLINGER, J., *Beiträge zur politischen, kirchlichen und Cultur-Geschichte der sechs letzten Jahrhunderts,* ii (Regensburg, 1863).

DUDA, B., 'Johannes Stojkovic de Ragusio, O.P.: doctrina de cognosc-ibilitate ecclesiae' in *Studia Antoniana,* ix (1958).

ECKERMANN, K., *Studien zur Geschichte des monarchischen Gedankens im 15. Jahrhundert* (Berlin, 1933).

ENGELS, O., 'Zur Konstanzer Konzilsproblematik in der konziliaren Historiographie des 15. Jahrhunderts' in Bäumer, ed. *Von Konstanz nach Trient,* (1972) 233-59.

ESCHMANN, T., 'Studies on the notion of society in St Thomas Aquinas' in *Medieval studies,* vi (1944), 1-42.

EUBEL, C., *Hierarchia catholica medii aevi,* ii (1431-1503) (Münster, 1914).

FEDELE, P., *Il probleme dell' anima communitatis nella dottrina canonica del consuetudine* (Milan, 1937).

FEINE, H., *Kirchliche Rechtsgeschichte, i: Die katholische Kirche* (Weimar, 1950).

FENTON, J., 'Scholastic definitions of the church' in *American ecclesiastical review*, cxi (1944), 56-69, 131-45, 212-28.

FERNANDEZ, L.S., *Castilla, el cisma y la crisis conciliar, 1378-1440* (Madrid, 1960).

FIGGIS, J.N., *Studies in political thought from Gerson to Grotius, 1414-1625* (Cambridge, 1916).

FIJALEK, J., *Mistrz Jakob za Paradyza i Uniwersytet Krakowski u okreie soboru bazylejskiego* (2 vols., Cracow, 1900).

FINK, K.A., 'Papsttum und Kirchenreform nach dem grossen Schisma' in *Theologishe Quartalschrift,* cxxvi (1946), 110-22.

'Zur Beurteilung des grossen abendländischen Schismas' in *ZK* lxxiii (1962), 335-43.

'Die konziliare Idee im Spätmittelalter' in *Vorträge und Forschungen,* ix (1964), 119-34.

'Die weltgeschichtliche Bedeutung des Konstanzer Konzil' in *Zeitschrift der Savigny-Stiftung für Rechtsgeschichte,* Kanon. Abt., li (1965). 1-23.

FLEURY, J. 'Le conciliarisme des canonistes au concile de Bâle d'après Panormitain' in *Mélanges Roger Secretan* (Montreux, 1964), 47-66.

FLICHE, A. *La réforme grégorienne* (Paris, 1950).

FLOROVSKY, G., *Bible, church, tradition: an Eastern Orthodox view (Collected works,* i) (Belmont, Mass., 1972).

FRANK, I.W. *Der antikonziliaristische Dominikaner Leonhard Huntpichler* (Vienna, 1976).

FRANZEN, A. and MÜLLER, W., edd., *Das Konzil von Konstanz, Beiträge zu seiner Geschichte und Theologie* (Freiburg, 1964a).

'Das Konzil der Einheit. Einigungsbemühungen und konziliare Gedanken auf dem Konstanzer Konzil. Die Dekrete "Haec Sancta" und "Frequens" in das Konzil von Konstanz' in KK (1964b), 69-112.

FROMHERZ, U., *Johannes von Segovia als Geschichtsschreiber des Konzils von Basel* (Basle, 1960).

GANDILLAC, M., *La philosophie de Nicholas de Cusa* (Paris, 1941).

GERZ VON BÜREN, V.. *La tradition de l'oeuvre de Jean Gerson chez les chartreux: la chartreuse de Bâle* (Paris, 1973).

GEWIRTH, A., *Marsilius of Padua: the Defender of the Peace,* i (New York, 1951).

'Philosophy and political thought in the fourteenth century' in F. Utley, ed. *The forward movement of the fourteenth century* (Columbus, Ohio, 1961), 125-64.

GIERKE, O. von, 'Über die Geschichte des Majoritätsprinzip' in *Essays in legal history,* ed. P. Vinogradoff (Oxford, 1913).

Johannes Althusius und die Entwicklung der naturrechtlichen Staats-theorien, trans. by B. Freyd as *The development of political theory* (New York, new ed., 1966).

Das deutsche Genossenschaftsrecht (4 vols., Graz, repr. 1954); trans. in part by F. Maitland as *Political theories of the Middle Age* (Cambridge, 1900); by E. Barker as *Natural law and the theory of society* (Cambridge, 1900); by F. Kolegar as 'The idea of corporation' in *Theories of society*, edd. T. Parsons and others (New York, 1965), 611-26.

GIESEY, R., 'The French estates and the *corpus mysticum regni*' in *Studies pres. to the internat. commission for the hist. of representative and parliamentary institutions*, xxiii (Louvain, 1960), 153-76.

GILL, J., *The Council of Florence* (Cambridge, 1959).

Eugenius IV, pope of Christian union (Westminster, Maryland, 1961).

'The fifth session of the council of Constance' in *Heythrop Journal*, v (1964), 131-43.

'The representation of the *universitas fidelium* in the councils of the conciliar period' in *SCH*, vii, edd. G. Cuming and D. Baker (Cambridge, 1971), 177-95.

GILLET, P., *La personnalité juridique en droit ecclésiastique* (Malines, 1927).

GILSON, E. *History of Christian philosophy in the Middle Ages* (London, 1955).

GONZALEZ, J., *El maestro Juan de Segovia y su biblioteca* (Madrid, 1944).

GOOCH, G.P., *Political thought in England from Bacon to Halifax* (London, repr. 1950).

English democratic ideas in the seventeenth century (Cambridge, 2nd. ed., 1954).

GOUGH, J.W., *The social contract, a critical study of its development* (Oxford, 2nd. ed., 1957).

GRABMANN, M., 'Studien über den Einfluss der aristotelischen Philosophie auf die mittelalterlichen Theorien über das Verhältnis von Kirche und Staat' *(Sitzungsber. d. bayerischen Akad. d. Wiss., phil-hist. Abt., ii)* (Munich, 1934).

GRASS, N., ed. *Cusanus Gedächtnisschrift* (Innsbruck, 1970).

GRILLMEIER, A., 'Konzil und Rezeption' in *Theologie und Philosophie* xlv (1970), 321-52.

HAJJAR, J., 'The synod in the Eastern Church' in *Concilium* viii (1965), no. 1, pp.30-4.

HALLER, J., 'Beiträge zur Geschichte des Basler Konzils' in *Zeitschrift für Geschichte des Oberrheins*, n.F., xvi (1901), 9-27, 207-45.

Papsttum und Kirchenreform: vier Kapitel zur Geschichte des augehenden

235

Mittelalters, i, (Berlin, 1903).

'Die Kirchenreform auf dem Konzil zu Basel' in *Korrespondenzblatt des Gesamtvereins der deutschen Geschichte- und Altertumsverein,* lviii (1910), 9-26.

HAMILTON, B., *Political thought in sixteenth-century Spain, a study of the political ideas of Vitoria, Soto, Suarez and Molina* (Oxford, 1963).

HANDBUCH DER KIRCHENGESCHICHTE, ed. H. Jedin (6 vols., Freiburg-Basle-Vienna, 3rd. ed., 1965-73).

HANNA, C., *Die südwestdeutschen Diözesen und das Baseler Konzil in den Jahren 1431 bis 1441* (Borna-Leipzig, 1929).

HAUBST, R., 'Johann von Segovia im Gesprach mit Nikolaus von Kues und Jean Germain über die Beweisbarkeit der göttlichen Dreieinigkeit und ihrer Verkündigung vor den Mohammedanern' in *Münchener theologische Zeitschrift,* ii (1951), 115-29.

'Zum Fortleben Alberts des grossen bei Heymerich von Kamp und Nikolaus von Kues' in *Studia Albertina,* Suppl. iv (Beiträge zur Geschichte der Philosophie und Theologie des Mittelalters) (Münster, 1952), 420-47.

HAUCK, A., 'Die Rezeption und Umbildung der allgemeinen Synode im Mittelalter' in *Historische Vierteljahrschrift,* x (1907), 465-82.

HÉFÈLE, C.J. and LECLERQ, H., *Histoire des conciles d'après les documents originaux* (French trans. from 2nd. ed.), vii (Paris, 1916).

HEIMPEL, H., *Studien zur Kirchen- und Reichsreform der 15. Jahrhunderts* in *SHA* (1929-30), i (Heidelberg, 1929).

Dietrich von Niem (Münster, 1932).

HEINZ-MOHR, G., *Nikolaus von Kues und die Konzilsbewegung* (Trier, 1963).

HEYMANN, F.G., *John Zizka and the Hussite revolution* (Princeton, 1955).

George of Bohemia; king of heretics (Princeton, 1965).

HÖDL, G., 'Zur Reichspolitik des Basler Konzils. Bischof Johannes Schele von Lübeck (1420-1439)' in *MIÖG* lxxv (1967), 46-65.

HOFMANN, G., *Papato, conciliarismo, patriarcato, 1438-9* (Miscellanea historica pontificiae, ii, no. 2) (Rome, 1940).

HORST, U., 'Grenzen der päpstlichen Autorität: konziliare Elemente in der Ekklesiologie des Johann Torquemada' in *Freiburger Zeitschrift für Philosophie und Theologie,* xv (1968), 367-402.

HOVE, A. van, *Prolegomena (ad codicem iuris canonici)* (Mechelen-Rome, 2nd. ed., 1945).

HUIZINGA, J. *The waning of the Middle Ages,* trans. F. Hopmann (London, 1955).

HÜRTEN, H., 'Die Mainzer Akzeptation von 1439' in *Archiv für mittelrheinische Geschichte,* xi (1959), 42-75.

'Zur Ekklesiologie der Konzilien von Konstanz und Basel' in *Theologische Revue,* lix (1963), 361-72.

INSTITUT D'HISTOIRE DE GENÈVE, ed., *Les universités européens du xive au xviie siècles* (Geneva, 1967).

JACOB, E.F., 'The Bohemians at the council of Basel, 1433' in *Prague essays,* ed. R. Seton-Watson (Oxford, 1949), 81-123.

Essays in the conciliar epoch (Manchester, 3rd. ed., 1963).

'Reflections upon the study of the general councils in the fifteenth century' in *SCH* i, edd. C. Dugmore and J. Duggan (London, 1964), 80-98.

'Giuliano Cesarini' in *Bulletin of the John Rylands library,* li (1968a), 104ff.

'The conciliar movement in recent study' in E.F. Jacob, *Essays in later medieval history* (Manchester, 1968b), 98-123.

'Theory and fact in the general councils of the fifteenth century' in *ibid.* (1968c), 124-40.

'Panormitanus and the council of Basle' in *Proceedings of the third internat. congress of medieval canon law,* ed. S. Kuttner (Vatican, 1971), 205-15.

JAROSCHKA, W., 'Thomas Ebendorfer als Theoretiker des Konziliarismus' in *MIÖG* lxii (1963), 87-98.

JEDIN, H., 'Giovanni Gozzadini, ein Konziliarist am Hofe Julius II' in *RQ* xlvii (1939), 193-267.

A history of the Council of Trent, i, trans. E. Graf (London, 1957).

Bischöfliches Konzil oder Kirchenparlament? Ein Beitrag zur Ekklesiologie der Konzilien von Konstanz und Basel (Basle-Stuttgart, 1965).

JÖCHER, C., *Allgemeines Gelehrten-Lexicon* (4 vols., Leipzig, 1750-1). *Supplement,* ed. J. Adeling (7 vols., Leipzig, 1784-1897).

KALLEN, G., *De auctoritate presidendi: Cusanus-Texte,* ii in *SHA* 1935-6, iii (Heidelberg, 1935).

KAMINSKY, H., *A history of the Hussite revolution* (Berkeley, 1967).

KANTOROWICZ, E., *The king's two bodies: a study in medieval political theology* (Princeton, 1957).

KAUFMANN, G., *Die Geschichte der deutschen Universitäten* (2 vols., Stuttgart, 1888-96).

KELLNER, H., 'Jakobus von Jüterbog, ein deutsche Theologe des fünfzehnten Jahrhunderts' in *Theologische Quartalschrift,* xlviii (1868), 315-48.

KELSEN, H., *Pure theory of law,* trans. M. Knight (Berkeley, 1967).

KEUSSEN, H., 'Ein kölner Traktat von c. 1440-9 über das Verhältnis der Glaubigen zur Zeit des Schismas' in *ZK,* xl (1921), 138-9.

Die Matrikel der Universität Köln, i (1389-1475) (Bonn, 1928).
'Die Stellung der Universität Köln im grossen Schisma und zu den Reform-konzilien' in *Annalen des historisches Vereins der Nordrhein,* cxv (1929), 225-54.

KLOTZNER, J., *Kardinal Dominikus Jacobazzi und sein Konzilswerk: ein Beitrag zur Geschichte der konziliare Idee* (Rome, 1948).

KNEER, A., 'Die Entstehung der konziliaren Theorie' in *RQ,* ersters Supplementheft (1893), 48-60.

KRCHNAK, A., *De vita et operibus Ioannis de Ragusio, O.P.* (Rome, 1960).

KÜCHLER, W., 'Alfons V von Aragon und das Basler Konzil' in *Gesammelte Aufsätze zur Kulturgeschichte Spaniens,* xxiii (1967), 131-46.

KÜNG, H., *Structures of the church,* trans. S. Attanasio (London, 1965).
Infallible? An enquiry, trans. E. Mosbacher (London, 1972).

KÜPPERS, W., 'Reception, Prolegomena to a systematic study' in *World council of churches studies* no. 5 (1961), pp.76-98.
ed., Report of *WCC* study group in *Study Encounter* x (1974), no. 2, pp.1ff.

KUTTNER, S., *Repertorium der Kanonistik* (Vatican city, 1937).

LADNER, P., 'Johannes von Segovias Stellung zur Präsidentenfrage des Basler Konzils' in *Zeitschrift für schweizerische Kirchengeschichte,* 1xii (1968), 1-113.
'Der Ablass-Traktat des Heymericus de Campo' in *ibid.,* 1xxi (1977), 93-140.

LAGARDE, G. de, 'Individualisme et corporatisme au moyen âge' in *Université de Louvain, Receuil de travaux d'hist. et de philol.,* xliv part 2 (1937), 1-60.
'Les théories representatives des xive-xve siècles et l'Église' in *Studies pres. to the internat. commission for the hist. of repres. and parliamentary institutions,* xviii (Louvain, 1958), 63-76.
'Ockham et le concile général' in *ibid.,* xxiii (Louvain, 1960), 83-94.
La naissance de l'esprit laique au déclin du moyen âge, v (new ed., Paris, 1963).

LAZARUS, P., *Das Basler Konzil, seine Berufung und seine Leitung, seine Gliederung und seine Behördenorganisation* (Berlin, 1912).

LE BRAS, G., *Les institutions de la Chrétieneté mediévale* (Paris, 1959).

LECLERQ, J., *Jean de Paris et l'ecclésiologie du xiiie siècle* (Paris, 1942).

LEFÈBVRE, C., 'L'enseignement de Nicolas de Tudeschis et l'autorité pontificale' in *Ephemerides iuris canonici,* xiv (1958), 312-39.

LEFF, G., *Heresy in the later Middle Ages: the relation of heterodoxy to dissent, c. 1250-1450* (2 vols., Manchester, 1967a).
'The apostolic ideal in later medieval ecclesiology' in *Journal of theological studies,* xviii (1967b), 58-82.

LEPSZY, K., ed., *Universitatis Iagelloniae 1364-1764 Historia,* i (Cracow, 1964).

LEWIS, E., 'Organic tendencies in medieval political thought' in *American political science review,* xxxii (1938), 849-76.
Medieval political ideas (2 vols., London 1954).

LEWIS, J.D., *The* Genossenschaft *theory of Otto von Gierke: a study in political thought,* in *University of Wisconsin studies in the social sciences and history,* vol. xxv (Madison, 1935).

LEXIKON FÜR THEOLOGIE UND KIRCHE, edd. M. Buchberger et al. (10 vols., Freiburg, 1957-65).

LHOTSKY, A., *Thomas Ebendorfer, ein österreichischer Geschichtsschreiber, Theologe und Diplomat des 15. Jahrhunderts* (Stuttgart, 1957).

LOOMIS, L.R., *The Council of Constance* (New York, 1961).

LOPEZ, M. Torres, 'Juan de Segovia y su donation de manuscritos a la Universidad de Salamanca' in *Anales de la asociacion para el progreso de las ciencias,* iv (1939), 947-64.

LUBAC, H. de, *Corpus mysticum, l'eucharistie et l'église au moyen âge* (Paris, 2nd ed., 1949).

MACEK, J. *The Hussite movement in Bohemia* (Prague, 2nd. ed., 1958).
'Der Konziliarismus in der böhmischen Reformation, besonders in der Politik Georgs von Podiebrad' in *ZK* lxxx (1969), 312-30.

MANTZKE, F.W., 'Die konziliaren Theorien des Mittelalters und die Anschauung Luthers zum Konzil' (Kiel, diss., 1965).

MARAVALL, J.A. *Las comunidadas de Castilla* (Madrid, 1963).

MARGULL, H., ed. *The councils of the church: history and analysis,* trans. W.F. Bense (Philadelphia, 1966).

MARONGIU, A., *Medieval parliaments, a comparative study,* trans. S. Woolf (London, 1968).

MARSCHALL, W., 'Ein Cyprianzitat im Schreiben des Konzils von Basel vom 20. Februar 1439 an die europäischen Gesandten' in Bäumer, ed., *Von Konstanz nach Trient,* 189ff.

MARTIMORT, A.G., *Le Gallicanisme de Bossuet* (Paris, 1953).

MARTIN, V., *Le Gallicanisme et la réforme catholique* (Paris, 1919).
'Comment s'est formé la doctrine de la superiorité du concile sur le pape' in *Revue des sciences religieuses,* xvii (1937), 212-43, 261-89, 404-27.
Les origines du Gallicanisme, ii (Paris, 1939).

MATTINGLEY, G., *Renaissance diplomacy* (London, 1965).

McGOWAN, J.P., *Pierre d'Ailly* (Washington, 1936).

McGRADE, A.S., *The political thought of William of Ockham: personal and institutional principles* (Cambridge, 1974).

McKEON, P., '*Concilium generale* and *studium generale.* The transformation of doctrinal regulations in the Middle Ages' in *CH* xxxv (1966), 24-34.

McNEILL, J.T., 'The emergence of conciliarism' in edd. J. Cate and E. Anderson, *Medieval and historiographical studies in honor of J.W. Thompson* (Chicago, 1938), 269-301.

Unitive Protestantism: the ecumenical spirit and its persistent expression (London, rev. ed., 1964).

'The relevance of conciliarism' in *The jurist*, xxxi (1971), 81-112.

MEERSSEMANN, G., *Geschichte des Albertismus*, ii: *Die erste Kölner Kontroversen* (Rome, 1935).

MEIER, L., *Die Werke der Erfürter Kartäusers Jakob von Jüterbog in ihrer handschriftliche Uberlieferung* (Münster, 1955).

MEIJKNECHT, A., 'Le concile de Bâle: aperçu général sur les sources' in *RHE*, lxv (1970), 465-73.

MERRIMAN, R., *The rise of the Spanish empire in the old world and the new*, i: *The Middle Ages* (New York, 1918).

MERZBACHER, G., 'Die ekklesiologische Konzeption des Kardinals Francesco Zabarella' in edd. A. Haidacher and H. Mayer, *Festschrift Pivec* (Innsbruck, 1966), 279-87.

MESNARD, P., *L'essor de la philosophie politique au xvième siècle* (Paris, 1936).

MEUTHEN, E., 'Nikolaus von Kues und der laie in der Kirche' in *HJ*, lxxxi (1962), 101-22.

'Kanonistik und Geschichtsverständnis. Über ein neuentdecktes Werk des Nikolaus von Kues: *De maioritate auctoritatis conciliorum supra auctoritatem papae*' in Bäumer, ed., *Von Konstanz nach Trient*, (1972), 147-70.

MICHAUD-QUANTIN, P., *Universitas: expressions du mouvement communautaire dans le moyen-âge latin* (Paris, 1970).

MISCELLANEA MEDIAEVALIA, ed. Thomas Institute, University of Cologne, viii (1971).

MOLITOR, E., *Die Reichsreformbestrebungen des 15. Jahrhunderts bis zum Tode Kaisers Friedrichs III* (Breslau, 1921).

MONTES, B.H., 'Obras de Juan de Segovia', in *Repertorio de Historia de las ciencias eclesiastica en España* (Salamanca, 1977) 267-347.

MORAWSKI, K., *Histoire de l'université de Cracovie*, ii, trans. P. Rougier (Paris-Cracow, 1903).

MORRALL, J., *Gerson and the great schism* (Manchester, 1960).

'Ockham and ecclesiology' in *Medieval studies pres. to A. Gwynn*, ed. J. Watt and others (Dublin, 1961), 481-91.

MOUGEL, D.A., *Denys le Chartreux, 1402-71: sa vie, son rôle* (Montreuil, 1896).

MULDER, W., 'Dionysius de Karthuizer en de conciliare Theorie' in *Die*

Katholiek, clxi (1912), 253-81.

MURE, G., *The philosophy of Hegel* (London, 1965).

NÖRR, K., *Kirche und Konzil bei Nicolaus de Tudeschis (Panormitanus)* (Cologne Graz, 1964).

OAKLEY, F., 'The *propositiones utiles* of Pierre d'Ailly: an epitome of conciliar thought' in *CH*, xxix (1960), 398ff.

'On the road from Constance to 1688' in *Journal of British studies*, i (1962), 1-32.

The political thought of Pierre d'Ailly: the voluntarist tradition (Yale, 1964a).

'Almain and Major: conciliar theory on the eve of the Reformation' in *American historical review*, lxx (1964b), 673-90.

'Figgis, Constance and the divines of Paris' in *American historical review*, lxxv (1969), 368-86.

'Conciliarism at the fifth Lateran Council?' in *CH*, xli (1972), 452-63.

OURLIAC, P., 'La sociologie du Concile de Bâle' in *RHE*, lvi (1961), 2-32.

PASCOE, L.B., *Jean Gerson: principles of church reform* (Leiden, 1973).

PELIKAN, J., *The Christian tradition*, i: *The emergence of the Catholic tradition (100-600)* (Chicago, 1971).

The Christian tradition, ii: *the spirit of Eastern Christendom (600-1700)* (Chicago, 1974).

PÉROUSE, G., *Le Cardinal Aleman, président du Concile de Bâle, et la fin du grand schisme* (Paris, 1905).

PETIT-DUTAILLIS, C., *Les communes françaises: caractères et évolution des origines au xviiie siècle* (Paris, 1947).

PICHLER, I.H., *Die Verbindlichkeit der Konstanzer Dekrete* (Vienna, 1967).

PITKIN, H.F., *The concept of representation* (Berkeley, 1967).

PLÖCHL, W.M., *Geschichte des Kirchenrechts*, i-ii (Munich-Vienna, 1953-5).

POCOCK, J., *Politics, language and time: essays on political thought and history* (London, 1972).

The Machiavellian moment: Florentine political thought and the Atlantic republican tradition (Princeton, 1975).

POSCH, A., *Die 'Concordantia Catholica' von Nikolaus von Cusa* (Paderborn, 1930).

POST, G., *Studies in medieval legal thought: public law and the state, 1100-1322* (Princeton, 1964).

POSTUMUS-MEYJES, G.H.M., *Jean Gerson: zijn kerkpolitiek en ecclesiolozie* ('s Gravenhage, 1963).

PREISWERK, E., *Der Einfluss Aragons auf dem Prozess des Basler Konzils gegen Papst Eugen IV* (Basle, 1902).

PREROVSKY, O., 'Le idee oligarchiche nei difensori di Clemente VII' in *Salesianum* xxii (1960), 383-408.

QUILLET, J., *Marsile de Padoue, Le Defenseur de la Paix* (Paris, 1968).

RAHNER, K. & RATZINGER, J., *The episcopate and the primacy* (Freiburg, 1962).

RASHDALL, H., *The universities of Europe in the Middle Ages*, edd. F. Powicke & A. Emden (3 vols., Oxford, 1936).

REIDLINGER, H., 'Hermeneutische Überlegungen zu den Konstanzer Dekreten' in *KK* (1964), 214-40.

REITER, E., 'Rezeption und Beachtung von Basler Dekreten in der Diözese Eichstatt unter Bischof Johann von Eych (1445-64)' in Bäumer, ed., *Von Konstanz nach Trient*, (1972), 215ff.

RIESENBERG, P.N., *Inalienability of sovereignty in medieval political thought* (New York, 1956).

RITTER, G., *Studien zur Spätscholastik*, iii in *SHA* 1926-7 (Heidelberg, 1927).

ROBERTI, M., 'Il *corpus mysticum* di S. Paolo nella storia della persona giuridica' in *Studi di storia e diritto in onore di Enrico Besta*, iv (Milan, 1939), 37-82.

ROBERTS, A.E., 'Pierre d'Ailly and the council of Constance: a study in "Ockhamite" theory and practice' in *Transactions of the royal hist. soc.*, 4th. ser., xviii (1935), 123-42.

ROPS, D., *The church in the seventeenth century*, trans. J. Buckingham (London, 1963).
The church in the eighteenth century. trans. J. Warrington (London, 1970).

RÖRIG, F., *The medieval town*, trans. D. Bryant. (London, 1967).

RUBINSTEIN, N., 'Marsilius of Padua and Italian political thought of his time', in *Europe in the late Middle Ages*, edd. J. Hale et al. (London, 1965).

RUEGER, Z., 'Gerson, the conciliar movement and the right of resistance (1642-4)' in *JHI* xxv (1964), 467-80.

SACRAMENTUM MUNDI: *an encyclopedia of theology*, edd. K. Rahner and others (6 vols., New York, 1968-70).

SÄGMÜLLER, J.B., 'Der Verfasser der Traktates *De modis uniendi ac reformandi ecclesiam in concilio universali* vom J. 1410' in *HJ* xiv (1893), 562-82.

SALVATORELLI, L. 'Le idee religiose di Fra Paolo Sarpi' in *Memorie dell'Accad naz. dei Lincei*, classi di scienze morali, storiche e filol., ser. 8, v (1954), 311-60.

SANTIAGO-OTERO, H., 'Juan de Segovia. Manuscritos de sus obras en la Biblioteca Nacional de Viena y en la Staatsbibliothek de Munich' in

Revista española de teologia, xxix (1969), 167-79.

'Juan de Sevogia. Algunos manuscritos de sus obras en la Biblioteca Vaticana' in *ibid.*, xxx (1970), 93-106.

SAVIGNY, F., *Geschichte des römischen Rechts im Mittelalter*, vi (Heidelberg, 1850).

SCHÄFER, C., *Die Staatslehre des Johannes Gerson* (Bielefeld, 1935).

SCHMIDINGER, H., 'Konziliarismus und Konzil im Spätmittelalter' in *Anima*, xv (1960), 308-18.

SCHNEYER, J.B., 'Baseler Konzilspredigten aus dem Jahre 1432' in Bäumer, ed., *Von Konstanz nach Trient* (1972), 139-46.

SCHNÖRR von CAROLSFELD, L., *Geschichte der juristische Person*, i: Universitas, corpus, collegium *im klassischen römischen Rechts* (Munich, 1933).

SCHOFIELD, A., 'The first English delegation to the council of Basel' in *JEH*, xii (1961), 167-96.

'England, the pope and the council of Basel, 1435-1449' in *CH*, xxxiii (1964), 248-78.

'The second English delegation to the council of Basel' in *JEH*, xvii (1966), 29-64.

'Ireland and the council of Basel' in *The Irish ecclesiastical record*, cvii (1967), 374-87.

'Some aspects of English representation at the council of Basel' in *SCH*, vii, edd. G. Cuming and D. Baker (Cambridge, 1971), 219-27.

SCHOLZ, R., *Die Publizistik zur Zeit Philipps des Schönen* (Stuttgart, 1903).

Unbekannte Kirchenpolitische Streitschriften aus der Zeit Ludwigs des Bayern, 1327-1354 (Rome, 1911-14).

'Eine Geschichte und Kritik der Kirchenverfassung vom Jahre 1406' in *Papsttum und Kaisertum im Mittelalter: Festchrfit M. P. Kehr* (Munich, 1926), 595-621.

Wilhelm von Ockham als politischer Denker und sein Breviloquium de principatu tyrannico (Stuttgart, 1952).

SCHULTE, J.F. von, *Die Stellung der Concilien, Päpste und Bischöfe* (Prague, 1871).

Die Geschichte der Quellen und Literatur des canonischen Rechts von Gratian bis auf die Gegenwart, ii (Stuttgart, 1877).

SCHWEIZER, J., *Nicolaus de Tudeschi, seine Tätigkeit am Basler Konzil* (Strasbourg, 1924).

SHAW, D., 'Thomas Livingstone, a conciliarist' in *Scottish church history society records*, xii (1955), 120-35.

SIGMUND, P., 'Cusanus' *Concordantia*, a re-interpretation' in *Political studies*, x (1962a), 180-97.

'The influence of Marsilius on fifteenth-century conciliarism' in *JHI* xxiii (1962b), 393-402.

Nicholas of Cusa and medieval political thought (Harvard, 1963).

SKINNER, Q., 'Meaning and understanding in the history of ideas' in *History and Theory* viii (1969), 3-51.

SOUTHERN, R.W., *Western views of Islam in the Middle Ages* (Cambr., Mass., 1962).

SPINKA, M., *John Hus' concept of the church* (Princeton, 1966).

STIEBER, J.W., *Pope Eugenius IV, the Council of Basel and the secular and ecclesiastical authorities in the Empire* (Leiden, 1978).

STÖCKLIN, A., 'Das Ende der mittelalterliche Konzilsbewegung' in *Zeitschrift für schweizerische Kirchengeschichte* xxxvii (1943), 8-30.

STUHR, F., *Die Organisation und Geschäftsordnung des pisaner und konstanzer Konzils* (Schwerin, 1891).

STUTT, H., *Die nordwestdeutschen Diözesen und das Baseler Konzil in den Jahren 1431 bis 1441* (Erlangen, 1928).

THILS, G., 'Le "tractatus de ecclesia" de Jean de Ragusa' in *Angelicum,* xvii (1940), 219-44.

TIERNEY, B., 'Ockham, the conciliar theory and the canonists' in *JHI* xv (1954), 40-70.

'Collegiality in the Middle Ages' in *Concilium,* vii (1965), 5-14.

Foundations of the conciliar theory: the contribution of the medieval canonists from Gratian to the great schism (Cambridge, repr. 1968).

'Hermeneutics and history: the problem of *Haec Sancta*' in edd. T. Sandquist and T. Powicke, *Essays in honor of Bertie Wilkinson* (Toronto, 1969), 354-70.

Origins of papal infallibility, 1150-1350: a study on the concepts of infallibility, sovereignty and tradition in the Middle Ages (Leiden, 1972).

'"Divided sovereignty" at Constance: a problem of medieval and early modern political theory' in *AHC* vii (1975), 238-56.

TOEWS, J. 'Pope Eugenius and the Concordat of Vienna (1448), an interpretation, in *CH* xxxiv (1965), 178ff.

TÖNNIES, F., *Gemeinschaft und Gesellschaft,* trans. C.P. Loomis as *Community and association* (London, 1974).

TROELTSCH, E., *The social teaching of the Christian churches,* trans. O. Wyon (2 vols., London, 1931).

ULLMANN, W., *Medieval papalism: the political theories of the medieval canonists* (London, 1949).

'De Bartoli sententia: *concilium representat mentem populi*' in *Bartolo da Sassoferrato, studi et documenta per il vi centenario,* ii (Milan, 1962), 703-33.

The growth of papal government in the Middle Ages: a study in the ideological relations of the clerical to the lay power (London, 3rd. ed., 1965).

The individual and society in the Middle Ages (London, 1967).

Principles of government and politics in the Middle Ages (London, 2nd. ed., 1966).

Origins of the great schism: a study in fourteenth-century ecclesiastical history (London, repr., 1972a).

'Julius II and the schismatic cardinals' in *SCH* ix (Cambridge, 1972b), 177-93.

Law and politics in the Middle Ages: an introduction to the sources of medieval political ideas (London, 1975).

'John Baconthorpe as a canonist' in *Church and government in the Middle Ages,* edd. C. Brooke and others (Cambridge, 1976), 223-46.

VALOIS, N., *La France et le grand schisme d'Occident* 2 vols., Paris, 1896).

Histoire de le Pragmatique Sanction de Bourges sous Charles VII (Paris, 1906).

Le pape et le concile (1378-1450). La crise religieuse du XVe siècle (2 vols., Paris, 1909).

VANSTEENBERGHE, E., *Le cardinal Nicolas de Cues (1401-1464)* (Lille, 1920).

VAUGHAN, R., *Philip the Good: the apogee of Burgundy* (London, 1972).

VERA-FAJARDO, G., *Le eclesiologia de Juan de Segovia en la crisis conciliar (1435-47)* (Vitoria, 1968).

VIGENER, F., *Bischofsamt und Papstgewalt* (Göttingen, 2nd ed., 1964).

VILLOSLADA, R.G., *La Universidad de Paris durante los estudios de Francisco de Vitoria, O.P. (1507-1522)* (Rome, 1938).

VOOGHT, P. de, *L'hérésie de Jean Hus* (Louvain, 1960a).

'Le conciliarisme aux conciles de Constance et de Bâle' in edd. B. Botte et al., *Le concile et les conciles* (Chevetogne, 1960b), 143-81.

'Le conciliarisme aux conciles de Constance et de Bâle: compléments et précisions' in *Irenikon,* xxxvi (1963), 61-75.

Les pouvoirs du concile et l'autorité du pape au concile de Constance (Paris, 1965).

'Gerson et le conciliarisme' in *RHE,* lxiii (1968), 857-67.

WALEY, D., *The Italian city-republics* (London, 1969).

WALSH, M., 'World council and world church' in *The Month,* 2nd. n.s., iii (1971), 35ff.

WALTERS, L., 'Andreas von Escobar, ein Vertreter der konziliaren Theorie am Anfange des 15. Jahrhunderts' (Münster, Diss., 1901).

WEBER, G., *Die selbständige Vermittlungspolitik der Kurfürsten im Konflikt zwischen Papst und Konzil, 1437-38* (Berlin, 1915).

WEBER, M., *General economic history*, trans. F. Knight (London, 1927). *The city*, trans. D. Martindale and G. Neuwirth (New York, 1958).

WENCK, K. 'Konrad von Gelnhausen und die Quellen der konziliaren Theorie' in *HZ* lxxvi (1896), 1-60.

WERMINGHOFF, A. *Nationalkirchliche Bestrebungen im deutschen Mittelalter* (Stuttgart, 1910).

WIDMER, B., *Enea Silvio Piccolomini in der sittlichen und politischen Entscheidung* (Basle, 1963).

WILKS, M., *'Papa est nomen iurisdictionis:* Augustinus Triumphus and the papal vicariate of Christ' in *Journal of theological studies,* viii (1957), 71-91, 256-71.

The problem of sovereignty in the later Middle Ages: the papal monarchy with Augustinus Triumphus and the publicists (Cambridge, 1963).

'The early Oxford Wyclif: papalist or nominalist?' in *SCH* v, ed. G. Cuming (Leiden, 1969), 69-98.

WILLAERT, L., *Après le concile de Trent: la restauration catholique. 1563-1648* (Paris, 1960).

WITTRAM, R., *Die französische Politik auf dem Basler Konzil während der Zeit seiner Blute* (Riga, 1927).

WOOLF, C., *Bartolus of Sassoferrato* (Cambridge, 1913).

WORLD COUNCIL OF CHURCHES (Faith and order) Studies, no. 5 (1961): *Councils and the church.*

WULF, M. de, 'L'individu et le groupe dans la scolastique du xiiie siècle' in *Revue néo-scolastique de philosophie,* xxii (1920), 341-57.

ZELLFELDER, A., *England und das Basler Konzil* (Berlin, 1913).

ZIMMERMANN, A., *Die kirchliche Verfassungskämpfe im XV Jahrhundert* (Breslau, 1882a).

'Juan de Segovia' (Breslau, diss., 1882b).

ZIMMERMANN, H., 'Die Absetzung de Päpste auf dem Konstanzer Konzil. Theorie und Praxis' in *KK* 113-37.

Papstabsetzungen des Mittelalters (Graz, 1968).

ZWÖLFER, R., 'Die Reform der Kirchenverfassung auf dem Konzil zu Basel' in *Basler Zeitschrift für Geschichte und Altertumskunde,* xxviii (1929), 144-247 and xxix (1930), 2-58.

INDEX OF TOPICS

247

INDEX OF NAMES